THE LETTERS OF
ROBERT BURNS

"You shall write whatever comes first,—what you see, what you read, what you hear, what you admire, what you dislike; trifles, bagatelles, nonsense, or, to fill up a corner, e'en put down a laugh at full length"—Burns.

"My life reminded me of a ruined temple: what strength, what proportion in some parts! what unsightly gaps, what prostrate ruin in others!"—Burns.

THE THOMSON LETTERS

BURNS'S LETTERS.

It is not perhaps generally known that the prose of Burns exceeds in quantity his verse. The world remembers him as a poet, and forgets or overlooks his letters. His place among the poets has never been denied—it is in the first rank; nor is he lowest, though little remembered, among letter-writers. His letters gave Jeffrey a higher opinion of him as a man than did his poetry, though on both alike the critic saw the seal and impress of genius. Dugald Stewart thought his letters objects of wonder scarcely less than his poetry. And Robertson, comparing his prose with his verse, thought the former the more extraordinary of the two. In the popular view of his genius there is, however, no denying the fact that his poetry has eclipsed his prose.

His prose consists mostly of letters, but it also includes a noble fragment of autobiography; three journals of observations made at Mossgiel, Edinburgh, and Ellisland respectively; two itineraries, the one of his border tour, the other of his tour in the Highlands; and historical notes to two collections of Scottish songs. A full enumeration of his prose productions would take account also of his masonic minutes, his inscriptions, a rather curious business paper drawn up by the poet-exciseman in prosecution of a smuggler, and of course his various prefaces, notably the dedication of his poems to the members of the Caledonian Hunt.

His letters, however, far exceed the sum of his other-prose writings. Close upon five hundred and forty have already been published. These are not all the letters he ever wrote. Where, for example, is the literary correspondence in which he engaged so enthusiastically with his Kirkoswald schoolfellows? "Though I had not three farthings' worth of business in the world, yet every post brought me as many letters as if I had been a broad-plodding son of daybook and ledger." Where are the letters which brought to the ploughman at Lochlie such a constant and copious stream of replies? The circumstances of his position will explain why they perished: he was then "a youth and all unknown to fame." It is even doubtful if the five hundred and forty published letters include all the letters of Burns that now exist. Scarcely a year passes but some epistolary scrap in the well-known handwriting is unearthed and ceremoniously added to the previous sum total, And yet, notwithstanding losses past or within recall, it is probable that we have long had the whole of Burns's most characteristic letters. It was inevitable that these should be preserved and published. His fame was so rooted in the popular regard in his lifetime, that a characteristic letter from his hand was sure to be received as something singularly precious. It must not be forgotten, however, that Burns's personality was so intense as to colour the smallest fragment of his correspondence, and it is on this account desirable that every note he penned that yet remains unpublished should be produced. It might give no new feature to our conception of his character; but it would help the shading—which, in the portraiture of any person, must chiefly be furnished by the minor and more commonplace actions of his everyday life.

The correspondence of Burns, as we have it, commences, presumably, near the close of his twenty-second year, and extends to all but exactly the middle of his thirty-eighth. The dates are a day somewhere at the end of 1780, and Monday, 18th July 1796. Between these limits lies the printed correspondence of sixteen years. The sum total of this correspondence allows about thirty-four letters to each year, but the actual distribution is very unequal, ranging from the minimum, in 1782, of one, a masonic letter addressed to Sir John Whitefoord of Ballochmyle, to the maximum number of ninety-two, in 1788, the great year of the Clarinda episode. It is in 1786, the year of the publication of his first volume at

Kilmarnock, the year of his literary birth, that his correspondence first becomes heavy. It rises at a leap from two letters in the preceding year to as many as forty-four. The phenomenal increase is partly explained by the success of his poems. He became a man that was worth the knowing, whose correspondence was worth preserving. The six years of his published correspondence previous to the discovery of his genius in 1786 are represented by only fourteen letters in all. But in those years his letters, though both numerous and prized above the common, were not considered as likely to be of future interest, and were therefore suffered to live or die as chance might determine. They mostly perished, the recipients thinking it hardly worth their while to be sae nice wi' Robin as to preserve them.

After the recognition of his power in 1786, the record of his preserved letters shews, for the ten years of his literary life, several fluctuations which admit of easy explanation. Commencing with 1787, the numbers are:—78, 92, 54, 33, 44, 31, 66, 30, 27, 24. The first of these years was totally severed from rural occupations, or business of any kind, if we except the publication of the first Edinburgh edition of his poems. It was a complete holiday year to him. He was either resident in Edinburgh, studying men and manners, or touring about the country, visiting those places which history, song, or scenery had made famous. Wherever he was, his fame brought him the acquaintance of a great many new people. His leisure and the novelty of his situation afforded him both opportunity and subject for an extensive correspondence. For a large part of the next year, 1788, he was similarly circumstanced, and the number of his letters was exceptionally increased by his entanglement with Mrs. M'Lehose. To her alone, in less than three months of this year, he wrote at least thirty-six letters,—considerably over one-third of the entire epistolary produce of the year. In 1789 we find the number of his letters fall to fifty-four. This was, perhaps, the happiest year of his life. He was now comfortably established as a farmer in a home of his own, busied with healthy rural work, and finding in the happy fireside clime which he was making for wife and weans "the true pathos and sublime" of human duty. He has still, however, time and inclination to write on the average one letter a week. For each of the next three years the average number is thirty-six. In 1793 the number suddenly goes up to sixty-six: the increase is due to the heartiness with which he took up the scheme of George Thomson to popularise and perpetuate the best old Scottish airs by fitting them with words worthy of their merits. He wrote, in this year, twenty-six letters in support of the scheme.

There is a sad falling off in Burns's ordinary correspondence in the last three years of his life. The amount of it scarcely touches twenty letters per year. Even the correspondence with Thomson, though on a subject so dear to the heart of Burns, rousing at once both his patriotism and his poetry, sinks to about ten letters per year, and is irregular at that. Burns was losing hope and health, and caring less and less for the world's favour and the world's friendships. He had lost largely in self-respect as well as in the respect of friends. The loss gave him little heart to write.

Burns's correspondents, as far as we know them, numbered over a hundred and fifty persons. The number is large and significant. Neither Gray, nor Cowper, nor Byron commanded so wide a circle. They had not the far-reaching sympathies of Burns. They were all more or less fastidious in their choice of correspondents. Burns, on the contrary, was as catholic, or as careless, in his friendships as his own *Caesar*—who

"Wad spend an hour caressin'
Ev'n wi' a tinkler gipsy's messan."

He moved freely up and down the whole social scale, blind to the imaginary distinctions of blood and title and the extrinsic differences of wealth, seeing true superiority in an honest manly heart, and bearing himself wherever he found it as an equal and a brother. His correspondents were of every social grade—peers and peasants; of every intellectual attainment—philosophers like Dugald Stewart, and simple swains like Thomas Orr; and of almost every variety of calling, from professional men of recognised eminence to obscure shopkeepers, cottars, and tradesmen. They include servant-girls, gentlewomen, and ladies of titled rank; country schoolmasters and college professors; men of law of all degrees, from poor John Richmond, a plain law-clerk with a lodging in the Lawnmarket, to the

Honourable Henry Erskine, Dean of the Faculty; farmers, small and large; lairds, large and small; shoemakers and shopkeepers; ministers, bankers, and doctors; printers, booksellers, editors; knights, earls—nay, a duke; factors and wine-merchants; army officers, and officers of Excise. His female correspondents were women of superior intelligence and accomplishments. They can lay claim to a large proportion of his letters. Mrs. McLehose takes forty-eight; Mrs. Dunlop, forty-two; Maria Riddell, eighteen; Peggy Chalmers, eleven. These four ladies received among them rather more than one-fourth of the whole of his published correspondence. No four of his male correspondents can be accredited with so many, even though George Thomson for his individual share claims fifty-six.

It is rather remarkable that so few of the letters are addressed to his own relatives. His cousin, James Burness of Montrose, and his own younger brother William receive, indeed, ten and eight respectively; but to his other brother Gilbert, with whom he was on the most affectionate and confidential terms, there fall but three; to his wife only two; one to his father; and none to either his sisters or his mother. A maternal uncle, Samuel Brown, is favoured with one—if, indeed, the old man was not scandalised with it—and there are two to James Armour, mason in Mauchline, his somewhat stony-hearted father-in-law.

Burns's letters exhibit quite as much variety of mood—seldom, of course, so picturesquely conveyed—as his poems. He is, in promiscuous alternation, refined, gross, sentimental, serious, humorous, indignant, repentant, dignified, vulgar, tender, manly, sceptical, reverential, rakish, pathetic, sympathetic, satirical, playful, pitiably self-abased, mysteriously self-exalted. His letters are confessions and revelations. They are as sincerely and spontaneously autobiographical of his inner life as the sacred lyrics of David the Hebrew. They were indited with as much free fearless abandonment. The advice he gave to young Andrew to keep something to himsel', not to be told even to a bosom crony, was a maxim of worldly prudence which he himself did not practice. He did not "reck his own rede." And, though that habit of unguarded expression brought upon him the wrath and revenge of the Philistines, and kept him in material poverty all his days, yet, prompted as it always was by sincerity, and nearly always by absolute truth, it has made the manhood of to-day richer, stronger, and nobler. The world to-day has all the more the courage of its opinions that Burns exercised as a right the freedom of sincere and enlightened speech—and suffered for his bravery.

The subjects of his letters are numerous, and, to a pretty large extent, of much the same sort as the subjects of his poems. Often, indeed, you have the anticipation of an image or a sentiment which his poetry has made familiar. You have a glimpse of green buds which afterwards unfold into fragrance and colour. This is an interesting connection, of which one or two examples may be given. So early as 1781 he wrote to Alison Begbie—"Once you are convinced I am sincere, I am perfectly certain you have too much goodness and humanity to allow an honest man to languish in suspense only because he loves you too well." Alison Begbie becomes Mary Morison, and the sentiment, so elegantly turned in prose for her, is thus melodiously transmuted for the lady-loves of all languishing lovers—

"O Mary, canst thou wreck his peace
Wha for thy sake would gladly dee,
Or canst thou break that heart of his
Wha's only faut is loving thee?
      If love for love thou wiltna gie,
At least be pity on me shown:
A thocht ungentle canna be
The thocht o' Mary Morison!"

Again, in the first month of 1783 he writes to Murdoch, the schoolmaster—"I am quite indolent about those great concerns that set the bustling busy sons of care agog; and if I have wherewith to answer for the present hour, I am very easy with regard to anything further. Even the last worst shift of the unfortunate and wretched does not greatly terrify me." Just one year later this sentiment was sent current in the well-known stanza concluding—

"But, Davie lad, ne'er fash your head
Though we hae little gear;
We're fit to win our daily bread
As lang's we're hale an' fier;
Mair speer na, nor fear na;
Auld age ne'er mind a fig,
The last o't, the warst o't,
Is only for to beg!"

Again, in the letter last referred to occurs the passage—"I am a strict economist, not indeed for the sake of the money, but one of the principal parts in my composition is a kind of pride, and I scorn to fear the face of any man living. Above everything I abhor as hell the idea of sneaking into a corner to avoid a dun." This is metrically rendered, in May 1786, in the following lines:—

"To catch dame Fortune's golden smile,
Assiduous wait upon her,
And gather gear by every wile
That's justified by honour:—
Not for to hide it in a hedge,
Nor for a train attendant,
But for the glorious privilege
Of being independent."

It would be easy to multiply examples: he is jostled in his letters by market-men before he is "hog-shouthered and jundied" by them in his verse; and the legends of Alloway Kirk are narrated in a letter to Grose before the immortal tale of Tam o'Shanter is woven for *The Antiquities of Scotland.*

There is nothing morbid or narrow in Burns's letters. They are frank and healthy. You can spend a day over them, and feel at the end of it as if you had been wandering at large through the freedom of nature. They seem to have been written in the open air. The first condition necessary to an appreciative understanding of them is to concern yourself with the sentiment. And, indeed, the strength and sincerity of the sentiment by-and-by draw you away to oblivion of the style, however much it may at first strike you as redundant and affected. They are not the letters of a literary man. They have nothing suggestive of the studious chamber and the midnight lamp. There is often a narrowness of idea in the merely literary man which limits his auditory to men of his peculiar pattern. To this narrowness Burns, with all his faults of style, was a stranger. His letters are the utterances of a man who refused to be imprisoned in any single department of human thought. He was no specialist, pinned to one standpoint, and making the width of the world commensurate with the narrowness of his own horizon. He moved about, he looked abroad; he had no pet subject, no restricted field of study; nature and human nature in their multitudinous phases and many retreats were his range, and he expressed his views as freely and vigorously as he took them.

The general tone of the letters is high. The subject is not seldom of supreme interest. Questions are discussed which are rarely discussed in ordinary correspondence. The writer rises above creeds and formularies and arbitrarily established rule. He speculates on a theology beyond the bounds of Calvinism, on a philosophy of the soul above the dialectics of the schoolmen, on a morality at variance with conventional law. He interrogates the intuitions of the mind and the intimations of nature in order that, if possible, he may learn something of the soul's origin, destiny, and supremest duty. But let us hear himself:—

4

(a) "I have ever looked on mankind in the lump to be nothing better   than a foolish, head-strong, credulous, unthinking mob; and their universal belief has ever had extremely little weight with me.... I am drawn by conviction like a Man, not by a halter like an Ass."

(b) "*'On Earth Discord! A gloomy Heaven above opening its jealous gates to the nineteen-thousandth part of the tithe of mankind! And below an inexorable Hell expanding its leviathan jaws for the vast residue of mortals!'* O doctrine comfortable and healing to the weary wounded soul of man! Ye sons and daughters of affliction, to whom day brings no pleasure and night yields no rest, be comforted! 'Tis one to but nineteen hundred housand that your situation will mend in this world, and 'tis nineteen hundred thousand to one, by the dogmas of theology, that you will be damned eternally in the world to come."

(c) "A pillar that bears us up amid the wreck of misfortune and   misery is to be found in those feelings and sentiments which, however   the sceptic may deny or the enthusiast disfigure them, are yet, I am convinced, original and component parts of the human soul; those; *senses of the mind*, if I may be allowed the expression, which link us to the awful obscure realities of an all-powerful and equally beneficent God and a world-to-come beyond death and the grave."

(d) "Can it be possible that when I resign this frail, feverish being I shall still find myself in conscious existence?... Shall I yet be warm in life, seeing and seen, enjoying and enjoyed? Ye venerable Sages and holy Flamens, is there probability in your conjectures, truth in your stories, of another world beyond death, or are they all alike baseless visions and fabricated fables? If there is another life, it must only be for the just, the benevolent, the amiable, and the humane; what a flattering idea then is a world to come! Would to God I as firmly believed it as I ardently wish it!... Jesus Christ, thou amiablest of characters! I trust thou art no impostor.... I trust that in Thee shall all the families of the earth be blessed."

(e) "From the seeming nature of the human mind, as well as from the evident imperfections in the administration of affairs, in both the natural and moral worlds, there must be a retributive scene of existence beyond the grave."

(f) "I never hear the loud solitary whistle of the curlew in a summer's noon, or the wild mixing cadence of a troop of grey plover in an autumn morning, without feeling an elevation of soul like the enthusiasm of Devotion or Poetry. Tell me, my dear friend, to what can this be owing? Are we a piece of machinery, that, like the Æolian harp, passive, takes the impression of the passing accident? Or do these workings argue something within us above the trodden clod?"

(g) "Gracious Heaven! why this disparity between our wishes and our powers? Why is the most generous wish to make others blest, impotent and ineffectual?... Out upon the world! say I, that its affairs are administered so ill."

(h) "At first glance, several of your propositions startled me as paradoxical. That the martial clangour of a trumpet had something in it vastly more grand, heroic, and sublime than the twingle-twangle of a jew's-harp; that the delicate flexure of a rose-twig, when the half-blown flower is heavy with the tears of the dawn, was infinitely more beautiful and elegant than the upright stub of a burdock; and that, from something innate and independent of all associations of ideas—these I had set down as irrefragable orthodox truths."[a]

(i) "O, I could curse circumstances, and the coarse tie of human laws which keeps fast what common-sense would loose, and which bars that happiness it cannot give—happiness which otherwise love and honour would warrant!"

(j) "If there is no man on earth to whom your heart and affections are justly due, it may savour of imprudence, but never of criminality, to bestow that heart and those affections where you please. The God of love meant and made those delicious attachments to be bestowed on somebody."

The inequalities of fortune, the pleasures of friendship, the miseries of poverty, the glories of independence, the privileges of wealth allied to generosity, the sin of ingratitude, and similar topics, are continually recurring to prove the elevation at which his spirit usually soared and surveyed mankind. It has been charged against him[b] that these subjects were not the food of his daily contemplation, but were lugged into his letters for the sake of effect, and that their clumsy introduction was frequently apologised for by the complaint that the writer had nothing else to write about. The frequent apologies here spoken of will be hard to find, and the critic's only reason for advancing the charge, for which he would fain find support in the fancied apologies of Burns, is that many of the letters "relate neither to facts nor feelings peculiarly connected with the author or his correspondent." This only means that a very large proportion of Burns's letters are not like the letters of ordinary men, and therefore do not satisfy the critic's idea or definition of a letter. They treat of themes that are not specially *à propos* of passing events, and therefore they are forced and affected. Few are likely to be imposed upon by such shallow reasoning. Another critic[c] avers that "while Burns says nothing of difficulties at all, he yet leaves an admirable letter, out of nothing, in your hands!" We may pit the one critic against the other, and so leave them, while we peruse the letters, and form an opinion for ourselves.

While both the verse and the prose of Burns are revelations, his letters reveal more than his poems the failings and frailties of the man. His poems, taken altogether, shew him at his best, as we wish to—and as we mainly do—remember him; a man to be loved, admired, even envied, and by no means pitied, for his soul, though often vexed with the irritations incidental to an obscure and toiling lot, has a strength and buoyancy which readily raise it to divine altitudes, where it might well be content to see and smile at the petty class distinctions and the paltry social tyranny from which those irritations chiefly spring. His letters, on the other hand, present him to us less frequently on those commanding altitudes. He is oftener careful and concerned about many things, groping occasionally in the world's ways for the world's gifts, and handicapped in the struggle for them by a contemptuous and half-hearted adoption of the world's methods of winning them.

The same personality that stands forth in the poems is everywhere present in all essential features in the letters. We have in the latter the same view of life, present and future; the same fierce contentment with honest poverty; the same aggressive independency of manhood; the same patriotism, susceptibility to female loveliness, love of sociality, undaunted likes and dislikes. The humour is the same, though often too elaborately expressed.[d] In one important respect, however, his letters fail to reflect that image of him which his poetry presents. It is remarkable that his descriptions of rural nature, and one might well add of rustic life, so full and plentiful in his verse, are so few and slight in his letters. He seems to have reserved these descriptions for his verse.

The best, because the most genuine, biography of Burns is furnished by his own writings. His letters will, if carefully studied, disprove many of the positions taken up so confidently by would-be interpreters of his history. It is not the purpose of this discursive paper to take up the details of the Clarinda episode; but philandering is scarcely the word by which to describe the mutual relations of the lovers. As for Mrs. M'Lehose, the severest thing that can with justice be said against her is that, if she maintained her virtue, she endangered her reputation. One remarkable position taken up by a recent writer[e] on the subject of Burns's amours is, that he never really loved any woman, and least of all Jean Armour. The letters would rather warrant the converse of his statement. They go to prove that while Burns's affections were more than oriental in their strength and liberality, they were especially centred upon Jean. He felt "a miserable blank in his heart with want of her;" "a rooted attachment for her;" "had no reason on her part to rue his marriage with her;" and "never saw where he could have made it better." If Burns was never really in love, it is more than probable that the whole world has been mistaking some other passion for it. It is this same writer who in one breath speaks of Burns philandering with Clarinda, and yet declaring his attachment to her in the best songs he ever wrote. Another error which the letters should correct is the belief expressed in some quarters that Burns was no longer capable of producing poetry after his fatal residence in Edinburgh. It was, as a matter of fact, subsequent to his residence in Edinburgh that he wrote the poems for which he is now, and for which he will be longest, famous—namely, his songs. The writer already referred to compares the composition of these songs to the carving of cherry-stones. They were, he says in effect, the amusement of a man who could do nothing better in literature! The world has agreed that they are the best things Burns has done; and rates him for their sake in the highest rank of its poets. The truth is that Burns came to Ellisland with numerous schemes of future poetical work, vigorous hopes of carrying some of them, and an inspiration and faculty of utterance unimpaired. It was in Dumfriesshire that he composed the most tenderly and melodiously seraphic of his lyrics—"To Mary in Heaven" and "Highland Mary;" the most powerful and popular of his narrative poems—"Tam O' Shanter;" the first of all patriotic odes—"Bruce's Address to his Army"; and the noblest manifesto of the rights and hopes of manhood—"A Man's a Man for a' that."

With one word on his style as a prose-writer this short paper must close. The most diverse opinions have been uttered on the subject. The critics trip up each other with charming independency. To Jeffrey they seemed to be "all composed as exercises and for display." Carlyle declared that they were written "for the most part with singular force and even gracefulness," and that when Burns wrote "to trusted friends on real interests, his style became simple, vigorous, expressive, sometimes even beautiful." Dr. Waddell prefers him to Cowper and Byron as a letter-writer. Scott, while allowing passages of great eloquence, found in the letters "strong marks of affectation, with a tincture of pedantry." Taine thinks "Burns brought ridicule on himself by imitating the men of the academy and the court." Lockhart thought, with Walker, that "he accommodated his style to the tastes" of his correspondents. And so on.

It is worth while to learn from Burns himself what he thought of his talent for prose-composition. And in the first place it is to be noted that he practised prose-composition before he took to poetry. At sixteen he was carrying on an extensive literary correspondence, which was virtually a competition in essay-writing. He kept copies of the letters he liked best, and was flattered to find that he was superior to his correspondents. He studied the essayists of Queen Anne's time, and formed his style upon theirs, and that of their most distinguished followers. Steele, Addison, Swift, Sterne, and Mackenzie were his models. He liked their rounded sentences, and caught their conventional phrases. He found delight in imitating them. He volunteered his services with the pen on behalf of his fellow-swains. He became the "Complete Letter-Writer" of his parish, and was proud of his function and his faculty. He was aware of his "abilities at a billet-doux." To the very last he had a high opinion of himself as a writer of letters. He speaks of one letter being in his "very best manner;" and of waiting for an hour of inspiration to write another that should be as good. He retained copies of about thirty of his longer letters, and had them bound for preservation.

The most serious, almost the only charge brought against the prose style of Burns is the charge of affectation more or less occasional. All the earlier critics make it or imply it, and with such an apparent show of proof that it has generally been believed. Later critics, while unable to deny the feature of his style which so looks like affectation, have explained it to such good effect as to make it appear a beauty; they have asked us to regard it as the happy result of a sympathetic mind adapting itself to the object of its address. This looks very like blaming Burns's correspondents for the badness of his style. There is some truth in the explanation, putting it even so extremely. But when this allowance is made, there still remains a wide and well-marked difference between his use of English prose and his mastery of Scottish verse. The latter is complete—it is the mastery of an originator of style. The former, on the other hand, is the attainment of a clever pupil when the sentiment is commonplace; when it is deep and vehement, it is often, in the language of Carlyle, "the effort of a man to express something which he has no organ fit for expressing." Common people, to whom niceties of style are unknown, and who read primarily or exclusively for the sake of the matter, perceive nothing of this affectation, and think scarcely less highly of Burns's letters than they do of his poetry.

J. LOGIE ROBERTSON.
7 LOCKHARTON TERRACE, SLATEFORD, EDINBURGH.

[a] This is really the exposure of an absurdity.
[b] By Jeffrey.
[c] Dr. Hately Waddell.

[d] See, for example, the *Cheese* Letter to Peter Hill, or the *Snail's-horns* Letter to Mrs. Dunlop.
[e] Mr. R. L. Stevenson.

GENERAL CORRESPONDENCE.
LETTERS
I.—To ELLISON OR ALISON BEGBIE (?)[1]

What you may think of this letter when you see the name that subscribes it I cannot know; and perhaps I ought to make a long preface of apologies for the freedom I am going to take; but as my heart means no offence, but, on the contrary, is rather too warmly interested in your favour,—for that reason I hope you will forgive me when I tell you that I most sincerely and affectionately love you. I am a stranger in these matters, A——, as I assure you that you are the first woman to whom I ever made such a declaration; so I declare I am at a loss how to proceed.

I have more than once come into your company with a resolution to say what I have just now told you; but my resolution always failed me, and even now my heart trembles for the consequence of what I have said. I hope, my dear A——, you will not despise me because I am ignorant of the flattering arts of courtship: I hope my inexperience of the work will plead for me. I can only say I sincerely love you, and there is nothing on earth I so ardently wish for, or that could possibly give me so much happiness, as one day to see you mine.

I think you cannot doubt my sincerity, as I am sure that whenever I see you my very looks betray me: and when once you are convinced I am sincere, I am perfectly certain you have too much goodness and humanity to allow an honest man to languish in suspense only because he loves you too well. And I am certain that in such a state of anxiety as I myself at present feel, an absolute denial would be a much preferable state.

[1] The original MS. of the foregoing letter is the property of John Adam, Esquire, Greenock, and the letter was first published in 1878. If it is a genuine love-letter, and not a mere exercise in love-letter writing, it was probably the first of the short series to Alison Begbie, who is supposed to have been the daughter of a small farmer, and who has been identified with the Mary Morison of the well-known lyric. The sentiment of the last paragraph of the letter agrees with the sentiment of the last stanza of the song.

II.-To ELLISON BEGBIE.
[LOCHLIE, 1780.]

MY DEAR E.,—I do not remember, in the course of your acquaintance and mine, ever to have heard your opinion on the ordinary way of falling in love, amongst people in our station in life; I do not mean the persons who proceed in the way of bargain, but those whose affection is really placed on the person.

Though I be, as you know very well, but a very awkward lover myself, yet, as I have some opportunities of observing the conduct of others who are much better skilled in the affair of courtship than I am, I often think it is owing to lucky chance, more than to good management, that there are not more unhappy marriages than usually are.

It is natural for a young fellow to like the acquaintance of the females, and customary for him to keep them company when occasion serves; some one of them is more agreeable to him than the rest; there is something, he knows not what, pleases him, he knows not how, in her company. This I take to be what is called love with the greater part of us; and I must own, my dear E., it is a hard game such a one as you have to play when you meet with such a lover. You cannot refuse but he is sincere, and yet though you use him ever so favourably, perhaps in a few months, or at farthest in a year or two, the same unaccountable fancy may make him as distractedly fond of another, whilst you are quite forgot. I am aware that perhaps the next time I have the pleasure of seeing you, you may bid me take my own lesson home, and tell me that the passion I have professed for you is perhaps one of those transient flashes I have been describing; but I hope, my dear E., you will do me the justice to believe me, when I assure you that the love I have for you is founded on the sacred principles of

8

virtue and honour, and by consequence so long as you continue possessed of those amiable qualities which first inspired my passion for you, so long must I continue to love you. Believe me, my dear, it is love like this alone which can render the marriage state happy. People may talk of flames and raptures as long as they please, and a warm fancy, with a flow of youthful spirits, may make them feel something like what they describe; but sure I am the nobler faculties of the mind with kindred feelings of the heart can only be the foundation of friendship, and it has always been my opinion that the married life was only friendship in a more exalted degree.

If you will be so good as to grant my wishes, and it should please Providence to spare us to the latest periods of life, I can look forward and see that, even then, though bent down with wrinkled age—even then, when all other worldly circumstances will be indifferent to me, I will regard my E. with the tenderest affection, and for this plain reason, because she is still possessed of those noble qualities, improved to a much higher degree, which first inspired my affection for her.

O! happy state, when souls each other draw,
Where love is liberty, and nature law.

I know, were I to speak in such a style to many a girl, who thinks herself possessed of no small share of sense, she would think it ridiculous—but the language of the heart is, my dear E., the only courtship I shall ever use to you.

When I look over what I have written, I am sensible it is vastly different from the ordinary style of courtship—but I shall make no apology—I know your good nature will excuse what your good sense may see amiss.

III.—TO ELLISON BEGBIE.
[LOCHLIE, 1780.]

I verily believe, my dear E., that the pure genuine feelings of love are as rare in the world as the pure genuine principles of virtue and piety. This, I hope, will account for the uncommon style of all my letters to you. By uncommon, I mean their being written in such a serious manner, which, to tell you the truth, has made me often afraid lest you should take me for some zealous bigot, who conversed with his mistress as he would converse with his minister. I don't know how it is, my dear; for though, except your company, there is nothing on earth gives me so much pleasure as writing to you, yet it never gives me those giddy raptures so much talked of among lovers. I have often thought, that if a well-grounded affection be not really a part of virtue, 'tis something extremely akin to it. Whenever the thought of my E. warms my heart, every feeling of humanity, every principle of generosity, kindles in my breast. It extinguishes every dirty spark of malice and envy, which are but too apt to infest me. I grasp every creature in the arms of universal benevolence, and equally participate in the pleasures of the happy, and sympathise with the miseries of the unfortunate. I assure you, my dear, I often look up to the Divine disposer of events with an eye of gratitude for the blessing which I hope He intends to bestow on me, in bestowing you. I sincerely wish that He may bless my endeavours to make your life as comfortable and happy as possible, both in sweetening the rougher parts of my natural temper, and bettering the unkindly circumstances of my fortune. This, my dear, is a passion, at least in my view, worthy of a man, and, I will add, worthy of a Christian. The sordid earth-worm may profess love to a woman's person, whilst, in reality, his affection is centred in her pocket; and the slavish drudge may go a-wooing as he goes to the horse-market, to choose one who is stout and firm, and as we say of an old horse, one who will be a good drudge and draw kindly. I disdain their dirty, puny ideas. I would be heartily out of humour with myself, if I thought I were capable of having so poor a notion of the sex, which were designed to crown the pleasures of society. Poor devils! I don't envy them their happiness who have such notions. For my part, I propose quite other pleasures with my dear partner.

IV.—TO ELLISON BEGBIE.
[LOCHLIE, 1781.]

MY DEAR E.,—I have often thought it a peculiarly unlucky circumstance in love, that though, in every other situation in life, telling the truth is not only the safest, but actually by far the easiest way of proceeding, a lover is never under greater difficulty in acting, or more puzzled for expression, than when his passion is sincere, and his intentions are honourable. I do not think that it is very difficult for a person of ordinary capacity to talk of love and fondness which are not felt, and to make vows of constancy and fidelity which are never intended to be performed, if he be villain enough to practice such detestable conduct; but to a man whose heart glows with the principles of integrity and truth, and who sincerely loves a woman of amiable person, uncommon refinement of sentiment, and purity of manners—to such a one, in such circumstances, I can assure you, my dear, from my own feelings at this present moment, courtship is a task indeed. There is such a number of foreboding fears and distrustful anxieties crowd into my mind when I am in your company, or when I sit down to write to you, that what to speak or what to write, I am altogether at a loss.

There is one rule which I have hitherto practised, and which I shall invariably keep with you, and that is, honestly to tell you the plain truth. There is something so mean and unmanly in the arts of dissimulation and falsehood, that I am surprised they can be used by any one in so noble, so generous a passion as virtuous love. No, my dear E., I shall never endeavour to gain your favour by such detestable practices. If you will be so good and so generous as to admit me for your partner, your companion, your bosom friend through life, there is nothing on this side of eternity shall give me greater transport; but I shall never think of purchasing your hand by any arts unworthy of a man, and, I will add, of a Christian. There is one thing, my dear, which I earnestly request of you, and it is this: that you would soon either put an end to my hopes by a peremptory refusal, or cure me of my fears by a generous consent.

It would oblige me much if you would send me a line or two when convenient. I shall only add, further, that if behaviour, regulated (though perhaps but very imperfectly) by the rules of honour and virtue, if a heart devoted to love and esteem you, and an earnest endeavour to promote your happiness; if these are qualities you would wish in a friend, in a husband, I hope you shall ever find them in your real friend and sincere lover.

V.-To ELLISON BEGBOE.
[LOCHLIE, 1781.]

I ought, in good manners, to have acknowledged the receipt of your letter before this time, but my heart was so shocked with the contents of it, that I can scarcely yet collect my thoughts so as to write you on the subject. I will not attempt to describe what I felt on receiving your letter. I read it over and over, again and again, and though it was in the politest language of refusal, still it was peremptory; "you were sorry you could not make me a return, but you wish me" what, without you, I never can obtain, "you wish me all kind of happiness." It would be weak and unmanly to say that without you I never can be happy; but sure I am, that sharing life with you would have given it a relish, that, wanting you, I can never taste.

Your uncommon personal advantages, and your superior good sense, do not so much strike me; these, possibly, in a few instances may be met with in others; but that amiable goodness, that tender feminine softness, that endearing sweetness of disposition, with all the charming offspring of a warm feeling heart—these I never again expect to meet with, in such a degree, in this world. All these charming qualities, heightened by an education much beyond anything I have ever met in any woman I ever dared to approach, have made an impression on my heart that I do not think the world can ever efface. My imagination has fondly flattered myself with a wish, I dare not say it ever reached a hope, that possibly I might one day call you mine. I had formed the most delightful images, and my fancy fondly brooded over them; but now I am wretched for the loss of what I really had no right to expect. I must now think no more of you as a mistress; still I presume to ask to be admitted as a friend. As such I wish to be allowed to wait on you, and as I expect to remove in a few days a little further off, and you, I suppose, will soon leave this place, I wish to see or hear from you soon; and if an expression should perhaps escape me, rather too warm for friendship, I hope you will pardon it in, my dear Miss—, (pardon me the dear expression for once) R. B.

VI.—TO HIS FATHER.

IRVINE, *December 27,* 1781.

HONOURED SIR,—I have purposely delayed writing in the hope that I should have the pleasure of seeing you on New Year's day; but work comes so hard upon us that I do not choose to be absent on that account, as well as for some other little reasons which I shall tell you at meeting. My health is nearly the same as when you were here, only my sleep is a little sounder, and on the whole I am rather better than otherwise, though I mend by very slow degrees. The weakness of my nerves has so debilitated my mind that I dare neither review my past wants nor look forward into futurity; for the least anxiety or perturbation in my breast produces most unhappy effects on my whole frame. Sometimes, indeed, when for an hour or two my spirits are a little lightened, I glimmer a little into futurity; but my principal, and indeed my only pleasurable, employment, is looking backwards and forwards in a moral and religious way; I am quite transported at the thought, that ere long, perhaps very soon, I shall bid an eternal adieu to all the pains, and uneasiness, and disquietudes of this weary life; for I assure you I am heartily tired of it; and, if I do not very much deceive myself, I could contentedly and gladly resign it.

The soul, uneasy, and confin'd at home,
Rests and expatiates in a life to come.

It is for this reason I am more pleased with the 15th, 16th, and 17th verses of the 7th chapter of Revelation[2] than with any ten times as many verses in the whole Bible, and would not exchange the whole noble enthusiasm with which they inspire me, for all that this world has to offer. As for this world, I despair of ever making a figure in it I am not formed for the bustle of the busy, nor the flutter of the gay. I shall never again be capable of entering into such scenes. Indeed, I am altogether unconcerned at the thoughts of this life. I foresee that poverty and obscurity probably await me, and I am in some measure prepared, and daily preparing, to meet them. I have but just time and paper to return you my grateful thanks for the lessons of virtue and piety you have given me, which were too much neglected at the time of giving them, but which I hope have been remembered ere it is yet too late. Present my dutiful respects to my mother, and my compliments to Mr. and Mrs. Muir; and with wishing you a merry New-year's day, I shall conclude.—I am, honoured Sir, your dutiful son,

ROBERT BURNESS.

P. S.—My meal is nearly out, but I am going to borrow till I get more.

[2] "Therefore are they before the throne of God, and serve him day and night in his temple; and he that sitteth on the throne shall dwell among them.

They shall hunger no more, neither thirst any more; neither shall the sun light on them, nor any heat.

For the Lamb, which is in the midst of the throne, shall feed them, and shall lead them unto living fountains of waters; and God shall wipe away all tears from their eyes."

VII.—To SIR JOHN WHITEFOORD, BART., OF BALLOCHMYLE.[3]

SIR,—We who subscribe this are both members of St. James's Lodge, Tarbolton, and one of us in the office of warden, and as we have the honour of having you for master of our lodge we hope you will excuse this freedom, as you are the proper person to whom we ought to apply. We look on our Mason Lodge to be a serious matter, both with respect to the character of masonry itself, and likewise as it is a charitable society. This last, indeed, does not interest you further than a benevolent heart is interested in the welfare of its fellow-creatures; but to us, sir, who are of the lower order of mankind, to have a fund in view on which we may with certainty depend to be kept from want, should we be in circumstances of distress, or old age—this is a matter of high importance.

We are sorry to observe that our lodge's affairs with respect to its finances have for a good while been in a wretched situation. We have considerable sums in bills which lie by without being paid, or put in execution, and many of our members never mind their yearly dues, or anything else belonging to the lodge. And since the separation[4] from St. David's we are not sure even of our existence as a lodge. There has been a dispute before the Grand Lodge, but how decided, or if decided at all, we know not.

For these and other reasons we humbly beg the favour of you, as soon as convenient, to call a meeting, and let us consider on some means to retrieve our wretched affairs.—We are, etc.

[3] The MS. of the foregoing joint letter in Burns's handwriting belongs to John Adam, Esquire, Greenock, and the letter was first published in 1878. Burns was first admitted in St. David's (Tarbolton) Lodge in July, 1781. At the separation preferred to he became a member of the new lodge, St. James's, of which, two years afterwards, he was depute-master.

[4] It was in June, 1782.

VIII.—To MR. JOHN MURDOCH, SCHOOL-MASTER, STAPLES INN BUILDINGS, LONDON.

LOCHLIE, *15th January*, 1783.

DEAR SIR,—As I have an opportunity of sending you a letter without putting you to that expense which any production of mine would but ill repay, I embrace it with pleasure, to tell you that I have not forgotten, or ever will forget, the many obligations I lie under to your kindness and friendship.

I do not doubt, Sir, but you will wish to know what has been the result of all the pains of an indulgent father, and a masterly teacher; and I wish I could gratify your curiosity with such a recital as you would be pleased with;—but that is what I am afraid will not be the case. I have, indeed, kept pretty clear of vicious habits; and in this respect, I hope, my conduct will not disgrace the education I have gotten; but as a man of the world, I am most miserably deficient. One would have thought that, bred as I have been, under a father who has figured pretty well as *un homme des affaires*, I might have been what the world calls a pushing active fellow; but to tell you the truth, Sir, there is hardly anything more my reverse. I seem to be one sent into the world to see and observe; and I very easily compound with the knave who tricks me of my money, if there be anything original about him which shows me human nature in a different light from anything I have seen before. In short, the joy of my heart is to "study men, their manners, and their ways;" and for this darling subject, I cheerfully sacrifice every other consideration. I am quite indolent about those great concerns that set the bustling, busy sons of care agog; and if I have to answer for the present hour, I am very easy with regard to anything further. Even the last, worst shift of the unfortunate and the wretched[5]does not much terrify me: I know that even then my talent for what countryfolks call "a sensible crack," when once it is sanctified by a hoary head, would procure me so much esteem that even then—I would learn to be happy. However, I am under no apprehensions about that; for though indolent, yet so far as an extremely delicate constitution permits, I am not lazy; and in many things, especially in tavern matters, I am a strict economist; not, indeed, for the sake of the money; but one of the principal parts in my composition is a kind of pride of stomach; and I scorn to fear the face of any man living: above every thing, I abhor as hell the idea of sneaking in a corner to avoid a dun—possibly some pitiful sordid wretch, whom in my heart I despise and detest. 'Tis this, and this alone, that endears economy to me.[6]

In the matter of books, indeed, I am very profuse. My favourite authors are of the sentimental kind, such as Shenstone, particularly his *Elegies;* Thomson; *Man of Feeling,*—a book I prize next to the Bible; *Man of the World;* Sterne, especially his *Sentimental Journey;* Macpherson's *Ossian*, etc.;—these are the glorious models after which I endeavour to form my conduct, and 'tis incongruous—'tis absurd to suppose that the man whose mind glows with sentiments lighted up at their sacred flame—the man whose heart distends with benevolence to all the human race—he "who can soar above this little scene of things"—can he descend to mind the paltry concerns about which the terrae-filial race fret, and fume, and vex themselves! O, how the glorious triumph swells my heart! I forget that I am a poor insignificant devil, unnoticed and unknown, stalking up and down fairs and markets, when I happen to be in them reading a page or two of mankind, and "catching the manners living as they rise," whilst the men of business jostle me on every side as an idle incumbrance in their way. But, I daresay, I have by this time tired your patience; so I shall conclude with begging you to give Mrs. Murdoch—not my compliments, for that is a mere commonplace story; but my warmest, kindest wishes for her welfare; and accept the same for yourself, from,—Dear Sir, yours, etc.

[5]"The last o't, the warst o't,
Is only for to beg."
—*First Epistle to Davie.*
[6]"For the glorious privilege
Of being independent."
—*Epistle to a Young Friend.*

IX.—To HIS COUSIN, MR. JAMES BURNESS, WRITER, MONTROSE.
LOCHLIE, *21st June, 1783.*

DEAR SIR,—My father received your favour of the both current, and as he has been for some months very poorly in health, and is in his own opinion (and, indeed, in almost every body's else) in a dying condition, he has only, with great difficulty, written a few farewell lines to each of his brothers-in-law. For this melancholy reason, I now hold the pen for him to thank you for your kind letter, and to assure you, Sir, that it shall not be my fault if my father's correspondence in the north die with him. My brother writes to John Caird,[6] and to him I must refer you for the news of our family.

I shall only trouble you with a few particulars relative to the wretched state of this country. Our markets are exceedingly high; oatmeal 17d. and 18d. per peck, and not to be got even at that price. We have indeed been pretty well supplied with quantities of white peas from England and elsewhere, but that resource is likely to fail us, and what will become of us then, particularly the very poorest sort, Heaven only knows. This country, till of late, was flourishing incredibly in the manufacture of silk, lawn, and carpet-weaving; and we are still carrying on a good deal in that way, but much reduced from what it was. We had also a fine trade in the shoe way, but now entirely ruined, and hundreds driven to a starving condition on account of it. Farming is also at a very low ebb with us. Our lands, generally speaking, are mountainous and barren; and our land-holders, full of ideas of farming gathered from the English and the Lothians, and other rich soils in Scotland, make no allowance for the odds of the quality of land, and consequently stretch us much beyond what in the event we will be found able to pay. We are also much at a loss for want of proper methods in our improvements of farming. Necessity compels us to leave our old schemes, and few of us have opportunities of being well informed in new ones. In short, my dear Sir, since the unfortunate beginning of this American war, and its as unfortunate conclusion, this country has been, and still is, decaying very fast. Even in higher life, a couple of Ayrshire noblemen, and the major part of our knights and squires, are all insolvent. A miserable job of a Douglas, Heron & Co.'s bank, which no doubt you have heard of, has undone numbers of them; and imitating English and French, and other foreign luxuries and fopperies, has ruined as many more. There is a great trade of smuggling carried on along our coasts, which, however destructive to the interests of the kingdom at large, certainly enriches this corner of it, but too often at the expense of our morals. However, it enables individuals to make, at least for a time, a splendid appearance; but Fortune, as is usual with her when she is uncommonly lavish of her favours, is generally even with them at last; and happy were it for numbers of them if she would leave them no worse than when she found them.

My mother sends you a small present of a cheese; 'tis but a very little one, as our last year's stock is sold off; but if you could fix on any correspondent in Edinburgh or Glasgow, we would send you a proper one in the season. Mrs. Black promises to take the cheese under her care so far, and then to send it to you by the Stirling carrier.

I shall conclude this long letter with assuring you that I shall be very happy to hear from you, or any of our friends in your country, when opportunity serves.

My father sends you, probably for the last time in this world, his warmest wishes for your welfare and happiness; and my mother and the rest of the family desire to inclose their kind compliments to you, Mrs. Burness, and the rest of your family, along with those of, dear Sir, your affectionate cousin,

X.-To MR. JAMES BURNESS, WRITER, MONTROSE.
LOCHLIE, 17th Feb. 1784.

DEAR COUSIN,—I would have returned you my thanks for your kind favour of the 13th of December sooner, had it not been that I waited to give you an account of that melancholy event, which, for some time past, we have from day to day expected.

On the 13th current I lost the best of fathers. Though, to be sure, we have had long warning of the impending stroke, still the feelings of nature claim their part, and I cannot recollect the tender endearments and parental lessons of the best of friends and ablest of instructors, without feeling what perhaps the calmer dictates of reason would partly condemn.

I hope my father's friends in your country will not let their connection in this place die with him. For my part I shall ever with pleasure—with pride, acknowledge my connection with those who were allied by the ties of blood and friendship to a man whose memory I shall ever honour and revere.

I expect, therefore, my dear Sir, you will not neglect any opportunity of letting me hear from you, which will very much oblige,—My dear Cousin, yours sincerely,
ROBERT BURNESS.

XI.—To MR. JAMES BURNESS, WRITER, MONTROSE.
MOSSGIEL, *3rd August* 1784.

MY DEAR SIR,—I ought in gratitude to have acknowledged the receipt of your last kind letter before this time, but, without troubling you with any apology, I shall proceed to inform you that our family are all in good health at present, and we were very happy with the unexpected favour of John Caird's[6a]company for nearly two weeks, and I must say it of him that he is one of the most agreeable, facetious, warm-hearted lads I was ever acquainted with.

We have been surprised with one of the most extraordinary phenomena in the moral world, which, I dare say, has happened in the course of this half century. We have had a party of Presbytery relief, as they call themselves, for some time in this country. A pretty thriving society of them has been in the burgh of Irvine for some years past, till about two years ago a Mrs. Buchan from Glasgow came among them, and began to spread some fanatical notions of religion among them, and in a short time made many converts; and among others their preacher, Mr. Whyte, who, upon that account, has been suspended and formally deposed by his brethren. He continued, however, to preach in private to his party, and was supported, both he, and their spiritual mother, as they affect to call old Buchan, by the contributions of the rest, several of whom were in good circumstances; till, in spring last, the populace rose and mobbed Mrs. Buchan, and put her out of the town; on which all her followers voluntarily quitted the place likewise, and with such precipitation that many of them never shut their doors behind them; one left a washing on the green, another a cow bellowing at the crib without food or anybody to mind her, and after several stages they are fixed at present in the neighbourhood of Dumfries. Their tenets are a strange jumble of enthusiastic jargon; among others, she pretends to give them the Holy Ghost by breathing on them, which she does with postures and practices that are scandalously indecent; they have likewise disposed of all their effects, and hold a community of goods, and live nearly an idle life, carrying on a great farce of pretended devotion in barns and woods, where they lodge and lie all together, and hold likewise a community of women, as it is another of their tenets that they can commit no moral sin. I am personally acquainted with most of them, and I can assure you the above mentioned are facts.

14

This, my dear Sir, is one of the many instances of the folly of leaving the guidance of sound reason and common sense in matters of religion.

Whenever we neglect or despise these sacred monitors, the whimsical notions of a perturbated brain are taken for the immediate influences of the Deity, and the wildest fanaticism, and the most inconsistent absurdities, will meet with abetters and converts. Nay, I have often thought, that the more out-of-the-way and ridiculous the fancies are, if once they are sanctified under the sacred name of religion, the unhappy mistaken votaries are the more firmly glued to them.

I expect to hear from you soon, and I beg you will remember me to all friends, and believe me to be, my dear Sir, your affectionate cousin,

ROBERT BURNESS.

P.S.—Direct to me at Mossgiel, parish of Mauchline, near Kilmarnock.

[6a] Probably John Caird, junior, as the father would be over sixty if he was about his wife's age, and she, Elspat Burnes, was born, we know, in 1725.

XII.—TO THOMAS ORR, PARK, KIRKOSWALD.

DEAR THOMAS,—I am much obliged to you for your last letter, though I assure you the contents of it gave me no manner of concern. I am presently so cursedly taken in with an affair of gallantry that I am very glad Peggy[7] is off my hand, as I am at present embarrassed enough[7a] without her. I don't choose to enter into particulars in writing, but never was a poor rakish rascal in a more pitiful taking. I should be glad to see you to tell you the affair.—Meanwhile I am your friend, ROBERT BURNESS.

MOSSGAVIL, 11*th Nov.* 1784.

[7] Peggy Thomson.

[7a] Birth of his illegitimate child by Elizabeth Paton, once a servant with his father at Lochlie.

XIII.-TO MISS MARGARET KENNEDY.[8]

[*A young lady of seventeen, when this letter was addressed to her, and on a visit to Mrs. Gavin Hamilton at Mauchline.*]

[*Probably Autumn,* 1785.]

MADAM,—Permit me to present you with the enclosed song as a small though grateful tribute for the honour of your acquaintance. I have in these verses attempted some faint sketch of your portrait in the unembellished simple manner of descriptive truth. Flattery I leave to your lovers whose exaggerating fancies may make them imagine you are still nearer perfection than you really are.

Poets, Madam, of all mankind, feel most forcibly the powers of beauty,—as, if they are really poets of nature's making, their feelings must be finer and their taste more delicate than most of the world. In the cheerful bloom of spring, or the pensive mildness of autumn, the grandeur of summer, or the hoary majesty of winter, the poet feels a charm unknown to the most of his species. Even the sight of a fine flower, or the company of a fine woman (by far the finest part of God's works below), has sensations for the poetic heart that the herd of men are strangers to. On this last account, Madam, I am, as in many other things, indebted to Mr. Hamilton's kindness in introducing me to you. Your lovers may view you with a wish—I look on you with pleasure; their hearts in your presence may glow with desire—mine rises with admiration.

That the arrows of misfortune, however they should, as incident to humanity, glance a slight wound, may never reach your heart; that the snares of villainy may never beset you in the road of life; that innocence may hand you by the path of honour to the dwelling of peace—is the sincere wish of him who has the honour to be, etc. R. B.

[8] Niece of Sir Andrew Cathcait, of Carleton. A melancholy interest attaches to her subsequent history. Burns's prayers for her happiness were unavailing.

XIV.—TO MISS ——, AYRSHIRE.[9]

[1785.]

MY DEAR COUNTRYWOMAN,—I am so impatient to show you that I am once more at peace with you, that I send you the book I mentioned, directly, rather than wait the uncertain time of my seeing you. I am afraid I have mislaid or lost Collins's Poems, which I promised to Miss Irvin. If I can find them I will forward them by you; if not, you must apologise for me.

I know you will laugh at it when I tell you that your piano and you together have played the deuce somehow about my heart. My breast has been widowed these many months, and I thought myself proof against the fascinating witchcraft; but I am afraid you will "feelingly convince me what I am.". I say, I am afraid, because I am not sure what is the matter with me. I have one miserable bad symptom,—when you whisper, or look kindly to another, it gives me a draught of damnation. I have a kind of wayward wish to be with you ten minutes by yourself, though what I would say, Heaven above knows, for I am sure I know not. I have no formed design in all this; but just, in the nakedness of my heart, write you down a mere matter-of-fact story. You may perhaps give yourself airs of distance on this, and that will completely cure me; but I wish you would not; just let us meet, if you please, in the old beaten way of friendship.

I will not subscribe myself your humble servant, for that is a phrase, I think, at least fifty miles off from the heart; but I will conclude with sincerely wishing that the Great Protector of innocence may shield you from the barbed dart of calumny, and hand you by the covert snare of deceit. R. B.

[9] Lady unidentified.

XV.—TO MR. JOHN RICHMOND, LAW CLERK, EDINBURGH.[10]
MOSSGIEL, *Feb. 17th,* 1786.

MY DEAR SIR,—I have not time at present to upbraid you for your silence and neglect; I shall only say I received yours with great pleasure. I have enclosed you a piece of rhyming ware for your perusal. I have been very busy with the muses since I saw you, and have composed, among several others, "The Ordination," a poem on Mr. M'Kinlay's being called to Kilmarnock; "Scotch Drink," a poem; "The Cottar's Saturday Night;" "An Address to the Devil," etc. I have likewise completed my poem on the "Dogs," but have not shown it to the world. My chief patron now is Mr. Aikin, in Ayr, who is pleased to express great approbation of my works. Be so good as send me Fergusson[11], by Connell, and I will remit you the money. I have no news to acquaint you with about Mauchline, they are just going on in the old way. I have some very important news with respect to myself, not the most agreeable—news that I am sure you cannot guess, but I shall give you the particulars another time. I am extremely happy with Smith;[11a] he is the only friend I have now in Mauchline. I can scarcely forgive your long neglect of me, and I beg you will let me hear from you regularly by Connell. If you would act your part as a friend, I am sure neither good nor bad fortune should estrange or alter me. Excuse haste, as I got yours but yesterday.—I am, my dear Sir, yours, ROBERT BURNESS.

[10] Three months before this letter was written Richmond was a clerk in the office of Mr. Gavin Hamilton, writer, Mauchline.

[11] Fergusson's *Poems.*

[11a] Keeper of a haberdashery store in Mauchline.

XVI.-TO MR. JAMES SMITH[12], SHOPKEEPER, MAUCHLINE.
[*Spring of* 1786.]

... Against two things I am fixed as fate,—staying at home, and owning her conjugally. The first, by Heaven, I will not do!—the last, by Hell, I will never do! A good God bless you, and make you happy up to the warmest weeping wish of parting friendship! ... If you see Jean tell her I will meet her, so help me God in my hour of need! R. B.

[12] The confidant of his amour with Jean Armour, daughter of James Armour, mason, Mauchline. Notwithstanding the blustering threat—for which Smith was probably more than half responsible—Burns was afterwards content to "own bonny Jean conjugally."

XVII.—TO MR. ROBERT MUIR, WINE MERCHANT, KILMARNOCK.
MOSSGIEL, 20*th March*, 1786.

DEAR SIR,—I am heartily sorry I had not the pleasure of seeing you as you returned through Mauchline; but as I was engaged, I could not be in town before the evening.

I here inclose you my "Scotch Drink," and "may the deil follow with a blessing for your edification." I hope, sometime before we hear the gowk, to have the pleasure of seeing you at Kilmarnock, when I intend we shall have a gill between us, in a mutchkin-stoup; which will be a great comfort and consolation to, dear Sir, your humble servant, ROBERT BURNESS.

XVIII.—To MR. JOHN BALLANTINE, BANKER, AYR. (?)
[*April* 1786.]

HONOURED SIR,—My proposals[12a] came to hand last night, and, knowing that you would wish to have it in your power to do me a service as early as any body, I enclose you half a sheet of them. I must consult you, first opportunity, on the propriety of sending my *quondam* friend, Mr. Aiken, a copy. If he is now reconciled to my character as an honest man, I would do it with all my soul; but I would not be beholden to the noblest being ever God created if he imagined me to be a rascal. *Apropos*, old Mr. Armour prevailed with him to mutilate that unlucky paper[12c] yesterday. Would you believe it? though I had not a hope, nor even a wish to make her mine after her conduct, yet when he told me the names were cut out of the paper, my heart died within me, and he cut my veins with the news. Perdition seize her falsehood! ROBERT BURNS.

[12a] Proposals for publishing his Scottish Poems by subscription.

[12b]Writer in Ayr.

[12c] The written acknowledgment of his marriage which Burns gave to Jean. She, influenced by her father, consented to destroy it.

XIX.—TO MR. M'WHINNIE, WRITER, AYR.
[MOSSGIEL, 17*th April* 1786.]

IT is injuring some hearts, those hearts that elegantly bear the impression of the good Creator, to say to them you give them the trouble of obliging a friend; for this reason, I only tell you that I gratify my own feelings in requesting your friendly offices with respect to the enclosed, because I know it will gratify yours to assist me in it to the utmost of your power.

I have sent you four copies, as I have no less than eight dozen, which is a great deal more than I shall ever need.

Be sure to remember a poor poet militant in your prayers He looks forward with fear[13] and trembling to that, to him, important moment which stamps the die with—with—with, perhaps, the eternal disgrace of, my dear Sir, your humble, afflicted, tormented, ROBERT BURNS.

[13] Cp. "Something cries *Hoolie! I rede ye, honest man, tak tent, ye'll show your folly!*"

XX.—TO JOHN ARNOT, ESQUIRE, OF DALQUATSWOOD.
[*April* 1786.]

SIR,—I have long wished for some kind of claim to the honour of your acquaintance, and since it is out of my power to make that claim by the least service of mine to you, I shall do it by asking a friendly office of you to me.—I should be much hurt, Sir, if any one should view my poor Parnassian Pegasus in the light of a spur-galled Hack, and think that I wish to make a shilling or two by him. I spurn the thought.

It may do, maun do, Sir, wi' them who

Maun please the great-folk for a wame-fou;

For me, sae laigh I needna boo

For, Lord be thankit! I can ploo;

And, when I downa yoke a naig,
Then, Lord be thankit! I can beg.

You will then, I hope, Sir, forgive my troubling you with the enclosed,[14] and spare a poor heart-crushed devil a world of apologies—a business he is very unfit for at any time, but at present, widowed as he is of every woman-giving comfort, he is utterly incapable of. Sad and grievous of late, Sir, has been my tribulation, and many and piercing my sorrows; and, had it not been for the loss the world would have sustained in losing so great a poet, I had ere now done as a much wiser man, the famous Achitophel of long-headed memory, did before me, when he "went home and set his house in order." I have lost, Sir, that dearest earthly treasure, that greatest blessing here below, that last, best gift which completed Adam's happiness in the garden of bliss; I have lost, I have lost—my trembling hand refuses its office, the frighted ink recoils up the quill,—I have lost a, a, a wife.
Fairest of God's creation, last and best,
Now art thou lost!

You have doubtless, Sir, heard my story, heard it with all its exaggerations; but as my actions, and my motives for action, are peculiarly like myself and that is peculiarly like nobody else, I shall just beg a leisure moment and a spare tear of you until I tell my own story my own way.

I have been all my life, Sir, one of the rueful-looking, long-visaged sons of disappointment. A damned star has always kept my zenith, and shed its hateful influence in the emphatic curse of the prophet—"And behold whatsoever he doth, it shall not prosper!" I rarely hit where I aim, and if I want anything, I am almost sure never to find it where I seek it. For instance, if my penknife is needed, I pull out twenty things—a plough-wedge, a horse nail, an old letter, or a tattered rhyme, in short, everything but my penknife; and that, at last, after a painful, fruitless search, will be found in the unsuspected corner of an unsuspected pocket, as if on purpose thrust out of the way. Still, Sir, I long had a wishing eye to that inestimable blessing, a wife.

... A young fellow, after a few idle commonplace stories from a gentleman in black ... no one durst say black was his eye; while I ... only wanting that ceremony, am made a Sunday's laughing-stock, and abused like a pickpocket. I was well aware, though, that if my ill-starred fortune got the least hint of my connubial wish, my scheme would go to nothing. To prevent this I determined to take my measures with such thought and fore-thought, such cautions and precautions, that all the malignant planets in the hemisphere should be unable to blight my designs .... Heaven and Earth! must I remember? my damned star wheeled about to the zenith, by whose baleful rays Fortune took the alarm.[15a] ... In short, Pharaoh at the Red Sea, Darius at Arbela, Pompey at Pharsalia, Edward at Bannockburn, Charles at Pultoway, Burgoyne at Saratoga—no prince, potentate, or commander of ancient or modern unfortunate memory ever got a more shameful or more total defeat. How I bore this can only be conceived. All powers of recital labour far, far behind. There is a pretty large portion of Bedlam in the composition of a poet at any time; but on this occasion I was nine parts and nine tenths, out of ten, stark staring mad. At first I was fixed in stuporific insensibility, silent, sullen, staring like Lot's wife besaltified in the plains of Gomorrha. But my second paroxysm chiefly beggars description. The rifted northern ocean, when returning suns dissolve the chains of winter, and loosening precipices of long-accumulated ice tempest with hideous crash the foaming deep,—images like these may give some faint shadow of what was the situation of my bosom. My chained faculties broke loose; my maddening passions, roused to tenfold fury, bore over their banks with impetuous, resistless force, carrying every check and principle before them. Counsel was an unheeded call to the passing hurricane; Reason a screaming elk in the vortex of Malstrom; and Religion a feebly-struggling beaver down the roarings of Niagara. I reprobated the first moment of my existence; execrated Adam's folly-infatuated wish for that goodly-looking but poison-breathing gift which had ruined him and undone me; and called on the womb of uncreated night to close over me and all my sorrows.

A storm naturally overblows itself. My spent passions gradually sunk into a lurid calm; and by degrees I have subsided into the time-settled sorrow of the sable-widower, who, wiping away the decent tear, lifts up his grief-worn eye to look-for another wife.

Such is the state of man; to-day he buds
His tender leaves of hope; to-morrow blossoms
And bears his blushing honours thick upon him;
The third day comes a frost, a killing frost,
And nips his root, and then he falls as I do.[15]

Such, Sir, has been the fatal era of my life. And it came to pass that when I looked for sweet, behold bitter; and for light, behold darkness.

But this is not all: already the holy beagles begin to snuff the scent, and I expect every moment to see them cast off, and hear them after me in full cry; but as I am an old fox, I shall give them dodging and doubling for it, and by and by I intend to earth among the mountains of Jamaica.

I am so struck, on a review, with the impertinent length of this letter, that I shall not increase it with one single word of apology, but abruptly conclude with assuring you that I am, Sir, yours and misery's most humble servant.

ROBERT BURNS.

[14] Proposals for publishing.

[15] Misquoted from Shakspeare's *Henry VIII*.

XXI.—To MR. DAVID BRICE, SHOEMAKER, GLASGOW.

MOSSGIEL, *June* 12*th*, 1786.

DEAR BRICE,—I received your message by G. Paterson, and as I am not very *throng* at present, I just write to let you know that there is such a worthless, rhyming reprobate as your humble servant still in the land of the living, though I can scarcely say in the place of hope. I have no news to tell you that will give me any pleasure to mention, or you to hear.

Poor, ill-advised, ungrateful Armour came home on Friday last. You have heard all the particulars of that affair, and a black affair it is. What she thinks of her conduct now I don't know; one thing I do know—she has made me completely miserable. Never man loved, or rather adored a woman more than I did her; and, to confess a truth between you and me, I do still love her to distraction after all, though I won't tell her so if I were to see her, which I don't want to do. My poor dear unfortunate Jean! how happy have I been in thy arms! It is not the losing her that makes me so unhappy, but for her sake I feel most severely: I foresee she is in the road to, I am afraid, eternal ruin.

May Almighty God forgive her ingratitude and perjury to me, as I from my very soul forgive her; and may His grace be with her and bless her in all her future life! I can have no nearer idea of the place of eternal punishment than what I have felt in my own breast on her account. I have tried often to forget her; I have run into all kinds of dissipation and riots, mason-meetings, drinking-matches, and other mischief, to drive her out of my head, but all in vain. And now for a grand cure; the ship is on her way home that is to take me out to Jamaica; and then, farewell, dear old Scotland! and farewell, dear ungrateful Jean! for never, never will I see you more.

You will have heard that I am going to commence poet in print; and to-morrow my work goes to the press. I expect it will be a volume of about two hundred pages—it is just the last foolish action I intend to do, and then turn a wise man as fast as possible.—Believe me to be, dear Brice, your friend and well-wisher. R. B.

XXII.—To MR. JOHN RICHMOND, EDINBURGH.

MOSSGIEL, 9*th July* 1786.

With the sincerest grief I read your letter. You are truly a son of misfortune. I shall be extremely anxious to hear from you how your health goes on; if it is in any way re-establishing, or if Leith promises well; in short, how you feel in the inner man.

19

No news worth anything; only godly Bryan was in the inquisition yesterday, and half the countryside as witnesses against him. He still stands out steady and denying; but proof was led yesternight of circumstances highly suspicious, almost *de facto*; one of the servant girls made oath that she upon a time rashly entered into the house, to speak in your cant, "in the hour of cause."

I have waited on Armour since her return home; not from the least view of reconciliation, but merely to ask for her health, and to you I will confess it, from a foolish hankering fondness, very ill placed indeed. The mother forbade me the house, nor did Jean show that penitence that might have been expected. However, the priest,[15a] I am informed, will give me a certificate as a single man, if I comply with the rules of the church, which for that very reason I intend to do.[16]

I am going to put on sackcloth and ashes this day. I am indulged so far as to appear in my own seat.*Peccavi, pater, miserere mei.* My book will be ready in a fortnight. If you have any subscribers, return them by Connell. The Lord stand with the righteous; amen, amen. R. B.

[15a] Rev. Mr. Auld—Daddie Auld.

[16] This accordingly he did.

XXIII—To MR. JOHN RICHMOND.

OLD ROME FOREST,[17] 30*th July* 1786.

MY DEAR RICHMOND,—My hour is now come—you and I will never meet in Britain more. I have orders, within three weeks at farthest, to repair aboard the *Nancy*, Captain Smith, from Clyde to Jamaica, and to call at Antigua. This, except to our friend Smith, whom God long preserve, is a secret about Mauchline. Would you believe it? Armour has got a warrant to throw me in jail till I find security for an enormous sum. This they keep an entire secret, but I got it by a channel they little dream of; and I am wandering from one friend's house to another, and, like a true son of the Gospel, "have nowhere to lay my head." I know you will pour an execration on her head, but spare the poor, ill-advised girl, for my sake; though may all the furies that rend the injured, enraged lover's bosom await her mother until her latest hour! I write in a moment of rage, reflecting on my miserable situation— exiled, abandoned, forlorn. I can write no more—let me hear from you by the return of the coach. I will write you ere I go.—I am, dear Sir, yours, here and hereafter, R. B.

[17] In the neighbourhood of Kilmarnock. Here he had deposited his travelling chest in the house of a relative.

XXIV.-To MR. JOHN KENNEDY.

KILMARNOCK, *August* 1786.

MY DEAR SIR—Your truly facetious epistle of the 3rd instant gave me much entertainment. I was only sorry I had not the pleasure of seeing you as I passed your way; but we shall bring up all our lee way on Wednesday, the 16th current, when I hope to have it in my power to call on you, and take a kind, very probably a last adieu, before I go for Jamaica; and I expect orders to repair to Greenock every day. I have at last made my public appearance, and am solemnly inaugurated into the numerous class.[18] Could I have got a carrier, you should have got a score of vouchers for my authorship; but, now you have them, let them speak for themselves.—

Farewell, dear friend! may guid luck hit you,

And 'mang her favourites admit you,

If e'er Detraction shore to smit you,

May nane believe him,

And ony Deil that thinks to get you,

Good LORD, deceive him,

R.B.

[18] The Kilmarnock Edition of his poems was published on 31st July.

XXV.—To HIS COUSIN, MR. JAMES BURNESS, WRITER, MONTROSE.

MOSSGIEL, *Tuesday Noon*, 26*th Sept.* 1786.

MY DEAR SIR,—I this moment receive yours—receive it with the honest hospitable warmth of a friend's welcome. Whatever comes from you always wakens up the better blood about my heart, which your kind little recollections of my parental friend carries as far as it will go. 'Tis there that man is blest! 'Tis there, my friend, man feels a consciousness of something within him above the trodden clod! The grateful reverence to the hoary earthly authors of his being, the burning glow when he clasps the woman of his soul to his bosom, the tender yearnings of heart for the little angels to whom he has given existence—these Nature has poured in milky streams about the human heart; and the man who never rouses them to action by the inspiring influences of their proper objects loses by far the most pleasurable part of his existence.

My departure is uncertain, but I do not think it will be till after harvest. I will be on very short allowance of time indeed, if I do not comply with your friendly invitation. When it will be I don't know, but if I can make my wish good I will endeavour to drop you a line some time before. My best compliments to Mrs. Burness; I should be equally mortified should I drop in when she is abroad, but of that, I suppose, there is little chance. What I have wrote, heaven knows. I have not time to review it, so accept of it in the beaten way of friendship. With the ordinary phrase, and perhaps rather more than the ordinary sincerity, I am, dear Sir, ever yours, R. B.

XXVI.-To MRS. STEWART, OF STAIR.[19]

[*Oct.* 1786.?]

MADAM,—The hurry of my preparations for going abroad has hindered me from performing my promise so soon as I intended. I have here sent you a parcel of songs, etc., which never made their appearance, except to a friend or two at most. Perhaps some of them may be no great entertainment to you, but of that I am far from being an adequate judge. The song to the time of "Ettrick Banks"[20] you will easily see the impropriety of exposing much even in manuscript. I think, myself, it has some merit, both as a tolerable description of one of nature's sweetest scenes, a July evening, and as one of the finest pieces of nature's workmanship, the finest indeed we know anything of, an amiable, beautiful young woman; but I have no common friend to procure me that permission, without which I would not dare to spread the copy.

I am quite aware, Madam, what task the world would assign me in this letter. The obscure bard, when any of the great condescend to take notice of him, should heap the altar with the incense of flattery. Their high ancestry, their own great and godlike qualities and actions, should be recounted with the most exaggerated description. This, Madam, is a task for which I am altogether unfit. Besides a certain disqualifying pride of heart, I know nothing of your connections in life, and have no access to where your real character is to be found—the company of your compeers: and more, I am afraid that even the most refined adulation is by no means the road to your good opinion.

One feature of your character I shall ever with grateful pleasure remember—the reception I got when I had the honour of waiting on you at Stair. I am little acquainted with politeness, but I know a good deal of benevolence of temper and goodness of heart. Surely did those in exalted stations know how happy they could make some classes of their inferiors by condescension and affability, they would never stand so high, measuring out with every look the height of their elevation, but condescend as sweetly as did Mrs. Stewart of Stair. R. B.

[19] Mrs. Stewart, of Stair, was the first person of note to discover in the Ayrshire ploughman a genius of the first order.

[20] The Bonnie Lass of Ballochmyle

XXVII.—TO MR. ROBERT AIKIN, WRITER, AYR.

[*Oct.* 1786.?]

SIR,—I was with Wilson, my printer, t'other day, and settled all our by-gone matters between us. After I had paid him all demands, I made him the offer of the second edition, on the hazard of being paid out of the first and readiest, which he declines. By his account, the paper of a thousand copies would cost about twenty-seven pounds, and the printing about fifteen or sixteen: he offers to agree to this for the printing, if I will advance for the paper, but this, you know, is out of my power; so farewell hopes of a second edition 'till I grow richer! an epocha which, I think, will arrive at the payment of the British national debt.

There is scarcely anything hurts me so much in being disappointed of my second edition, as not having it in my power to show my gratitude to Mr. Ballantine, by publishing my poem of "The Brigs of Ayr." I would detest myself as a wretch, if I thought I were capable in a very long life of forgetting the honest, warm, and tender delicacy with which he enters into my interests. I am sometimes pleased with myself in my grateful sensations; but I believe, on the whole, I have very little merit in it, as my gratitude is not a virtue, the consequence of reflection, but sheerly the instinctive emotion of my heart, too inattentive to allow worldly maxims and views to settle into selfish habits.

I have been feeling all the various rotations and movements within, respecting the Excise. There are many things plead strongly against it; the uncertainty of getting soon into business; the consequences of my follies, which may perhaps make it impracticable for me to stay at home; and, besides, I have for some time been pining under secret wretchedness, from causes which you pretty well know—the pang of disappointment, the sting of pride, with some wandering stabs of remorse, which never fail to settle on my vitals like vultures, when attention is not called away by the calls of society, or the vagaries of the muse. Even in the hour of social mirth, my gaiety is the madness of an intoxicated criminal under the hands of the executioner. All these reasons urge me to go abroad, and to all these reasons I have only one answer—the feelings of a father. This, in the present mood I am in, overbalances everything that can be laid in the scale against it.

You may perhaps think it an extravagant fancy, but it is a sentiment which strikes home to my very soul: though sceptical in some points of our current belief, yet, I think, I have every evidence for the reality of a life beyond the stinted bourne of our present existence; if so, then, how should I, in the presence of that tremendous Being, the Author of existence, how should I meet the reproaches of those who stand to me in the dear relation of children, whom I deserted in the smiling innocency of helpless infancy? O, thou great unknown Power!—thou Almighty God! who has lighted up reason in my breast, and blessed me with immortality!—I have frequently wandered from that order and regularity necessary for the perfection of Thy works, yet Thou hast never left me nor forsaken me!

Since I wrote the foregoing sheet, I have seen something of the storm of mischief thickening over my folly-devoted head. Should you, my friends, my benefactors, be successful in your applications for me, perhaps it may not be in my power, in that way, to reap the fruit of your friendly efforts. What I have written in the preceding pages, is the settled tenor of my present resolution; but should inimical circumstances forbid me closing with your kind offer, or enjoying it only threaten to entail farther misery——

To tell the truth, I have little reason for this last complaint; as the world, in general, has been kind to me fully up to my deserts. I was, for some time past, fast getting into the pining, distrustful snarl of the misanthrope. I saw myself alone, unfit for the struggle of life, shrinking at every rising cloud in the chance-directed atmosphere of fortune, while, all defenceless, I looked about in vain for a cover. It never occurred to me, at least never with the force it deserved, that this world is a busy scene, and man, a creature destined for a progressive struggle; and that, however I might possess a warm heart and inoffensive manners (which last, by the by, was rather more than I could well boast) still, more than these passive qualities, there was something to be done. When all my school-fellows and youthful compeers (those misguided few excepted who joined, to use a Gentoo phrase, the "hallachores" of the human race) were striking off with eager hope and earnest intent, in some one or other of the many paths of busy life, I was "standing idle in the market-place," or only left the chase of the butterfly from flower to flower, to hunt fancy from whim to whim.

You see, Sir, that if to know one's errors were a probability of mending them, I stand a fair chance: but, according to the reverend Westminster divines, though conviction must precede conversion, it is very far from always implying it.

XXVIII.—TO DR. MACKENZIE, MAUCHLINE; INCLOSING HIM VERSES ON DINING WITH LORD DAER.

Wednesday Morning [1st Nov. 1786].

DEAR SIR,—I never spent an afternoon among great folks with half that pleasure as when, in company with you, I had the honour of paying my devoirs to that plain, honest, worthy man, the professor[21] I would be delighted to see him perform acts of kindness and friendship, though I were not the object; he does it with such a grace. I think his character, divided into ten parts, stands thus,—four parts Socrates—four parts Nathaniel—and two parts Shakespeare's Brutus.

The following verses were really extempore, but a little corrected since. They may entertain you a little with the help of that partiality with which you are so good as to favour the performances of, dear Sir, your very humble servant, R. B.

[21] Dugald Stewart, Professor of Moral Philosophy in the University of Edinburgh.

XXIX.—TO MRS. DUNLOP, OF DUNLOP.

Nov. 1786.

MADAM,—I am truly sorry I was not at home yesterday, when I was so much honoured with your order for my copies, and incomparably more by the handsome compliments you are pleased to pay my poetic abilities. I am fully persuaded that there is not any class of mankind so feelingly alive to the titillations of applause as the sons of Parnassus; nor is it easy to conceive how the heart of the poor bard dances with rapture, when those, whose character in life gives them a right to be polite judges, honour him with their approbation. Had you been thoroughly acquainted with me, Madam, you could not have touched my darling heart-chord more sweetly, than by noticing my attempts to celebrate your illustrious ancestor, the saviour of his country.

Great patriot hero! ill-requited chief!

The first book I met with in my early years which I perused with pleasure was *The Life of Hannibal*, the next was *The History of Sir William Wallace*: for several of my early years I had few other authors; and many a solitary hour have I stole out, after the laborious vocations of the day, to shed a tear over their glorious, but unfortunate stories. In those boyish days I remember, in particular, being struck with that part of Wallace's story, where these lines occur—
"Syne to the Leglen wood, when it was late,
To make a silent and a safe retreat."
I chose a fine summer Sunday, the only day my line of life allowed, and walked half-a-dozen of miles to pay my respects to the Leglen wood, with as much devout enthusiasm as ever pilgrim did to Loretto; and as I explored every den and dell where I could suppose my heroic countryman to have lodged, I recollect (for even then I was a rhymer) that my heart glowed with a wish to be able to make a song on him in some measure equal to his merits. R. B.

XXX.—TO MISS ALEXANDER.

MOSSGIEL, 18*th Nov.* 1786.

MADAM,—Poets are such *outré* beings, so much the children of wayward fancy and capricious whim, that I believe the world generally allows them a larger latitude in the laws of propriety than the sober sons of judgment and prudence. I mention this as an apology for the liberties that a nameless stranger has taken with you in the inclosed poem, which he begs leave to present you with. Whether it has poetical merit any way worthy of the theme, I am not the proper judge: but it is the best my abilities can produce; and what to a good heart will, perhaps, be a superior grace, it is equally sincere as fervent.

The scenery was nearly taken from real life, though I dare say, Madam, you do not recollect it, as I believe you scarcely noticed the poetic *reveur* as he wandered by you. I had roved out as chance directed, in the favourite haunts of my muse, on the banks of the Ayr, to view nature in all the gaiety of the vernal year. The evening sun was flaming over the distant western hills; not a breath stirred the crimson opening blossom, or the verdant-spreading leaf. It was a golden moment for a poetic heart. I listened to the feathered warblers, pouring their harmony on every hand, with a congenial kindred regard, and frequently turned out of my path, lest I should disturb their little songs, or frighten them to another station. Surely, said I to myself, he must be a wretch indeed, who, regardless of your harmonious endeavour to please him, can eye your elusive flights to discover your secret recesses, and to rob you of all the property nature gives you—your dearest comforts, your helpless nestlings. Even the hoary hawthorn twig that shot across the way, what heart at such a time but must have been interested in its welfare, and wished it preserved from the rudely-browsing cattle, or the withering eastern blast? Such was the scene, and such the hour, when, in a corner of my prospect, I spied one of the fairest pieces of nature's workmanship that ever crowned a poetic landscape, or met a poet's eye, those visionary bards excepted, who hold commerce with aerial beings! Had Calumny and Villainy taken my walk, they had at that moment sworn eternal peace with such an object.

What an hour of inspiration for a poet! It would have raised plain dull historic prose into metaphor and measure.

The inclosed song was the work of my return; and perhaps it but poorly answers what might have been expected from such a scene.—I have the honour to be, Madam, your most obedient and very humble servant,

R. B.

P.S.—Well, Mr. Burns, and *did* the lady give you the desired permission? No; she was too fine a lady to *notice* so plain a compliment. As to her great brothers, whom I have since met in life on more equal terms[22] of respectability—why should I quarrel with their want of attention to me? When fate swore that their purses should be full, nature was equally positive that their heads should be empty. Men of their fashion were surely incapable of being unpolite? Ye canna mak a silk-purse o' a sow's lug.

R. B., 1792.

[22] As Depute Master of St. James's Lodge, Burns admitted Claude Alexander, Esq., of Ballochmyle, an honorary member, in July 1789.

XXXI.—IN THE NAME OF THE NINE.

Amen.

WE, Robert Burns, by virtue of a warrant from Nature, bearing date the twenty-fifth day of January, Anno Domini one thousand seven hundred and fifty-nine,[23] Poet Laureat, and Bard-in-Chief, in and over the districts and countries of Kyle, Cunningham, and Carrick, of old extent,—To our trusty and well-beloved William Chalmers and John M'Adam, students and practitioners in the ancient and mysterious science of confounding right and wrong.

RIGHT TRUSTY,—Be it known unto you, That whereas in the course of our care and watchings over the order and police of all and sundry the manufacturers, retainers, and vendors of poesy; bards, poets, poetasters, rhymers, jinglers, songsters, ballad-singers, etc., etc., etc., etc., male and female—We have discovered a certain nefarious, abominable, and wicked song or ballad, a copy whereof we have here inclosed; Our Will therefore is, that Ye pitch upon and appoint the most execrable individual of that most execrable species known by the appellation, phrase, and nickname of The Deil's Yell Nowte,[24] and after having caused him to kindle a fire at the Cross of Ayr, ye shall, at noontide of the day, put into the said wretch's merciless hands the said copy of the said nefarious and wicked song, to be consumed by fire in presence of all beholders, in abhorrence of, and terrorem to, all such compositions and composers. And this in no wise leave ye undone, but have it executed in every point as this our mandate bears, before the twenty-fourth current, when in person We hope to applaud your faithfulness and zeal.

Given at Mauchline this twentieth day of November, Anno Domini one thousand seven hundred and eighty-six. God save the Bard!

[23] His birthday.

24

XXXII.—TO JAMES DALRYMPLE, ESQ., ORANGEFIELD.

[30*th Nov*. 1786.]

DEAR SIR,—I suppose the devil is so elated with his success with you, that he is determined by a *coup de main* to complete his purposes on you all at once, in making you a poet. I broke open the letter you sent me; hummed over the rhymes; and as I saw they were extempore, said to myself, they were very well; but when I saw at the bottom a name that I shall ever value with grateful respect, "I gapit wide, but naething spak." I was nearly as much struck as the friends of Job, of affliction-bearing memory, when they sat down with him seven days and seven nights, and spake not a word.

I am naturally of a superstitious cast, and as soon as my wonder-scared imagination regained its consciousness, and resumed its functions, I cast about what this mania of yours might portend. My foreboding ideas had the wide stretch of possibility; and several events, great in their magnitude, and important in their consequences, occurred to my fancy. The downfall of the conclave, or the crushing of the Cork rumps; a ducal coronet to Lord George Gordon, and the protestant interest; or St Peter's keys to .....

You want to know how I come on. I am just in *statu quo*, or, not to insult a gentleman with my Latin, in "auld use and wont." The noble Earl of Glencairn took me by the hand to-day, and interested himself in my concerns, with a goodness like that benevolent Being whose image he so richly bears. He is a stronger proof of the immortality of the soul than any that philosophy ever produced. A mind like his can never die. Let the worshipful squire H. L., or the reverend Mass J. M. go into their primitive nothing. At best, they are but ill-digested lumps of chaos, only one of them strongly tinged with bituminous particles and sulphureous effluvia. But my noble patron, eternal as the heroic swell of magnanimity, and the generous throb of benevolence, shall look on with princely eye at "the war of elements, the wreck of matter, and the crash of worlds." R. B.

XXXIII.-To SIR JOHN WHITEFOORD.

EDINBURGH, 1*st Dec*. 1786.

SIR,—Mr. McKenzie in Mauchline, my very warm and worthy friend, has informed me how much you are pleased to interest yourself in my fate as a man, and—what to me is incomparably dearer-my fame as a poet. I have, Sir, in one or two instances, been patronised by those of your character in life, when I was introduced to their notice by social friends to them, and honoured acquaintances to me; but you are the first gentleman in the country whose benevolence and goodness of heart has interested him for me, unsolicited and unknown. I am not master enough of the etiquette of these matters to know, nor did I stay to inquire, whether formal duty bade or cold propriety disallowed my thanking you in this manner, as I am convinced, from the light in which you kindly view me, that you will do me the justice to believe this letter is not the manoeuvre of the needy sharping author, fastening on those in upper life who honour him with a little notice of him or his works. Indeed, the situation of poets is generally such, to a proverb, as may, in some measure, palliate that prostitution of heart and talents they have at times been guilty of. I do not think that prodigality is, by any means, a necessary concomitant of a poetic turn, but I believe a careless, indolent inattention to economy is almost inseparable from it; then there must be in the heart of every bard of nature's making a certain modest sensibility, mixed with a kind of pride, which will ever keep him out of the way of those windfalls of fortune, which frequently light on hardy impudence and foot-licking servility. It is not easy to imagine a more helpless state than his whose poetic fancy unfits him for the world, and whose character as a scholar gives him some pretensions to the *politesse* of life, yet is as poor as I am. For my part, I thank heaven my star has been kinder: learning never elevated my ideas above the peasant's shed, and I have an independent fortune at the plough-tail.

I was surprised to hear[25] that any one who pretended in the least to the manners of the gentleman should be so foolish, or worse, as to stoop to traduce the morals of such a one as I am, and so inhumanly cruel, too, as to meddle with that late most unfortunate, unhappy part of my story. With a tear of gratitude I thank you, Sir, for the warmth with which you interposd in behalf of my conduct. I am, I acknowledge, too frequently the sport of whim, caprice, and passion; but reverence to God, and integrity to my fellow-creatures, I hope I shall ever preserve. I have no return, Sir, to make you for your goodness, but one—a return which I am persuaded will not be unacceptable—the honest warm wishes of a grateful heart for your happiness, and every one of that lovely flock who stand to you in a filial relation. If ever Calumny aims the poisoned shaft at them, may friendship be by to ward the blow! R. B.

[25] From Dr. Mackenzie, Burns's friend, and medical attendant of the family of Sir John.

XXXIV.—To MR, GAVIN HAMILTON, MAUCHLINE.

EDINBURGH, *Dec. 7th*, 1786,

HONOURED SIR,—I have paid every attention to your commands, but can only say what perhaps you will have heard before this reach you, that Muirkirklands were bought by a John Gordon, W.S., but for whom I know not; Mauchlands, Haugh Miln, etc., by a Frederick Fotheringham, supposed to be for Ballochmyle Laird, and Adam-hill and Shawood were bought for Oswald's folks. This is so imperfect an account, and will be so late ere it reach you, that were it not to discharge my conscience I would not trouble you with it; but after all my diligence I could make it no sooner nor better.

For my own affairs, I am in a fair way of becoming as eminent as Thomas à Kempis or John Bunyan; and you may expect henceforth to see my birthday inserted among the wonderful events in the poor Robin's and Aberdeen Almanacks, along with the black Monday and the battle of Bothwell Bridge. My Lord Glencairn and the Dean of Faculty, Mr. H. Erskine, have taken me under their wing; and by all probability I shall soon be the tenth worthy, and the eighth wise man of the world. Through my lord's influence, it is inserted in the records of the Caledonian Hunt, that they universally, one and all, subscribe for the second edition. My subscription bills come out to-morrow, and you shall have some of them next post. I have met in Mr. Dalrymple, of Orangefield, what Solomon emphatically calls, "a friend that sticketh closer than a brother." The warmth with which he interests himself in my affairs is of the same enthusiastic kind which you, Mr. Aikin, and the few patrons that took notice of my earlier poetic days, showed for the poor unlucky devil of a poet.

I always remember Mrs. Hamilton and Miss Kennedy in my poetic prayers, but you both in prose and verse.

May cauld ne'er catch you, but a hap,
Nor hunger but in plenty's lap!
Amen!
R. B.

XXXV.—To MR. JOHN BALLANTINE, BANKER, AT ONE TIME PROVOST OF AYR.

EDINBURGH, 13*th December* 1786.

MY HONOURED FRIEND,—I would not write you till I could have it in my power to give you some account of myself and my matters, which, by the by, is often no easy task. I arrived here on Tuesday was se'nnight[26], and have suffered ever since I came to town with a miserable headache and stomach complaint, but am now a good deal better. I have found a worthy warm friend in Mr. Dalrymple, of Orangefield, who introduced me to Lord Glencairn, a man whose worth and brotherly kindness to me I shall remember when time shall be no more. By his interest it is passed in the "Caledonian Hunt," and entered in their books, that they are to take each a copy of the second edition, for which they are to pay one guinea. I have been introduced to a good many of the *noblesse*, but my avowed patrons and patrones es are, the Duchess of Gordon—the Countess of Glencairn, with my Lord and Lady Betty[27]—the Dean of Faculty—Sir John Whitefoord. I have likewise warm friends among the literati; Professors Stewart, Blair, and Mr. Mackenzie—the Man of Feeling. An unknown hand left ten guineas for the Ayrshire bard with Mr. Sibbald, which I got. I since have discovered my generous unknown friend to be Patrick Miller, Esq., brother to the Justice Clerk; and drank a glass of claret with him, by invitation, at his own house yesternight. I am nearly agreed with Creech to print my book, and I suppose I will begin on Monday. I will send a subscription bill or two, next post; when I intend writing my first kind patron, Mr. Aikin. I saw his son to-day, and he is very well.

Dugald Stewart, and some of my learned friends, put me in the periodical paper called the *Lounger*,[28] a copy of which I here enclose you. I was, Sir, when I was first honoured with your notice, too obscure; now I tremble lest I should be ruined by being dragged too suddenly into the glare of polite and learned observation.

I shall certainly, my ever honoured patron, write you an account of my every step; and better health and more spirits may enable me to make it something better than this stupid matter-of-fact epistle.—I have the honour to be, good Sir, your ever grateful humble servant, R. B.

If any of my friends write me, my direction is care of Mr. Creech, Bookseller.

[26] A mistake for "a fortnight."

[27] Cunningham

[28] The paper here alluded to was written by Mackenzie, the celebrated author of *The Man of Feeling*.

XXXVI.—TO MR. ROBERT MUIR.

EDINBURGH, *Dec.* 20*th*, 1786.

MY DEAR FRIEND,—I have just time for the carrier, to tell you that I received your letter, of which I shall say no more but what a lass of my acquaintance said of her bastard wean; she said she "didna ken wha was the father exactly, but she suspected it was some o' thae bonny blackguard smugglers, for it was like them." So I only say, your obliging epistle was like you. I enclose you a parcel of subscription bills. Your affair of sixty copies is also like you; but it would not be like me to comply.

Your friend's notion of my life has put a crotchet in my head of sketching it in some future epistle to you. My compliments to Charles and Mr. Parker. R. B.

XXXVII.—TO MR. WILLIAM CHALMERS, WRITER, AYR.

EDINBURGH, *Dec.* 27*th*, 1786.

MY DEAR FRIEND,—I confess I have sinned the sin for which there is hardly any forgiveness—ingratitude to friendship, in not writing you sooner; but of all men living, I had intended to have sent you an entertaining letter; and by all the plodding, stupid powers, that in nodding conceited majesty preside over the dull routine of business—a heavily-solemn oath this!—I am and have been, ever since I came to Edinburgh, as unfit to write a letter of humour, as to write a commentary on the Revelation of St. John the Divine, who was banished to the Isle of Patmos by the cruel and bloody Domitian, son to Vespasian and brother to Titus, both emperors of Rome, and who was himself an emperor, and raised the second or third persecution, I forget which, against the Christians, and after throwing the said apostle John, brother to the apostle James, commonly called James the Greater, to distinguish him from another James, who was on some account or other known by the name of James the Less—after throwing him into a cauldron of boiling oil from which he was miraculously preserved, he banished the poor son of Zebedee to a desert island in the Archipelago where he was gifted with the second sight, and saw as many wild beasts as I have seen since I came to Edinburgh; which, a circumstance not uncommon in story-telling, brings me back to where I set out.

To make you some amends for what, before you reach this paragraph, you will have suffered, I enclose you two poems I have carded and spun since I passed Glenbuck.

One blank in the address to Edinburgh—"Fair B——," is heavenly Miss Burnet, daughter to Lord Monboddo, at whose house I have had the honour to be more than once. There has not been anything nearly like her in all the combinations of beauty, grace, and goodness the great Creator has formed, since Milton's Eve on the first day of her existence.

My direction is—care of Andrew Bruce, merchant, Bridge Street. R. B.

XXXVIII.—To THE EARL OF EGLINGTON.

EDINBURGH, *January* 1787.

MY LORD,—As I have but slender pretensions to philosophy, I cannot rise to the exalted ideas of a citizen of the world, but have all those national prejudices, which I believe glow peculiarly strong in the breast of a Scotchman. There is scarcely anything to which I am so fully alive as the honour and welfare of my country; and as a poet, I have no higher enjoyment than singing her sons and daughters. Fate had cast my station in the veriest shades of life; but never did a heart pant more ardently than mine to be distinguished; though till very lately I looked in vain on every side for a ray of light. It is easy then to guess how much I was gratified with the countenance and approbation of one of my country's most illustrious sons, when Mr. Wauchope called on me yesterday on the part of your lordship. Your munificence, my lord, certainly deserves my very grateful acknowledgments; but your patronage is a bounty peculiarly suited to my feelings. I am not master enough of the etiquette of life to know, whether there be not some impropriety in troubling your lordship with my thanks, but my heart whispered me to do it. From the emotions of my inmost soul I do it. Selfish ingratitude I hope I am incapable of; and mercenary servility, I trust, I shall ever have so much honest pride as to detest. R. B.

XXXIX.—TO MR. JOHN BALLANTINE.

EDINBURGH, *Jan.* 14*th* 1787.

MY HONOURED FRIEND,—It gives me a secret comfort to observe in myself that I am not yet so far gone as Willie Gaw's Skate, "past redemption;" for I have still this favourable symptom of grace, that when my conscience, as in the case of this letter, tells me I am leaving something undone that I ought to do, it teases me eternally till I do it.

I am still "dark as was Chaos" in respect to futurity. My generous friend, Mr. Patrick Miller, has been talking with me about a lease of some farm or other in an estate called Dalswinton, which he has lately bought near Dumfries. Some life-rented embittering recollections whisper me that I will be happier anywhere than in my old neighbourhood, but Mr. Miller is no judge of land; and though I daresay he means to favour me, yet he may give me, in his opinion, an advantageous bargain that may ruin me. I am to take a tour by Dumfries as I return, and have promised to meet Mr. Miller on his lands some time in May.

I went to a mason-lodge yesternight, where the Most Worshipful Grand Master Chartres, and all the Grand Lodge of Scotland visited. The meeting was numerous and elegant; all the different lodges about town were present, in all their pomp. The Grand Master, who presided with great solemnity and honour to himself as a gentleman and mason, among other general toasts gave "Caledonia, and Caledonia's Bard, Brother Burns," which rung through the whole assembly with multiplied honours and repeated acclamations. As I had no idea such a thing would happen, I was downright thunderstruck, and, trembling in every nerve, made the best return in my power. Just as I had finished, some of the grand officers said so loud that I could hear with a most comforting accent, "Very well, indeed!" which set me something to rights again.

I have just now had a visit from my landlady,[29] who is a staid, sober, piously-disposed, vice-abhorring widow, coming on her climacteric; she is at present in great tribulation respecting some daughters of Belial who are on the floor immediately above. My landlady, who, as I have said, is a flesh-disciplining godly matron, firmly believes her husband is in heaven; and, having been very happy with him on earth, she vigorously and perseveringly practises such of the most distinguished Christian virtues as attending church, railing against vice, etc., that she may be qualified to meet him in that happy place where the ungodly shall never enter. This, no doubt, requires some strong exertions of self-denial in a hale, well-kept widow of forty-five; and as our floors are low and ill-plastered, we can easily distinguish our laughter-loving, night-rejoicing neighbours when they are eating, drinking, singing, etc. My worthy landlady tosses sleepless and unquiet, "looking for rest and finding none," the whole night. Just now she told me—though by-the-by she is sometimes dubious that I am, in her own phrase, "but a rough an' roun' Christian,"—that "we should not be uneasy or envious because the wicked enjoy the good things of this life, for the jades would one day lie in hell," etc., etc.

I have to-day corrected my 152nd page. My best good wishes to Mr. Aikin.—I am ever, dear Sir, your much indebted humble servant, R. B.

[29] Mrs. Carfrae, Baxter's Close, Lawnmarket, Edinburgh, according to John Richmond, law clerk.

XL.—TO MRS. DUNLOP.
EDINBURGH, 15*th January* 1787.

MADAM,—Yours of the 9th current, which I am this moment honoured with, is a deep reproach to me for ungrateful neglect. I will tell you the real truth, for I am miserably awkward at a fib—I wished to have written to Dr. Moore before I wrote to you; but, though every day since I received yours of December 30th, the idea, the wish to write to him has constantly pressed on my thoughts, yet I could not for my soul set about it. I know his fame and character, and I am one of "the sons of little men." To write him a mere matter-of-fact affair, like a merchant's order, would be disgracing the little character I have; and to write the author of *The View of Society and Manners* a letter of sentiment—I declare every artery runs cold at the thought. I shall try, however, to write to him to-morrow or next day. His kind interposition on my behalf I have already experienced, as a gentleman waited on me the other day, on the part of Lord Eglinton, with ten guineas, by way of subscription, for two copies of my next edition.

The word you object to in the mention I have made of my glorious countryman and your immortal ancestor, is indeed borrowed from Thomson; but it does not strike me as an improper epithet. I distrusted my own judgment on your finding fault with it, and applied for the opinion of some of the literati here, who honour me with their critical strictures, and they all allowed it to be proper. The song you ask I cannot recollect, and I have not a copy of it. I have not composed anything on the great Wallace, except what you have seen in print; and the inclosed, which I will print in this edition.[30] You will see I have mentioned some others of the name. When I composed my "Vision," long ago, I had attempted a description of Kyle, of which the additional stanzas are a part as it originally stood. My heart glows with a wish to be able to do justice to the merits of the "saviour of his country," which sooner or later I shall at least attempt.

You are afraid I shall grow intoxicated with my prosperity as a poet; alas! Madam, I know myself and the world too well. I do not mean any airs of affected modesty; I am willing to believe that my abilities deserve some notice; but in a most enlightened, informed age and nation, when poetry is and has been the study of men of the first natural genius, aided with all the powers of polite learning, polite books, and polite company—to be dragged forth to the full glare of learned and polite observation, with all my imperfections of awkward rusticity and crude unpolished ideas on my head—I assure you, Madam, I do not dissemble when I tell you I tremble for the consequences. The novelty of a poet in my obscure situation, without any of those advantages which are reckoned necessary for that character, at least at this time of day, has raised a partial tide of public notice which has borne me to a height, where I am absolutely, feelingly certain, my abilities are inadequate to support me; and too surely do I see that time when the same tide will leave me, and recede, perhaps, as far below the mark of truth. I do not say this in the ridiculous affectation of self-abasement and modesty. I have studied myself, and know what ground I occupy; and however a friend or the world may differ from me in that particular, I stand for my own opinion, in silent resolve, with all the tenaciousness of property. I mention this to you once for all to disburthen my mind, and I do not wish to hear or say more about it. But

When proud fortune's ebbing tide recedes,

you will bear me witness, that when my bubble of fame was at the highest I stood unintoxicated, with the inebriating cup in my hand, looking forward with rueful resolve to the hastening time, when the blow of Calumny should dash it to the ground, with all the eagerness of vengeful triumph.

Your patronising me and interesting yourself in my fame and character as a poet, I rejoice in; it exalts me in my own idea; and whether you can or cannot aid me in my subscription is a trifle. Has a paltry subscription-bill any charms to the heart of a bard, compared with the patronage of the descendant of the immortal Wallace? R. B.

[30] Stanza in the "Vision," beginning, "By stately tower or palace fair," and ending with the first Duan.

XLI—TO DR. MOORE.[31]
EDINBURGH, *Jan.* 1787.

SIR,—Mrs. Dunlop has been so kind as to send me extracts of letters she has had from you, where you do the rustic bard the honour of noticing him and his works. Those who have felt the anxieties and solicitudes of authorship, can only know what pleasure it gives to be noticed in such a manner, by judges of the first character. Your criticisms, Sir, I receive with reverence: only I am sorry they mostly came too late: a peccant passage or two that I would certainly have altered, were gone to the press.

The hope to be admired for ages is, in by far the greater part of those even who are authors of repute, an unsubstantial dream. For my part, my first ambition was, and still my strongest wish is, to please my compeers, the inmates of the hamlet, while ever-changing language and manners shall allow me to be relished and understood. I am very willing to admit that I have some poetical abilities; and as few, if any, writers, either moral or poetical, are intimately acquainted with the classes of mankind among whom I have chiefly mingled, I may have seen men and manners in a different phasis from what is common, which may assist originality of thought. Still I know very well the novelty of my character has by far the greatest share in the learned and polite notice I have lately had; and in a language where Pope and Churchill have raised the laugh, and Shenstone and Gray drawn the tear; where Thomson and Beattie have painted the landscape, and Lyttelton and Collins described the heart, I am not vain enough to hope for distinguished poetic fame. R. B.

[31] Father of the hero of Coruña, and author of *Zeluco*, etc.

XLII.—To THE REV. G. LAWRIE, NEWMILNS, NEAR KILMARNOCK.
EDINBURGH, *Feb. 5th,* 1787.

REVEREND AND DEAR SIR,—When I look at the date of your kind letter, my heart reproaches me severely with ingratitude in neglecting so long to answer it. I will not trouble you with any account, by way of apology, of my hurried life and distracted attention: do me the justice to believe that my delay by no means proceeded from want of respect. I feel, and ever shall feel for you, the mingled sentiments of esteem for a friend and reverence for a father.

I thank you, Sir, with all my soul, for your friendly hints, though I do not need them so much as my friends are apt to imagine. You are dazzled with newspaper accounts and distant reports; but, in reality, I have no great temptation to be intoxicated with the cup of prosperity. Novelty may attract the attention of mankind awhile; to it I owe my present *eclat*; but I see the time not far distant when the popular tide which has borne me to a height of which I am, perhaps, unworthy, shall recede with silent celerity, and leave me a barren waste of sand, to descend at my leisure to my former station. I do not say this in the affectation of modesty; I see the consequence is unavoidable, and am prepared for it. I had been at a good deal of pains to form a just, impartial estimate of my intellectual powers before I came here: I have not added, since I came to Edinburgh, anything to the account; and I trust I shall take every atom of it back to my shades, the coverts of my unnoticed early years.

In Dr. Blacklock, whom I see very often, I have found what I would have expected in our friend, a clear head and an excellent heart.

By far the most agreeable hours I spend in Edinburgh must be placed to the account of Miss Lawrie and her pianoforte. I cannot help repeating to you and Mrs. Lawrie a compliment that Mr. Mackenzie, the celebrated "Man of Feeling," paid to Miss Lawrie, the other night, at the concert. I had come in at the interlude, and sat down by him till I saw Miss Lawrie in a seat not very far distant, and went up to pay my respects to her. On my return to Mr. Mackenzie he asked me who she was; I told him 'twas the daughter of a reverend friend of mine in the west country. He returned, there were something very striking, to his idea, in her appearance. On my desiring to know what it was, he was pleased to say, "She has a great deal of the elegance of a well-bred lady about her, with all the sweet simplicity of a country girl."

My compliments to all the happy inmates of St. Margaret's.—I am, my dear Sir, yours, most gratefully,

ROBERT BURNS.

XLIII.-To THE EARL OF BUCHAN.[32]

MY LORD,—The honour your lordship has done me, by your notice and advice in yours of the 1st instant, I shall ever gratefully remember:—

Praise from thy lips 'tis mine with joy to boast,

They best can give it who deserve it most.

Your lordship touches the darling chord of my heart, when you advise me to fire my muse at Scottish story and Scottish scenes. I wish for nothing more than to make a leisurely pilgrimage through my native country; to sit and muse on those once hard-contended fields, where Caledonia, rejoicing, saw her bloody lion borne through broken ranks to victory and fame; and, catching the inspiration, to pour the deathless names in song. But, my lord, in the midst of these enthusiastic reveries, a long-visaged, dry moral-looking phantom strides across my imagination, and pronounces these emphatic words:—

"I, Wisdom, dwell with Prudence. Friend, I do not come to open the ill-closed wounds of your follies and misfortunes, merely to give you pain: I wish through these wounds to imprint a lasting lesson on your heart. I will not mention how many of my salutary advices you have despised: I have given you line upon line and precept upon precept; and while I was chalking out to you the straight way to wealth and character, with audacious effrontery you have zigzagged across the path, contemning me to my face; you know the consequences. It is not yet three months since home was so hot for you, that you were on the wing for the western shore of the Atlantic, not to make a fortune, but to hide your misfortune.

"Now that your dear-loved Scotia puts it in your power to return to the situation of your forefathers, will you follow these will-o'-wisp meteors of fancy and whim, till they bring you once more to the brink of ruin? I grant that the utmost ground you can occupy is but half a step from the veriest poverty; but still it is half a step from it. If all that I can urge be ineffectual, let her who seldom calls to you in vain, let the call of pride prevail with you. You know how you feel at the iron gripe of ruthless oppression: you know how you bear the galling sneer of contumelious greatness. I hold you out the conveniences, the comforts of life, independence and character, on the one hand; I tender you servility, dependence, and wretchedness on the other. I will not insult your understanding by bidding you make a choice."

This, my lord, is unanswerable. I must return to my humble station, and woo my rustic muse in my wonted way at the plough-tail. Still, my lord, while the drops of life warm my heart, gratitude to that dear-loved country in which I boast my birth, and gratitude to those her distinguished sons, who have honoured me so much with their patronage and approbation, shall, while stealing through my humble shades, ever distend my bosom, and at times, as now, draw forth the swelling tear.

R. B.

[32] The Earl of Buchan was the very pink of parsimonious patrons.— MOTHERWELL.

XLIV.—TO MR. JAMES CANDLISH,[33]STUDENT IN PHYSIC, GLASGOW COLLEGE.

EDINBURGH, *March* 21*st*, 1787.

MY EVER DEAR OLD ACQUAINTANCE,—I was equally surprised and pleased at your letter, though I dare say you will think, by my delaying so long to write to you, that I am so drowned in the intovirarion of good fortune as to be indifferent to old, and once dear connections. The truth is, I was determined to write a good letter, full of argument, amplification, erudition, and, as Bayes says, *all that.* I thought of it, and thought of it, and, by my soul, I could not; and, lest you should mistake the cause of my silence, I just sit down to tell you so. Don't give yourself credit, though, that the strength of your logic scares me; the truth is, I never mean to meet you on that ground at all. You have shown me one thing which was to be demonstrated: that strong pride of reasoning, with a little affectation of singularity, may mislead the best of hearts. I likewise, since you and I were first acquainted, in the pride of despising old women's stories, ventured in "the daring path Spinosa trod;" but experience of the weakness, not the strength of human powers, made me glad to grasp at revealed religion.

I am still, in the Apostle Paul's phrase, "the old man with his deeds," as when we were sporting about the "Lady Thorn." I shall be four weeks here yet at least: and so I shall expect to hear from you; welcome sense, welcome nonsense.—I am, with the warmest sincerity, R. B.

[33] Mr. Candlish married Miss Smith, one of the six *belles* of Mauchline. Their son was the Rev. Dr. Candlish, of Free St. George's Church, Edinburgh.

XLV.—TO MR. PETER STUART, EDITOR OF "THE STAR," LONDON.

EDINBURGH, 1787.

MY DEAR SIR,—You may think, and too justly, that I am a selfish, ungrateful fellow, having received so many repeated instances of kindness from you, and yet never putting pen to paper to say thank you; but if you knew what a devil of a life my conscience has led me on that account, your good heart would think yourself too much avenged. By the by, there is nothing in the whole frame of man which seems to be so unaccountable as that thing called conscience. Had the troublesome yelping cur powers efficient to prevent a mischief, he might be of use; out at the beginning of the business, his feeble efforts are, to the workings of passion, as the infant frosts of an autumnal morning to the unclouded fervour of the rising sun; and no sooner are the tumultuous doings of the wicked deed over, than amidst the bitter native consequences of folly in the very vortex of our horrors, up starts conscience, and harrows us with the feelings of the damned.

I have inclosed you, by way of expiation, some verse and prose, that, if they merit a place in your truly entertaining miscellany, you are welcome to. The prose extract is literally as Mr. Sprott sent it me.

The inscription on the stone is as follows:—

"HERE LIES ROBERT FERGUSSON, POET,

Born, September 5th, 1751—Died, 16th October 1774.

No sculptured marble here, nor pompous lay,
'No storied urn nor animated bust;'
This simple stone directs pale Scotia's way
To pour her sorrows o'er her poet's dust."

On the other side of the stone is as follows:—

"By special grant of the managers to Robert Burns, who erected this stone, this burial place is to remain for ever sacred to the memory of Robert Fergusson."

XLVI—TO MRS. DUNLOP.

EDINBURGH, *March* 22*nd*, 1787.

MADAM,—I read your letter with watery eyes. A little, very little while ago, I had scarce a friend but the stubborn pride of my own bosom; now I am distinguished, patronised, befriended by you. Your friendly advices—I will not give them the cold name of criticisms—I receive with reverence. I have made some small alterations in what I before had printed. I have the advice of some very judicious friends among the literati here, but with them I sometimes find it necessary to claim the privilege of thinking for myself. The noble Earl of Glencairn, to whom I owe more than to any man, does me the honour of giving me his strictures; his hints, with respect to impropriety or indelicacy, I follow implicitly.

You kindly interest yourself in my future views and prospects; there I can give you no light. It is all

Dark as was Chaos ere the infant sun
Was roll'd together, or had tried his beams
Athwart the gloom profound.

The appellation of a Scottish bard is by far my highest pride; to continue to deserve it is my most exalted ambition. Scottish scenes and Scottish story are the themes I could wish to sing. I have no dearer aim than to have it in my power, unplagued with the routine of business, for which Heaven knows I am unfit enough, to make leisurely pilgrimages through Caledonia; to sit on the fields of her battles; to wander on the romantic banks of her rivers; and to muse by the stately towers or venerable ruins, once the honoured abodes of her heroes.

But these are all Utopian thoughts: I have dallied long enough with life; 'tis time to be in earnest. I have a fond, an aged mother to care for: and some other bosom ties perhaps equally tender. Where the individual only suffers by the consequences of his own thoughtlessness, indolence, or folly, he may be excusable; nay, shining abilities, and some of the nobler virtues, may half sanctify a heedless character; but where God and nature have intrusted the welfare of others to his care; where the trust is sacred, and the ties are dear, that man must be far gone in selfishness, or strangely lost to reflection, whom these connections will not rouse to exertion.

I guess that I shall clear between two and three hundred pounds by my authorship;[34] with that sum I intend, so far as I may be said to have any intention, to return to my old acquaintance, the plough; and, if I can meet with a lease by which I can live, to commence farmer. I do not intend to give up poetry; being bred to labour, secures me independence, and the muses are my chief, sometimes have been my only enjoyment. If my practice second my resolution, I shall have principally at heart the serious business of life; but while following my plough, or building up my shocks, I shall cast a leisure glance to that dear, that only feature of my character, which gave me the notice of my country, and the patronage of a Wallace.

Thus, honoured Madam, I have given you the bard, his situation, and his views, native as they are in his own bosom. R. B.

[34] The proceeds amounted to more—some £500 or so.

XLVII—TO MRS. DUNLOP.
EDINBURGH, 15*th April* 1787.

MADAM,—There is an affectation of gratitude which I dislike. The periods of Johnson and the pauses of Sterne may hide a selfish heart. For my part, Madam, I trust I have too much pride for servility, and too little prudence for selfishness. I have this moment broken open your letter, but

Rude am I in speech,
And therefore little can I grace my cause
In speaking for myself—

so I shall not trouble you with any fine speeches and hunted figures. I shall just lay my hand on my heart and say, I hope I shall ever have the truest, the warmest sense of your goodness.

I come abroad, in print, for certain on Wednesday. Your orders I shall punctually attend to; only, by the way, I must tell you that I was paid before for Dr. Moore's and Miss Williams's copies, through the medium of Commissioner Cochrane in this place, but that we can settle when I have the honour of waiting on you.

Dr. Smith[35] was just gone to London the morning before I received your letter to him. R. B.

[35] Adam Smith, the celebrated author of *The Wealth of Nations*.

XLVIII.—TO DR. MOORE.

EDINBURGH, 23rd *April* 1787.

I received the books, and sent the one you mentioned to Mrs. Dunlop. I am ill skilled in beating the coverts of imagination for metaphors of gratitude. I thank you, Sir, for the honour you have done me and to my latest hour will warmly remember it. To be highly pleased with your book, is what I have in common with the world; but to regard these volumes as a mark of the author's friendly esteem, is a still more supreme gratification.

I leave Edinburgh in the course of ten days or a fortnight, and after a few pilgrimages over some of the classic ground of Caledonia, Cowden Knowes, Banks of Yarrow, Tweed, etc., I shall return to my rural shades, in all likelihood never more to quit them. I have formed many intimacies and friendships here, but I am afraid they are all of too tender a construction to bear carriage a hundred and fifty miles. To the rich, the great, the fashionable, the polite, I have no equivalent to offer; and I am afraid my meteor appearance will by no means entitle me to a settled correspondence with any of you, who are the permanent lights of genius and literature.

My most respectful compliments to Miss Williams. If once this tangent flight of mine were over, and I were returned to my wonted leisurely motion in my old circle, I may probably endeavour to return her poetic compliment in kind. R. B.

XLIX.—TO MRS. DUNLOP.

EDINBURGH, 30th *April* 1787.

—Your criticisms, Madam, I understand very well, and could have wished to have pleased you better. You are right in your guess that I am not very amenable to counsel. Poets, much my superiors, have so flattered those who possessed the adventitious qualities of wealth and power, that I am determined to flatter no created being, either in prose or verse.

I set as little by princes, lords, clergy, critics, etc., as, all these respective gentry do by my bardship. I know what I may expect from the world, by-and-bye—illiberal abuse, and perhaps contemptuous neglect.

I am happy, Madam, that some of my own favourite pieces are distinguished by your particular approbation. For my "dream,"[36] which has unfortunately incurred your loyal displeasure, I hope, in four weeks, or less, to have the honour of appearing, at Dunlop, in its defence in person. R. B.

[36] The well-known poem, beginning, "Guid morning to your Majesty." Mrs. Dunlop had recommended its omission, in the second edition, on the score of prudence.

L—To MR. WILLIAM NICOL, CLASSICAL MASTER, HIGH SCHOOL, EDINBURGH.

CARLISLE, *June* 1, 1787.

KIND, HONEST-HEARTED WILLIE.—I'm sitten down here, after seven-and-forty miles' ridin', e'en as forjesket and forniaw'd as a forfoughten cock, to gie ye some notion o' my land lowper-like stravaguin sin the sorrowfu' hour that I sheuk hands and parted wi' auld Reekie.

My auld, ga'd gleyde o' a meere has huchyall'd up hill and down brae, in Scotland and England, as teugh and birnie as a very deil wi' me. It's true, she's as poor's a sang-maker and as hard's a kirk, and tipper-taipers when she taks the gate, first like a lady's gentlewoman in a minuwae, or a hen on a het girdle; but she's a yauld, poutherie Girran for a' that, and has a stomack like Willie Stalker's meere that wad hae disgeested tumbler-wheels, for she'll whip me aff her five stimparts o' the best aits at a down-sittin and ne'er fash her thumb. When ance her ring-banes and spavies, her crucks and cramps, are fairly soupl'd, she beets to, beets to, and aye the hindmost hour the tightest. I could wager her price to a thretty pennies, that for twa or three wooks ridin' at fifty miles a day, the deil-stickit a five gallopers acqueesh Clyde and Whithorn could cast saut on her tail.

I hae dander'd owre a' the kintra frae Dunbar to Selcraig, and hae forgather'd wi' mony a guid fallow, and mony a weelfar'd hizzie. I met wi' twa dink quines in particlar, ane o' them a sonsie, fine, fodgel lass, baith braw and bonnie; the tither was a clean-shankit, straught, tight, weel-far'd winch, as blythe's a lintwhite on a flowerie thorn, and as sweet and modest's a new blawn plumrose in a hazle shaw. They were baith bred to mainers by the beuk, and onie ane o' them had as muckle smeddum and rumblegumtion as the half o' some presbyteries that you and I baith ken.

I was gaun to write ye a lang pystle, but, Gude forgie me, I gat mysel sae notouriously fou the day after kail-time that I can hardly stoiter but and ben.

My best respecks to the guidwife and a' our common friens, especiall Mr. and Mrs. Cruikshank, and the honest guidman o' Jock's Lodge.[37]

I'll be in Dumfries the morn gif the beast be to the fore, and the branks bide hale.

Gude be wi' you, Willie! Amen!

R. B.

[37] Louis Cauvin, teacher of French.

LI.-To MR. WILLIAM NICOL.

MAUCHLINE, *June* 18, 1787.

My dear friend,—I am now arrived safe in my native country, after a very agreeable jaunt, and have the pleasure to find all my friends well. I breakfasted with your greyheaded, reverend friend, Mr. Smith; and was highly pleased, both with the cordial welcome he gave me, and his most excellent appearance and sterling good sense.

I have been with Mr. Miller at Dalswinton, and am to meet him again in August. From my view of the lands, and his reception of my bardship, my hopes in that business are rather mended; but still they are but slender.

I am quite charmed with Dumfries folks—Mr. Burnside, the clergyman, in particular, is a man whom I shall ever gratefully remember; and his wife, Gude forgie me! I had almost broke the tenth commandment on her account. Simplicity, elegance, good sense, sweetness of disposition, good humour, kind hospitality, are the constituents of her manner and heart; in short—but if I say one word more about her, I shall be directly in love with her.

I never, my friend, thought mankind very capable of anything generous; but the stateliness of the patricians in Edinburgh, and the servility of my plebeian brethren (who, perhaps, formerly eyed me askance) since I returned home, have nearly put me out of conceit altogether with my species. I have bought a pocket Milton which I carry perpetually about with me, in order to study the sentiments—the dauntless magnanimity, the intrepid, unyielding independence, the desperate daring, and noble defiance of hardship in that great personage, SATAN. 'Tis true, I have just now a little cash; but I am afraid the star that hitherto has shed its malignant, purpose-blasting rays full in my zenith; that noxious planet, so baneful in its influence to the rhyming tribe—I much dread it is not yet beneath my horizon. Misfortune dodges the path of human life; the poetic mind finds itself miserably deranged in, and unfit for the walks of business; add to all, that thoughtless follies and hare-brained whims, like so many *ignes fatui*, eternally diverging from the right line of sober discretion, sparkle with step-bewitching blaze in the idly-gazing eyes of the poor heedless Bard, till, pop, "he falls like Lucifer, never to hope again." God grant this may be an unreal picture with respect to me! but should it not, I have very little dependence on mankind. I will close my letter with this tribute my heart bids me pay you—the many ties of acquaintance and friendship which I have, or think I have in life, I have felt along the lines, and damn them, they are almost all of them of such frail contexture, that I am sure they would not stand the breath of the least adverse breeze of fortune; but from you, my ever dear Sir, I look with confidence for the Apostolic love that shall wait on me "through good report and bad report"—the love which Solomon emphatically says "is strong as death." My compliments to Mrs. Nicol and all the circle of our common friends.

P.S.—I shall be in Edinburgh about the latter end of July.

R. B.

LII.-To MR. ROBERT AINSLIE
[38]

ARROCHAR, 28*th June* 1787.

My dear sir,—I write this on my tour through a country where savage streams tumble over savage mountains, thinly overspread with savage flocks, which sparingly support as savage inhabitants. My last stage was Inverary—to-morrow night's stage Dumbarton. I ought sooner to have answered your kind letter, but you know I am a man of many sins. R. B. [38] A young writer in Edinburgh.

LIII.—TO MR. JAMES SMITH, LINLITHGOW, FORMERLY OF MAUCHLINE
June 30th, 1787.

MY DEAR FRIEND,—On our return, at a Highland gentleman's hospitable mansion, we fell in with a merry party, and danced till the ladies left us, at three in the morning. Our dancing was none of the French or English insipid formal movements; the ladies sung Scotch songs like angels, at intervals; then we flew at *Bab at the Bowster, Tullochgorum, Loch Erroch Side,*[39] etc., like midges sporting in the mottie sun, or craws prognosticating a storm in a hairst day. When the dear lasses left us, we ranged round the bowl till the good-fellow hour of six; except a few minutes that we went out to pay our devotions to the glorious lamp of day peering over the towering top of Benlomond. We all kneeled; our worthy landlord's son held the bowl; each man a full glass in his hand; and I, as priest, repeated some rhyming nonsense, like Thomas-a-Rhymer's prophecies, I suppose. After a small refreshment of the gifts of Somnus, we proceeded to spend the day on Lochlomond, and reached Dumbarton in the evening. We dined at another good fellow's house, and, consequently, pushed the bottle; when we went out to mount our horses we found ourselves "No vera fou but gaylie yet." My two friends and I rode soberly down the Loch side, till by came a Highlandman at the gallop, on a tolerably good horse, but which had never known the ornaments of iron or leather. We scorned to be out-galloped by a Highlandman, so off we started, whip and spur. My companions, though seemingly gaily mounted, fell sadly astern; but my old mare, Jenny Geddes, one of the Rosinante family, she strained past the Highlandman in spite of all his efforts with the hair halter: just as I was passing him, Donald wheeled his horse, as if to cross before me to mar my progress, when down came his horse, and threw his rider's breekless a—— in a clipt hedge; and down came Jenny Geddes over all, and my hardship between her and the Highlandman's horse. Jenny Geddes trode over me with such cautious reverence, that matters were not so bad as might well have been expected; so I came off with a few cuts and bruises, and a thorough resolution to be a pattern of sobriety for the future.

I have yet fixed on nothing with respect to the serious business of life. I am, just as usual, a rhyming, mason-making, raking, aimless, idle fellow. However, I shall somewhere have a farm soon. I was going to say, a wife too; but that must never be my blessed lot. I am but a younger son of the house of Parnassus, and like other younger sons of great families, I may intrigue, if I choose to run all risks, but must not marry.

I am afraid I have almost ruined one source, the principal one indeed, of my former happiness; that eternal propensity I always had to fall in love. My heart no more glows with feverish rapture. I have no paradisiacal evening interviews, stolen from the restless cares and prying inhabitants of this weary world. I have only ——. This last is one of your distant acquaintances, has a fine figure, and elegant manners; and in the train of some great folks whom you know, has seen the politest quarters in Europe. I do like her a deal; but what piques me is her conduct at the commencement of our acquaintance. I frequently visited her when I was in ——, and after passing regularly the intermediate degrees between the distant formal bow and the familiar grasp round the waist, I ventured, in my careless way, to talk of friendship in rather ambiguous terms; and after her return to ——, I wrote to her in the same style. Miss, construing my words farther, I suppose, than even I intended, flew off in a tangent of female dignity and reserve, like a mounting lark in an April morning; and wrote me an answer which measured me out very completely what an immense way I had to travel before I could reach the climate of her favour. But I am an old hawk at the sport, and wrote her such a cool, deliberate, prudent reply, as brought my bird from her aerial towerings, pop down at my foot, like Corporal Trim's hat.

As for the rest of my acts, and my wars, and all my wise sayings, and why my mare was called Jenny Geddes, they shall be recorded in a few weeks hence at Linlithgow, in the chronicles of your memory, by

R. B.

[39] Scotch tunes.

LIV.-To MR. JOHN RICHMOND.

MOSSGIEL, 7th *July* 1787.

MY DEAR RICHMOND,-I am all impatience to hear of your fate since the old confounder of right and wrong has turned you out of place, by his journey to answer his indictment at the bar of the other world. He will find the practice of the court so different from the practice in which he has for so many years been thoroughly hackneyed, that his friends, if he had any connections truly of that kind, which I rather doubt, may well tremble for his sake. His chicane, his left-handed wisdom, which stood so firmly by him, to such good purpose, here, like other accomplices in robbery and plunder, will, now the piratical business is blown, in all probability turn king's evidences, and then the devil's bagpiper will touch him off "Bundle and go!"

If he has left you any legacy, I beg your pardon for all this; if not, I know you will swear to every word I said about him.

I have lately been rambling over by Dumbarton and Inverary, and running a drunken race on the side of Loch Lomond with a wild Highlandman; his horse, which had never known the ornaments of iron or leather, zig-zagged across before my old spavin'd hunter, whose name is Jenny Geddes, and down came the Highlandman, horse and all, and down came Jenny and my bardship; so I have got such a skinful of bruises and wounds, that I shall be at least four weeks before I dare venture on my journey to Edinburgh.

Not one new thing under the sun has happened in Mauchline since you left it. I hope this will find you as comfortably situated as formerly, or, if heaven pleases, more so; but, at all events, I trust you will let me know of course how matters stand with you, well or ill. 'Tis but poor consolation to tell the world when matters go wrong; but you know very well your connection and mine stands on a different footing.—I am ever, my dear friend, yours,

R. B.

LV.—TO MR. ROBERT AINSLIE.

MAUCHLINE, *23rd July* 1787.

MY DEAR AINSLIE,-There is one thing for which I set great store by you as a friend, and it is this, that I have not a friend upon earth, besides yourself, to whom I can talk nonsense without forfeiting some degree of his esteem. Now, to one like me, who never cares for speaking anything else but nonsense, such a friend as you is an invaluable treasure. I was never a rogue, but have been a fool all my life; and, in spite of all my endeavours, I see now plainly that I shall never be wise. Now it rejoices my heart to have met with such a fellow as you, who, though you are not just such a hopeless fool as I, yet I trust you will never listen so much to temptation as to grow so very wise that you will in the least disrespect an honest fellow because he is a fool. In short, I have set you down as the staff of my old age, when the whole list of my friends will, after a decent share of pity, have forgot me.

Though in the morn comes sturt and strife,
Yet joy may come at noon;
And I hope to live a merry, merry life
When a' thir days are done.

Write me soon, were it but a few lines, just to tell me how that good, sagacious man your father is,—that kind, dainty body your mother,—that strapping chiel your brother Douglas-and my friend Rachel, who is as far before Rachel of old, as she was before her blear-eyed sister Leah.

R. B.

LVI-To DR. MOORE.
MAUCHLINE, 2nd August 1787.

SIR,-For some months past I have been rambling over the country, but I am now confined with some lingering complaints, originating, as I take it, in the stomach. To divert my spirits a little in this miserable fog of ennui, I have taken a whim to give you a history of myself. My name has made some little noise in this country; you have done me the honour to interest yourself very warmly in my behalf; and I think a faithful account of what character of a man I am, and how I came by that character, may perhaps amuse you in an idle moment. I will give you an honest narrative, though I know it will be often at my own expense; for I assure you, Sir, I have, like Solomon, whose character, excepting in the trifling affair of wisdom, I sometimes think I resemble,—I have, I say, like him, turned my eyes to behold madness and folly, and like him, too, frequently shaken hands with their intoxicating friendship. After you have perused these pages, should you think them trifling and impertinent, I only beg leave to tell you, that the poor author wrote them under some twitching qualms of conscience, arising from a suspicion that he was doing what he ought not to do: a predicament he has more than once been in before.

I have not the most distant pretensions to assume that character which the pye-coated guardians of escutcheons call a gentleman. When at Edinburgh last winter, I got acquainted in the herald's office; and, looking through that granary of honours, I there found almost every name in the kingdom; but for me,
My ancient but ignoble blood
Has crept thro' scoundrels ever since the flood.

Gules, purpure, argent, etc., quite disowned me.

My father was in the north of Scotland the son of a farmer, and was thrown by early misfortunes on the world at large, where, after many years' wanderings and sojournings, he picked up a pretty large quantity of observation and experience, to which I am indebted for most of my little pretensions to wisdom. I have met with few who understood men, their manners, and their ways, equal to him; but stubborn, ungainly integrity, and headlong, ungovernable irascibility are disqualifying circumstances; consequently, I was born a very poor man's son. For the first six or seven years of my life, my father was gardener to a worthy gentleman of small estate in the neighbourhood of Ayr. Had he continued in that station, I must have marched off to be one of the little underlings about a farm house; but it was his dearest wish and prayer to have it in his power to keep his children under his own eye, till they could discern between good and evil; so, with the assistance of his generous master, my father ventured on a small farm on his estate. At those years, I was by no means a favourite with anybody. I was a good deal noted for a retentive memory, a stubborn sturdy something in my disposition, and an enthusiastic idiot piety. I say idiot piety, because I was then but a child. Though it cost the schoolmaster some thrashings, I made an excellent English scholar; and by the time I was ten or eleven years of age, I was a critic in substantives, verbs, and particles. In my infant and boyish days, too, I owed much to an old woman who resided in the family, remarkable for her ignorance, credulity, and superstition. She had, I suppose, the largest collection in the country of tales and songs concerning devils, ghosts, fairies, brownies, witches, warlocks, spunkies, kelpies, elf-candles, dead-lights, wraiths, apparitions, cantraips, giants, enchanted towers, dragons, and other trumpery. This cultivated the latent seeds of poetry, but had so strong an effect on my imagination, that to

this hour, in my nocturnal rambles, I sometimes keep a sharp look out in suspicious places; and though nobody can be more sceptical than I am in such matters, yet it often takes an effort of philosophy to shake off these idle terrors. The earliest composition that I recollect taking pleasure in was "The Vision of Mirza," and a hymn of Addison's, beginning, "How are thy servants blest, O Lord!" I particularly remember one half-stanza which was music to my boyish ear—
"For though on dreadful whirls we hung
High on the broken wave—"

I met with these pieces in Manson's English Collection, one of my school-books. The first two books I ever read in private, and which gave me more pleasure than any two books I ever read since, were the *Life of Hannibal*, and the *History of Sir William Wallace*. Hannibal gave my young ideas such a turn, that I used to strut in rapture up and down after the recruiting drum and bag-pipe, and wish myself tall enough to be a soldier; while the story of Wallace poured a Scottish prejudice into my veins which will boil along there, till the flood-gates of life shut in eternal rest.

Polemical divinity about this time was putting the country half mad, and I, ambitious of shining in conversation parties on Sundays, between sermons, at funerals, etc., used a few years afterwards to puzzle Calvinism with so much heat and indiscretion, that I raised a hue and cry of heresy against me, which has not ceased to this hour.

My vicinity to Ayr was of some advantage to me. My social disposition, when not checked by some modifications of spirited pride, was like our catechism definition of infinitude, without bounds or limits. I formed several connections with other younkers, who possessed superior advantages; the youngling actors who were busy in the rehearsal of parts, in which they were shortly to appear on the stage of life, where, alas! I was destined to drudge behind the scenes. It is not commonly at this green stage that our young gentry have a just sense of the immense distance between them and their ragged play-fellows. It takes a few dashes into the world, to give the young great man that proper, decent, unnoticing disregard for the poor, insignificant, stupid devils, the mechanics and peasantry around him, who were, perhaps, born in the same village. My young superiors never insulted the clouterly appearance of my plough-boy carcase, the two extremes of which were often exposed to all the inclemencies of all the seasons. They would give me stray volumes of books; among them, even then, I could pick up some observations; and one, whose heart, I am sure, not even the "Munny Begum" scenes have tainted, helped me to a little French. Parting with these my young friends and benefactors, as they occasionally went off for the East or West Indies, was often to me a sore affliction; but I was soon called to more serious evils. My father's generous master died; the farm proved a ruinous bargain; and to clench the misfortune, we fell into the hands of a factor, who sat for the picture I have drawn of one in my tale of "Twa Dogs." My father was advanced in life when he married; I was the eldest of seven children, and he, worn out by early hardships, was unfit for labour. My father's spirit was soon irritated, but not easily broken. There was a freedom in his lease in two years more, and to weather these two years, we retrenched our expenses. We lived very poorly: I was a dexterous ploughman for my age; and the next eldest to me was a brother (Gilbert), who could drive a plough very well, and help me to thrash the corn. A novel-writer might, perhaps, have viewed these scenes with some satisfaction, but so did not I; my indignation yet boils at the recollection of the scoundrel factor's insolent threatening letters, which used to set us all in tears.

This kind of life—the cheerless gloom of a hermit with the unceasing moil of a galley-slave, brought me to my sixteenth year; a little before which period I first committed the sin of rhyme. You know our country custom of coupling a man and woman together as partners in the labours of harvest. In my fifteenth autumn, my partner was a bewitching creature, a year younger than myself. My scarcity of English denies me the power of doing her justice in that language, but you know the Scottish idiom: she was a "bonnie, sweet, sonsie lass." In short, she, altogether unwittingly to herself, initiated me in that delicious passion, which, in spite of acid disappointment, gin-horse prudence, and book-worm philosophy, I hold to be the first of human joys, our dearest blessing here below! How she caught the contagion I cannot tell; you medical people talk much of infection from breathing the same air, the touch, etc.; but I never expressly said I loved her. Indeed, I did not know myself why I liked so much to loiter behind with her, when returning in the evening from our labours; why the tones of her voice made my heart-strings thrill like an Aeolian harp; and particularly why my pulse beat such a furious ratan, when I looked and fingered over her little hand to pick out the cruel nettle-stings and thistles. Among her other love-inspiring qualities, she sung sweetly; and it was her favourite reel to which I attempted giving an embodied vehicle in rhyme. I was not so presumptuous as to imagine that I could make verses like printed ones, composed by men who had Greek and Latin; but my girl sung a song which was said to be composed by a small country laird's son, on one of his father's maids, with whom he was in love; and I saw no reason why I might not rhyme as well as he; for, excepting that he could smear sheep, and cast peats, his father living in the moorlands, he had no more scholar-craft than myself.

Thus with me began love and poetry; which at times have been my only, and till within the last twelve months, have been my highest enjoyment. My father struggled on till he reached the freedom in his lease, when he entered on a larger farm, about ten miles farther in the country. The nature of the bargain he made was such as to throw a little ready money into his hands at the commencement of his lease, otherwise the affair would have been impracticable. For four years we lived comfortably here, but a difference commencing between him and his landlord as to terms, after three years tossing and whirling in the vortex of litigation, my father was just saved from the horrors of a jail, by a consumption, which, after two years' promises, kindly stepped in, and carried him away, to where the wicked cease from troubling, and where the weary are at rest!

It is during the time that we lived on this farm that my little story is most eventful. I was, at the beginning of this period, perhaps the most ungainly awkward boy in the parish— no *solitaire* was less acquainted with the ways of the world. What I knew of ancient story was gathered from Salmon's and Guthrie's Geographical Grammars; and the ideas I had formed of modern manners, of literature, and criticism, I got from the *Spectator*. These, with Pope's Works, some Plays of Shakespeare, Tull and Dickson on Agriculture, *The Pantheon*, Locke's *Essay on the Human Understanding,* Stackhouse's *History of the Bible,* Justice's *British Gardener's Directory*, Boyle's *Lectures*, Allan Ramsays's Works, Taylor's*Scripture Doctrine of Original Sin, A Select Collection of English Songs,* and Hervey's *Meditations,* had formed the whole of my reading. The collection of songs was my *vade mecum.* I pored over them, driving my cart, or walking to labour, song by song, verse by verse; carefully noting the true tender, or sublime, from affectation and fustian. I am convinced I owe to this practice much of my critic-craft, such as it is.

In my seventeenth year, to give my manners a brush, I went to a country dancing-school. My father had an unaccountable antipathy against these meetings, and my going was, what to this moment I repent, in opposition to his wishes. My father, as I said before, was subject to strong passions; from that instance of disobedience in me, he took a sort of dislike to me, which, I believe, was one cause of the dissipation which marked my succeeding years. I say dissipation, comparatively with the strictness, and sobriety, and regularity of presbyterian country life; for though the will-o'-wisp meteors of thoughtless whim were almost the sole lights of my path, yet early ingrained piety and virtue kept me for several years afterwards within the line of innocence. The great misfortune of my life was to want an aim. I had felt early some stirrings of ambition, but they were the blind gropings of Homer's Cyclops round the walls of his cave. I saw my father's situation entailed on me perpetual labour. The only two openings by which I could enter the temple of fortune were the gate of niggardly economy, or the path of little chicaning bargain-making. The first is so contracted an aperture I never could squeeze myself into it—the last I always hated—there was contamination in the very entrance! Thus abandoned of aim or view in life, with a strong appetite for sociability, as well from native hilarity as from a pride of observation and remark; a constitutional melancholy or hypochondriasm that made me fly solitude; add to these incentives to social life, my reputation for bookish knowledge, a certain wild logical talent, and a strength of thought something like the rudiments of good sense; and it will not seem surprising that I was generally a welcome guest where I visited, or any great wonder that always, where two or three met together, there was I among them. But far beyond all other impulses of my heart, was *un penchant à l'adorable moitié du genre humain*. My heart was completely tinder, and was eternally lighted up by some goddess or other; and, as in every other warfare in this world, my fortune was various; sometimes I was received with favour, and sometimes I was mortified with a repulse. At the plough, scythe, or reap-hook, I feared no competitor, and thus I set absolute want at defiance; and as I never cared further for my labours than while I was in actual exercise, I spent the evenings in the way after my own heart. A country lad seldom carries on a love adventure without an assisting confidant. I possessed a curiosity, zeal, and intrepid dexterity that recommended me as a proper second on these occasions; and I dare say I felt as much pleasure in being in the secret of half the loves of the parish of Tarbolton, as ever did statesman in knowing the intrigues of half the courts of Europe. The very goose-feather in my hand seems to know instinctively the well-worn path of my imagination, the favourite theme of my song, and is with difficulty restrained from giving you a couple of paragraphs on the love-adventures of my compeers, the humble inmates of the farm-house and cottage; but the grave sons of science, ambition, or avarice, baptise these things by the name of follies. To the sons and daughters of labour and poverty they are matters of the most serious nature: to them the ardent hope, the stolen interview, the tender farewell, are the greatest and most delicious parts of their enjoyments.

Another circumstance in my life which made some alteration in my mind and manners, was, that I spent my nineteenth summer on a smuggling coast, a good distance from home, at a noted school, to learn mensuration, surveying, dialling, etc., in which I made a pretty good progress. But I made a greater progress in the knowledge of mankind. The contraband trade was at that time very successful, and it sometimes happened to me to fall in with those who carried it on. Scenes of swaggering riot and roaring dissipation were, till this time, new to me: but I was no enemy to social life. Here, though I learned to fill my glass, and to mix without fear in a drunken squabble, yet I went on with a high hand with my geometry, till the sun entered Virgo, a month which is always a carnival in my bosom, when a charming fillette, who lived next door to the school, overset my trigonometry, and set me off at a tangent from the spheres of my studies. I, however, struggled on with my sines and cosines for a few days more; but stepping into the garden one charming noon, to take the sun's altitude, there I met my angel,
Like Proserpine gathering flowers,
Herself a fairer flower.
It was in vain to think of doing any more good at school.

The remaining week I staid I did nothing but craze the faculties of my soul about her, or steal out to meet her; and the two last nights of my stay in the country, had sleep been a mortal sin, the image of this modest and innocent girl had kept me guiltless.

I returned home very considerably improved. My reading was enlarged with the very important edition of Thomson's and Shenstone's Works; I had seen human nature in a new phasis; and I engaged several of my schoolfellows to keep up a literary correspondence with me. This improved me in composition. I had met with a collection of letters by the wits of Queen Anne's reign, and I pored over them most devoutly. I kept copies of any of my own letters that pleased me, and a comparison between them and the composition of most of my correspondents flattered my vanity. I carried this whim so far, that though I had not three-farthings' worth of business in the world, yet almost every post brought me as many letters as if I had been a broad plodding son of day-book and ledger.

My life flowed on much in the same course till my twenty-third year. *Vive l'amour, et vive la bagatelle*, were my sole principles of action. The addition of two more authors to my library gave me great pleasure; Sterne and Mackenzie—*Tristram Shandy* and the *Man of Feeling* were my bosom favourites. Poesy was still a darling walk for my mind, but it was only indulged in according to the humour of the hour. I had usually half-a-dozen or more pieces on hand: I took up one or other, as it suited the momentary tone of the mind, and dismissed the work as it bordered on fatigue. My passions, when once lighted up, raged like so many devils, till they got vent in rhyme; and then the conning over my verses, like a spell, soothed all into quiet! None of the rhymes of those days are in print, except "Winter, a Dirge," the eldest of my printed pieces; "The Death of Poor Maillie," "John Barleycorn," and songs first, second, and third. Song second was the ebullition of that passion which ended the forementioned school business.

My twenty-third year was to me an important era. Partly through whim, and partly that I wished to set about doing something in life, I joined a flax-dresser in a neighbouring town (Irvine), to learn his trade. This was an unlucky affair. My partner was a scoundrel of the first water; and to finish the whole, as we were giving a welcome carousal to the New Year, the shop took fire and burnt to ashes, and I was left, like a true poet, not worth a sixpence.

I was obliged to give up this scheme; the clouds of misfortune were gathering thick round my father's head; and, what was worst of all, he was visibly far gone in a consumption; and, to crown my distresses, a *belle fille*, whom I adored, and who had pledged her soul to meet me in the field of matrimony, jilted me, with peculiar circumstances of mortification. The finishing evil that brought up the rear of this infernal file, was my constitutional melancholy being increased to such a degree that for three months I was in a state of mind scarcely to be envied by the hopeless wretches who have got their mittimus—"Depart from me, ye cursed."

From this adventure I learned something of a town life; but the principal thing which gave my mind a turn was a friendship I formed with a young fellow, a very noble character, but a hapless son of misfortune.[40] He was the son of a simple mechanic; but a great man in the neighbourhood taking him under his patronage, gave him a genteel education, with a view of bettering his situation in life. The patron dying just as he was ready to launch out into the world, the poor fellow, in despair, went to sea; where, after a variety of good and ill fortune, a little before I was acquainted with him he had been sent on shore by an American privateer, on the wild coast of Connaught, stripped of everything. I cannot quit this poor fellow's story without adding, that he is at this time master of a large West-India-man belonging to the Thames.

His mind was fraught with independence, magnanimity, and every manly virtue. I loved and admired him to a degree of enthusiasm, and of course strove to imitate him.

In some measure I succeeded; I had pride before, but he taught it to flow in proper channels. His knowledge of the world was vastly superior to mine, and I was all attention to learn. He was the only man I ever saw who was a greater fool than myself where woman was the presiding star; but he spoke of illicit love with the levity of a sailor, which hitherto I had regarded with horror. Here his friendship did me a mischief, and the consequence was, that soon after I resumed the plough, I wrote the "Poet's Welcome." My reading only increased while in this town by two stray volumes of *Pamela*, and one of *Ferdinand Count Fathom*, which gave me some idea of novels. Rhyme, except some religious pieces that are in print, I had given up; but meeting with Fergusson's Scottish Poems, I strung anew my wildly-sounding lyre with emulating vigour. When my father died, his all went among the hell-hounds that prowl in the kennel of justice; but we made a shift to collect a little money in the family amongst us, with which, to keep us together, my brother and I took a neighbouring farm. My brother wanted my hair-brained imagination, as well as my social and amorous madness; but in good sense, and every sober qualification, he was far my superior.

I entered on this farm with a full resolution, "Come, go to, I will be wise!" I read farming books; I calculated crops; I attended markets; and, in short, in spite of the devil, and the world, and the flesh, I believe I should have been a wise man; but the first year, from unfortunately buying bad seed, the second from a late harvest, we lost half our crops. This overset all my wisdom, and I returned "like the dog to his vomit, and the sow that was washed, to her wallowing in the mire."

I now began to be known in the neighbourhood as a maker of rhymes. The first of my poetic offspring that saw the light was a burlesque lamentation on a quarrel between two reverend Calvinists, both of them *dramatis personæ* in my "Holy Fair". I had a notion myself that the piece had some merit; but, to prevent the worst, I gave a copy of it to a friend, who was very fond of such things, and told him that I could not guess who was the author of it, but that I thought it pretty clever. With a certain description of the clergy, as well as laity, it met with a roar of applause. "Holy Willie's Prayer" next made its appearance, and alarmed the kirk-session so much, that they held several meetings to look over their spiritual artillery, if haply any of it might be pointed against profane rhymers. Unluckily for me, my wanderings led me on another side, within point-blank shot of their heaviest metal. This is the unfortunate story that gave rise to my printed poem, "The Lament." This was a most melancholy affair, which I cannot yet bear to reflect on, and had very nearly given me one or two of the principal qualifications for a place among those who have lost the chart, and mistaken the reckoning of rationality. I gave up my part of the farm to my brother; in truth it was only nominally mine; and made what little preparation was in my power for Jamaica. But before leaving my native country for ever, I resolved to publish my poems. I weighed my productions as impartially as was in my power; I thought they had merit; and it was a delicious idea that I should be called a clever fellow, even though it should never reach my ears—a poor negro-driver—or perhaps a victim to that inhospitable clime, and gone to the world of spirits! I can truly say, that, *pauvre inconnu* as I then was, I had pretty nearly as high an idea of myself and of my works as I have at this moment, when the public has decided in their favour. It ever was my opinion that the mistakes and blunders, both in a rational and religious point of view, of which we see thousands daily guilty, are owing to their ignorance of themselves. To know myself, had been all along my constant study. I weighed myself alone; I balanced myself with others; I watched every means of information, to see how much ground I occupied as a man, and as a poet; I studied assiduously Nature's design in my formation—where the lights and shades in my character were intended. I was pretty confident my poems would meet with some applause; but at the worst, the roar of the Atlantic would deafen the voice of censure, and the novelty of West Indian scenes make me forget neglect. I threw off six hundred copies, of which I had got subscriptions for about three hundred and fifty. My vanity was highly gratified by the reception I met with from the public; and besides, I pocketed, all expenses deducted, nearly twenty pounds. This sum came very seasonably, as I was thinking of indenting myself, for want of money to procure my passage. As soon as I was master of nine guineas, the price of wafting me to the torrid zone, I took a steerage passage in the first ship that was to sail from the Clyde, for

Hungry ruin had me in the wind.

I had been for some days skulking from covert to covert, under all the terrors of a jail; as some ill-advised people had uncoupled the merciless pack of the law at my heels. I had taken the last farewell of my few friends; my chest was on the road to Greenock; I had composed the last song I should ever measure in Caledonia—"The gloomy night is gathering fast," when a letter from Dr. Blacklock to a friend of mine overthrew all my schemes, by opening new prospects to my poetic ambition. The doctor belonged to a set of critics, for whose applause I had not dared to hope. His opinion, that I would meet with encouragement in Edinburgh for a second edition, fired me so much, that away I posted for that city, without a single acquaintance or a single letter of introduction. The baneful star that had so long shed its blasting influence in my zenith, for once made a revolution to the nadir; and a kind Providence placed me under the patronage of one of the noblest of men, the Earl of Glencairn. *Oubliez moi, grand Dieu, si jamais je l'oublie!*

I need relate no farther. At Edinburgh I was in a new world; I mingled among many classes of men, but all of them new to me, and I was all attention to "catch" the characters, and "the manners living as they rise."

You can now, Sir, form a pretty near guess of what sort of a wight he is whom for some time you have honoured with your correspondence. That whim and fancy, keen sensibility and riotous passions, may still make him zigzag in his future path of life is very probable; but come what will, I shall answer for him the most determinate integrity and honour. And though his evil star should again blaze in his meridian with tenfold more direful influence, he may reluctantly tax friendship with pity, but with no more.

My most respectful compliments to Miss Williams.[41] The very elegant and friendly letter she honoured me with a few days ago I cannot answer at present, as my presence is required at Edinburgh for a week or so, and I set off to-morrow.

I enclose you *Holy Willie* for the sake of giving you a little further information of the affair than Mr. Creech[42] could do. An elegy I composed the other day on Sir James H. Blair, if time allow, I will transcribe. The merit is just mediocre.

If you will oblige me so highly, and do me so much honour as now and then to drop me a line, please direct to me at Mauchline. With the most grateful respect, I have the honour to be, Sir, your very humble servant, ROBERT BURNS.[43]

[40] Richard Brown.

[41] A young poetical lady, though not a poetess.

[42] His Edinburgh publisher; a bookseller, afterwards Lord Provost of the city.

[43] The foregoing biographical letter brings us down to Burns's 29th year.

LVIL.—To MR. ARCHIBALD LAWRIE.[44]

EDINBURGH, 14*th August* 1787.

MY DEAR SIR,—Here am I. That is all I can tell you of that unaccountable being, myself. What I am doing no mortal can tell; what I am thinking, I myself cannot tell; what I am usually saying is not worth telling. The clock is just striking—one, two, three, four...twelve, forenoon; and here I sit in the attic storey, the garret, with a friend on the right hand of my standish, a friend whose kindness I shall largely experience at the close of this line—there, thank you!—a friend, my dear Lawrie, whose kindness often makes me blush—a friend who has more of the milk of human kindness than all the human race put together, and what is highly to his honour, peculiarly a friend to the friendless as often as they come his way; in short, Sir, he is wthout the least alloy a universal philanthropist, and his much-beloved name is a bottle of good old Port!

In a week, if whim and weather serve, I set out for the north, a tour to the Highlands.

I ate some Newhaven broth—in other words, boiled mussels—with Mr. Farquharson's family t'other day. Now I see you prick up your ears. They are all well, and mademoiselle is particularly well. She begs her respects to you all—along with which please present those of your humble servant. I can no more. I have so high a veneration, or rather idolatrization, for the clerical character, that even a little *futurum esse*priestling, with his *penna pennæ*, throws an awe over my mind in his presence, and shortens my sentences into single ideas.

Farewell, and believe me to be ever, my dear Sir, yours,
ROBERT BURNS.

[44] Son, and successor, to the minister of Loudon.

LVIII.—To MR. ROBERT MUIR, KILMARNOCK.

STIRLING, 26*th August* 1787.

MY DEAR SIR,—I intended to have written you from Edinburgh, and now write you from Stirling to make an excuse. Here am I, on my way to Inverness, with a truly original, but very worthy man, a Mr. Nicol, one of the masters of the High-school in Edinburgh. I left Auld Reekie yesterday morning, and have passed, besides by-excursions, Linlithgow, Borrowstounness, Falkirk, and here am I undoubtedly. This morning I knelt at the tomb of Sir John the Graham, the gallant friend of the immortal Wallace; and two hours ago I said a fervent prayer for old Caledonia over the hole in a blue whinstone, where Robert de Bruce fixed his royal standard on the banks of Bannockburn and just now, from Stirling Castle, I have seen by the setting sun the glorious prospect of the windings of Forth through the rich carse of Stirling, and skirting the equally rich carse of Falkirk. The crops are very strong, but so very late that there is no harvest except a ridge or two perhaps in ten miles, all the way I have travelled from Edinburgh.

I left Andrew Bruce[45] and family all well. I will be at least three weeks in making my tour, as I shall return by the coast, and have many people to call for.

My best compliments to Charles, our dear kinsman and fellow-saint; and Messrs. W. and H. Parkers. I hope Hughoc[46] is going on and prospering with God and Miss M'Causlin.

If I could think on anything sprightly, I should let you hear every other post; but a dull, matter-of-fact business like this scrawl, the less and seldomer one writes the better.

Among other matters-of-fact I shall add this, that I am and ever shall be, my dear Sir, your obliged,

ROBERT BURNS.

[45] A shopkeeper on the North Bridge, Edinburgh.

[46] The wee Hughoc mentioned in "Poor Maillie."

LIX.—TO MR. GAVIN HAMILTON.

STIRLING, *28th August* 1787.

MY DEAR SIR,—Here am I on my way to Inverness. I have rambled over the rich, fertile carses of Falkirk and Stirling, and am delighted with their appearance: richly waving crops of wheat, barley, etc., but no harvest at all yet, except, in one or two places, an old-wife's ridge. Yesterday morning I rode from this town up the meandering Devon's banks, to pay my respects to some Ayrshire folks at Harvieston. After breakfast, we made a party to go and see the famous Caudron-linn, a remarkable cascade in the Devon, about five miles above Harvieston; and after spending one of the most pleasant days I ever had in my life, I returned to Stirling in the evening. They are a family, Sir, though I had not had any prior tie, though they had not been the brother and sisters of a certain generous friend of mine, I would never forget them. I am told you have not seen them these several years, so you can have very little idea of what these young folks are now. Your brother[47] is as tall as you are, but slender rather than otherwise; and I have the satisfaction to inform you that he is getting the better of those consumptive symptoms which I suppose you know were threatening him. His make, and particularly his manner, resemble you, but he will have a still finer face. (I put in the word still, to please Mrs. Hamilton.) Good sense, modesty, and at the same time a just idea of that respect that man owes to man, and has a right in his turn to exact, are striking features in his character; and, what with me is the Alpha and the Omega, he has a heart that might adorn the breast of a poet! Grace has a good figure, and the look of health and cheerfulness, but nothing else remarkable in her person. I scarcely ever saw so striking a likeness as is between her and your little Beenie; the mouth and chin particularly. She is reserved at first; but as we grew better acquainted, I was delighted with the native frankness of her manner, and the sterling sense of her observation. Of Charlotte I cannot speak in common terms of admiration: she is not only beautiful but lovely. Her form is elegant; her features not regular, but they have the smile of sweetness, and the settled complacency of good nature in the highest degree; and her complexion, now that she has happily recovered her wonted health, is equal to Miss Burnet's. After the exercises of our riding to the Falls, Charlotte was exactly Dr. Donne's mistress:—

Her pure and eloquent blood
Spoke in her cheeks, and so distinctly wrought,
That one would almost say her body thought.

Her eyes are fascinating; at once expressive of good sense, tenderness, and a noble mind.

I do not give you all this account, my good Sir, to flatter you. I mean it to reproach you. Such relations the first peer in the realm might own with pride; then why do you not keep up more correspondence with these so amiable young folks? I had a thousand questions to answer about you. I had to describe the little ones with the minuteness of anatomy. They were highly delighted when I told them that John[48] was so good a boy, and so fine a scholar, and that Willie was going on still very pretty; but I have it in commission to tell her from them, that beauty is a poor silly bauble without she be good. Miss Chalmers I had left in Edinburgh, but I had the pleasure of meeting with Mrs. Chalmers, only Lady Mackenzie being rather a little alarmingly ill of a sore throat somewhat marred our enjoyment.

I shall not be in Ayrshire for four weeks. My most respectful compliments to Mrs. Hamilton, Miss Kennedy, and Doctor Mackenzie. I shall probably write him from some stage or other.—I am ever; Sir, yours most gratefully,

ROBT. BURNS.

[47] Step-brother, more correctly.

[48] This is the "Wee Curlie Johnnie" mentioned in Burns's *Dedication to Gavin Hamilton, Esq.*

LX.—To MR. WALKER, BLAIR OF ATHOLE.[49]
INVERNESS, *5th September* 1787.

MY DEAR SIR,—I have just time to write the foregoing,[50] and to tell you that it was (at least most part of it) the effusion of an half-hour I spent at Bruar. I do not mean it was extempore, for I have endeavoured to brush it up as well as Mr. Nicol's chat, and the jogging of the chaise, would allow. It eases my heart a good deal, as rhyme is the coin with which a poet pays his debts of honour or gratitude. What I owe to the noble family of Athole, of the first kind, I shall ever proudly boast; what I owe of the last, so help me God in my hour of need! I shall never forget.

The "little angel-band!" I declare I prayed for them very sincerely today at the Fall of Fyers. I shall never forget the fine family-piece I saw at Blair; the amiable, the truly noble duchess, with her smiling little seraph in her lap, at the head of the table; the lovely "olive plants," as the Hebrew bard finely says, round the happy mother; the beautiful Mrs. G——; the lovely, sweet Miss C., etc. I wish I had the powers of Guido to do them justice! My Lord Duke's kind hospitality—markedly kind indeed; Mr. Graham of Fintry's charms of conversation; Sir W. Murray's friendship. In short, the recollection of all that polite, agreeable company raises an honest glow in my bosom.

R. B.

[49] Mr. Walker was tutor to the children of the Duke of Athole. He afterwards became Professor of Humanity in the University of Glasgow.

[50] The Humble Petition of Bruar Water.

LXI.—To His BROTHER, MR. GILBERT BURNS, MOSSGIEL.
EDINBERG, *17th September* 1787.

My Dear Sir,—I arrived here safe yesterday evening after a tour of twenty-two days, and travelling near six hundred miles, windings included. My farthest stretch was about ten miles beyond Inverness. I went through the heart of the Highlands by Crieff, Taymouth, the famous seat of Lord Breadalbane, down the Tay, among cascades and druidical circles of stones, to Dunkeld, a seat of the Duke of Athole; thence across Tay, and up one of his tributary streams to Blair of Athole, another of the duke's seats, where I had the honour of spending nearly two days with his grace and family; thence many miles through a wild country among cliffs grey with eternal snows, and gloomy savage glens, till I crossed Spey and went down the stream through Strathspey, so famous in Scottish music; Badenoch, etc., till I reached Grant Castle, where I spent half a day with Sir James Grant and family; and then crossed the country for Fort George, but called by the way at Cawdor, the ancient seat of Macbeth; there I saw the identical bed in which tradition says king Duncan was murdered: lastly, from Fort George to Inverness.

I returned by the coast through Nairn, Forres, and so on, to Aberdeen, thence to Stonehive, where James Burness, from Montrose, met me by appointment. I spent two days among our relations, and found our aunts, Jean and Isabel, still alive, and hale old women. John Cairn, though born the same year with our father, walks as vigorously as I can: they have had several letters from his son in New York. William Brand is likewise a stout old fellow; but further particulars I delay till I see you, which will be in two or three weeks. The rest of my stages are not worth rehearsing; warm as I was for Ossian's country, where I had seen his very grave, what cared I for fishing-towns or fertile carses? I slept at the famous Brodie of Brodie's one night, and dined at Gordon Castle next day, with the Duke, Duchess, and family. I am thinking to cause my old mare to meet me, by means of John Ronald, at Glasgow; but you shall hear farther from me before I leave Edinburgh. My duty and many compliments from the north to my mother; and my brotherly compliments to the rest. I have been trying for a berth for William,[51] but am not likely to be successful. Farewell. R. B.

[51] Their youngest brother, afterwards a journeyman saddler.

LXII.—TO MR. PATRICK MILLER,[52]DALSWINTON.
EDINBURGH, *20th Oct.*, 1787.

SIR,—I was spending a few days at Sir William Murray's, Ochtertyre, and did not get your obliging letter till to-day I came to town. I was still more unlucky in catching a miserable cold, for which the medical gentlemen have ordered me into close confinement under pain of death—the severest of penalties. In two or three days, if I get better, and if I hear at your lodgings that you are still at Dalswinton, I will take a ride to Dumfries directly. From something in your last, I would wish to explain my idea of being your tenant. I want to be a farmer in a small farm, about a plough-gang, in a pleasant country, under the auspices of a good landlord. I have no foolish notion of being a tenant on easier terms than another. To find a farm where one can live at all is not easy—I only mean living soberly, like an old-style farmer, and joining personal industry. The banks of the Nith are as sweet poetic ground as any I ever saw; and besides, Sir, 'tis but justice to the feelings of my own heart and the opinion of my best friends, to say that I would wish to call you landlord sooner than any landed gentleman I know. These are my views and wishes; and in whatever way you think best to lay out your farms I shall be happy to rent one of them. I shall certainly be able to ride to Dalswinton about the middle of next week, if I hear that you are not gone.—I have the honour to be, Sir, your obliged humble servant,

  ROBERT BURNS.

[52] His future landlord, at Ellisland.

LXIII.-To REV. JOHN SKINNER.

Edinburgh, *October 25th*, 1787.

Reverend and Venerable Sir,—Accept, in plain, dull prose, my most sincere thanks for the best poetical compliment I ever received. I assure you, Sir, as a poet, you have conjured up an airy demon of vanity in my fancy, which the best abilities in your other capacity would be ill able to lay. I regret, and while I live I shall regret, that when I was in the north I had not the pleasure of paying a younger brother's dutiful respect to the author of the best Scotch song ever Scotland saw—"Tullochgorum's my delight!" The world may think slightingly of the craft of song-making if they please; but, as Job says—"O that mine adversary had written a book!"—let them try. There is a certain something in the old Scotch songs, a wild happiness of thought and expression, which peculiarly marks them, not only from English songs, but also from the modern efforts of song-wrights, in our native manner and language. The only remains of this enchantment, these spells of the imagination, rest with you. Our true brother, Ross of Lochlee, was likewise "owre cannie"—a "wild warlock"—but now he sings among the "sons of the morning."

I have often wished, and will certainly endeavour, to form a kind of common acquaintance among all the genuine sons of Caledonian song. The world, busy in low prosaic pursuits, may overlook most of us; but "reverence thyself." The world is not our *peers* so we challenge the jury. We can lash that world, and find ourselves a very great source of amusement and happiness independent of that world.

There is a work[53] going on in Edinburgh, just now, which claims your best assistance. An engraver in this town has set about collecting and publishing all the Scotch songs, with the music, that can be found. Songs in the English language, if by Scotchmen, are admitted, but the music must all be Scotch. Drs. Beattie and Blacklock are lending a hand, and the first musician in town presides over that department. I have been absolutely crazed about it, collecting old stanzas, and every information remaining respecting their origin, authors, etc., etc. This last is but a very fragment business; but at the end of his second number—the first is already published—a small account will be given of the authors, particularly to preserve those of latter times. Your three songs, "Tullochgorum," "John of Badenyon," and "Ewie wi' the crookit Horn," go in this second number. I was determined, before I got your letter, to write you, begging that you would let me know where the editions of these pieces may be found as you would wish them to continue in future times: and if you would be so kind to this undertaking as send any songs, of your own or others, that you would think proper to publish, your name will be inserted among the other authors. "Nill ye, will ye," one-half of Scotland already give your songs to other authors. Paper is done. I beg to hear from you; the sooner the better, as I leave Edinburgh in a fortnight or three weeks.—I am, with the warmest sincerity, Sir, your obliged humble Servant, R. B.

[53] Johnson's *Musical Museum*.

LXIV.—To Miss MARGARET CHALMERS, HARVIESTON. (AFTERWARDS MRS. HAY, OF EDINBURGH.)

Oct. 26, 1787.

I send Charlotte the first number of the songs; I would not wait for the second number; I hate delays in little marks of friendship, as I hate dissimulation in the language of the heart. I am determined to pay Charlotte a poetic compliment, if I could hit on some glorious old Scotch air, in number second.[54] You will see a small attempt on a shred of paper in the book; but though Dr. Blacklock commended it very highly, I am not just satisfied with it myself. I intend to make it a description of some kind: the whining cant of love, except in real passion, and by a masterly hand, is to me as insufferable as the preaching cant of old Father Smeaton, whig-minister at Kilmaurs. Darts, flames, cupids, loves, graces, and all that farrago, are just a Mauchline—a senseless rabble.

I got an excellent poetic epistle yesternight from the old, venerable author of "Tullochgorum," "John of Badenyon," etc. I suppose you know he is a clergyman. It is by far the finest poetic compliment I ever got. I will send you a copy of it.

I go on Thursday or Friday to Dumfries, to wait on Mr. Miller about his farms. Do tell that to Lady Mackenzie, that she may give me credit for a little wisdom. "I, Wisdom, dwell with Prudence." What a blessed fireside! How happy should I be to pass a winter evening under their venerable roof! and smoke a pipe of tobacco, or drink water-gruel with them! What solemn, lengthened, laughter-quashing gravity of phiz! What sage remarks on the good-for-nothing sons and daughters of indiscretion and folly! And what frugal lessons, as we straitened the fireside circle, on the uses of the poker and tongs!

Miss N. is very well, and begs to be remembered in the old way to you. I used all my eloquence, all the persuasive flourishes of the hand, and heart-melting modulation of periods in my power, to urge her out to Harvieston, but all in vain. My rhetoric seems quite to have lost its effect on the lovely half of mankind. I have seen the day—but this is "a tale of other years." In my conscience I believe that my heart has been so oft on fire that it is absolutely vitrified. I look on the sex with something like the admiration with which I regard the starry sky in a frosty December night. I admire the beauty of the Creator's workmanship; I am charmed with the wild but graceful eccentricity of their motions, and—wish them good-night. I mean this with respect to a certain passion *dont j'at eu l'honneur d'etre un miserable esclave.* As for friendship, you and Charlotte have given me pleasure, permanent pleasure, "which the world cannot give, nor take away," I hope, and which will outlast the heavens and the earth.

R. B.

[54] Of the Scots *Musical Museum*.

LXV.—To MRS. DUNLOP OF DUNLOP HOUSE, STEWARTON.

Edin., 4*th Nov.* 1787.

Madam,— ... When you talk of correspondence and friendship to me, you do me too much honour; but, as I shall soon be at my wonted leisure and rural occupation, if any remark on what I have read or seen, or any new rhyme that I may twist, be worth the while ... you shall have it with all my heart and soul. It requires no common exertion of good sense and philosophy in persons of elevated rank to keep a friendship properly alive with one much their inferior. Externals, things wholly extraneous of the man, steal upon the hearts and judgments of almost, if not altogether, all mankind; nor do I know more than one instance of a man who fully regards all the world as a stage and all the men and women merely players, and who (the dancing-school bow excepted) only values these players, the *dramatis personæ* who build cities and who rear hedges, who govern provinces or superintend flocks, *merely as they act their parts.* For the honour of Ayrshire this man is Professor Dugald Stewart of Catrine. To him I might perhaps add another instance, a Popish bishop, Geddes of Edinburgh.... I ever could ill endure those ... beasts of prey who foul the hallowed ground of religion with their nocturnal prowlings; and if the prosecution against my worthy friend, Dr. McGill, goes on, I shall keep no measure with the savages, but fly at them with the *faucons* of ridicule, or run them down with the bloodhounds of satire as lawful game wherever I start them.

I expect to leave Edinburgh in eight or ten days, and shall certainly do myself the honour of calling at Dunlop House as I return to Ayrshire.—I have the honour to be, Madam, your obliged humble Servant,

ROBERT BURNS.

LXVI.—To MR. JAMES HOY,[55]GORDON CASTLE.

Edinburg, 6th November 1787.

Dear Sir,—I would have wrote you immediately on receipt of your kind letter, but a mixed impulse of gratitude and esteem whispered to me that I ought to send you something by way of return. When a poet owes anything, particularly when he is indebted for good offices, the payment that usually recurs to him—the only coin, indeed, in which he is probably conversant—is rhyme. Johnson sends the books by the fly, as directed, and begs me to inclose his most grateful thanks: my return I intended should have been one or two poetic bagatelles which the world have not seen, or, perhaps, for obvious seasons, cannot see. These I shall send you before I leave Edinburgh. They may make you laugh a little, which, on the whole, is no bad way of spending one's precious hours and still more precious breath. At any rate, they will be, though a small, yet a very sincere mark of my respectful esteem for a gentleman whose farther acquaintance I should look upon as a peculiar obligation.

The Duke's song, independent totally of his dukeship, charms me. There is I know not what of wild happiness of thought and expression peculiarly beautiful in the old Scottish song style, of which his Grace, old venerable Skinner, the author of "Tullochgorum," etc., and the late Ross, at Lochlee, of true Scottish poetic memory, are the only modern instances that I recollect, since Ramsay, with his contemporaries, and poor Bob Fergusson, went to the world of deathless existence and truly immortal song. The mob of mankind, that many-headed beast, would laugh at so serious a speech about an old song; but, as Job says, "O that mine adversary had written a book!" Those who think that composing a Scotch song is a trifling business—let them try.

I wish my Lord Duke would pay a proper attention to the Christian admonition, "Hide not your candle under a bushel," but "let your light shine before men." I could name half-a-dozen Dukes that I guess are a deal worse employed; nay, I question if there are half-a-dozen better: perhaps there are not half that scanty number whom Heaven has favoured with the tuneful, happy, and, I will say, glorious gift.—I am, dear Sir, your obliged humble servant, R. B.

[55] Librarian to the Duke of Gordon.

LXVII.-To THE EARL OF GLENCAIRN.

Edinburg, (End of 1787.)

My Lord,—I know your lordship will disapprove of my ideas in a request I am going to make to you; but I have weighed, long and seriously weighed, my situation, my hopes, and turn of mind, and am fully fixed to my scheme, if I can possibly effectuate it. I wish to get into the Excise: I am told that your lordship's interest will easily procure me the grant from the commissioners; and your lordship's patronage and goodness, which have already rescued me from obscurity, wretchedness, and exile, embolden me to ask that interest. You have likewise put it in my power to save the little tie of home that sheltered an aged mother, two brothers, and three sisters from destruction. There, my lord, you have bound me over to the highest gratitude.

My brother's farm is but a wretched lease, but I think he will probably weather out the remaining seven years of it; and after the assistance which I have given, and will give him, to keep the family together, I think, by my guess, I shall have rather better than two hundred pounds, and instead of seeking, what is almost impossible at present to find, a farm that I can certainly live by, with so small a stock, I shall lodge this sum in a banking-house, a sacred deposit, excepting only the calls of uncommon distress or necessitous old age.

These, my lord, are my views: I have resolved from the maturest deliberation; and now I am fixed, I shall leave no stone unturned to carry my resolve into execution. Your lordship's patronage is the strength of my hopes; nor have I yet applied to anybody else. Indeed my heart sinks within me at the idea of applying to any other of the great who have honoured me with their countenance. I am ill-qualified to dog the heels of greatness with the impertinence of solicitation, and tremble nearly as much at the thought of the cold promise as the cold denial; but to your lordship I have not only the honour, the comfort, but the pleasure of being your lordship's much obliged and deeply indebted humble servant,

R. B.

LXVIII—To Miss CHALMERS.
Edinburgh, *Nov.* 21, 1787.

I have one vexatious fault to the kindly, welcome, well-filled sheet which I owe to your and Charlotte's goodness—it contains too much sense, sentiment, and good spelling. It is impossible that even you two, whom, I declare to my God, I will give credit for any degree of excellence the sex are capable of attaining-it is impossible you can go on to correspond at that rate; so, like those who, Shenstone says, retire because they have made a good speech, I shall, after a few letters, hear no more of you. I insist that you shall write whatever comes first—what you see, what you read, what you hear, what you admire, what you dislike, trifles, bagatelles, nonsense; or, to fill up a corner, e'en put down a laugh at full length. Now, none of your polite hints about flattery; I leave that to your lovers, if you have or shall have any; though, thank heaven, I have found at last two girls who can be luxuriantly happy in their own minds and with one another, without that commonly necessary appendage to female bliss—A LOVER.

Charlotte and you are just two favourite resting-places for my soul in her wanderings through the weary, thorny wilderness of this world. God knows, I am ill-fitted for the struggle: I glory in being a poet, and I want to be thought a wise man—I would fondly be generous, and I wish to be rich. After all, I am afraid I am a lost subject. "Some folk hae a hantle o' faults, and I'm but a ne'er-do-well".

Afternoon.—To close the melancholy reflections at the end of last sheet, I shall just add a piece of devotion, commonly known in Carrick by the title of the "Wabster's grace":—
Some say we're thieves, and e'en sae are we,
Some say we lie, and e'en sae do we!
Gude forgie us, and I hope sae will he!
Up and to your looms, lads.
R. B.

LXIX.—TO MISS CHALMERS.
Edinburgh, *Dec.* 12, 1787.

I am here under the care of a surgeon, with a bruised limb extended on a cushion, and the tints of my mind vieing with the livid horror preceding a midnight thunderstorm. A drunken coachman was the cause of the first, and incomparably the lightest evil; misfortune, bodily constitution, hell, and myself have formed a "quadruple alliance" to guarantee the other. I got my fall on Saturday, and am getting slowly better.

I have taken tooth and nail to the Bible, and am got through the five books of Moses, and half way in Joshua. It is really a glorious book. I sent for my bookbinder today, and ordered him to get me an octavo Bible in sheets, the best paper and print in town, and bind it with all the elegance of his craft.

I would give my best song to my worst enemy—I mean the merit of making it—to have you and Charlotte by me. You are angelic creatures, and would pour oil and wine into my wounded spirit.

I inclose you a proof copy of the "Banks of the Devon", which present with my best wishes to Charlotte. The "Ochil Hills"[56] you shall probably have next week for yourself. None of your fine speeches!

R. B.

[56] The song in honour of Miss Chalmers, beginning, "Where, braving angry winter's storms".

LXX.—TO MISS CHALMERS.

Edinburgh, 19*th Dec.* 1787.

I begin this letter in answer to yours of the 17th current, which is not yet cold since I read it. The atmosphere of my soul is vastly clearer than when I wrote you last. For the first time, yesterday I crossed the room on crutches. It would do your heart good to see my hardship, not on my poetic, but on my oaken stilts; throwing my best leg with an air! and with as much hilarity in my gait and countenance, as a May frog leaping across the newly-harrowed ridge, enjoying the fragrance of the refreshed earth, after the long-expected shower!

I can't say I am altogether at my ease when I see anywhere in my path that meagre, squalid, famine-faced spectre, poverty; attended as he always is, by iron-fisted oppression, and leering contempt; but I have sturdily withstood his buffetings many a hard-laboured day already, and still my motto is—I DARE! My worst enemy is *moi même*. I lie so miserably open to the inroads and incursions of a mischievous, light-armed, well-mounted banditti, under the banners of imagination, whim, caprice, and passion; and the heavy-armed veteran regulars of wisdom, prudence, and forethought move so very, very slow, that I am almost in a state of perpetual warfare, and, alas! frequent defeat. There are just two creatures I would envy, a horse in his wild state traversing the forests of Asia, or an oyster on some of the desert shores of Europe. The one has not a wish without enjoyment, the other has neither wish nor fear.

R. B.

LXXI.—TO MR. RICHARD BROWN, IRVINE.

Edinburgh, 30*th Dec.* 1787.

My Dear Sir,—I have met with few things in life which have given me more pleasure, than Fortune's kindness to you since those days in which we met in the vale of misery; as I can honestly say, that I never knew a man who more truly deserved it, or to whom my heart more truly wished it. I have been much indebted, since that time, to your story and sentiments for steeling my mind against evils, of which I have had a pretty decent share. My will-o'-wisp fate you know: do you recollect a Sunday we spent together in Eglinton woods? You told me, on my repeating some verses to you, that you wondered I could resist the temptation of sending verses of such merit to a magazine. It was from this remark I derived that idea of my own pieces, which encouraged me to endeavour at the character of a poet. I am happy to hear that you will be two or three months at home. As soon as a bruised limb will permit me I shall return to Ayrshire, and we shall meet; "and faith, I hope we'll not sit dumb, nor yet cast out!"

I have much to tell you "of men, their manners, and their ways," perhaps a little of the other sex. Apropos, I beg to be remembered to Mrs. Brown. There, I doubt not, my dear friend, but you have found substantial happiness. I expect to find you something of an altered but not a different man; the wild, bold, generous young fellow composed into the steady affectionate husband, and the fond careful parent. For me, I am just the same will-o'-wisp being I used to be. About the first and fourth quarters of the moon, I generally set in for the trade wind of wisdom; but about the full and change, I am the luckless victim of mad tornadoes, which blow me into chaos. Almighty love still reigns and revels in my bosom; and I am at this moment ready to hang myself for a young Edinburgh widow,[57] who has wit and wisdom more murderously fatal than the assassinating stiletto of the Sicilian bandit, or the poisoned arrow of the savage African. My Highland dirk, that used to hang beside my crutches, I have gravely removed into a neighbouring closet, the key of which I cannot command, in case of spring-tide paroxysms. My best compliments to our friend Allan. Adieu!

R. B.

[57] The earliest allusion to Clarinda (Mrs. M'Lehose). Her husband was alive, in the West Indies.

LXXII—TO MRS. DUNLOP.
Edinburg, *January* 21, 1788.

After six weeks' confinement, I am beginning to walk across the room. They have been six horrible weeks; anguish and low spirits made me unfit to read, write, or think.

I have a hundred times wished that one could resign life as an officer resigns a commission; for I would not take in any poor, ignorant wretch by selling out. Lately I was a sixpenny private, and, God knows, a miserable soldier enough; now I march to the campaign, a starving cadet; a little more conspicuously wretched.

I am ashamed of all this; for though I do want bravery for the warfare of life, I could wish, like some other soldiers, to have as much fortitude or cunning as to dissemble or conceal my cowardice.

As soon as I can bear the journey, which will be, I suppose, about the middle of next week, I leave Edinburgh; and soon after I shall pay my grateful duty at Dunlop House. R. B.

LXXIII.—TO MRS. DUNLOP.
EDINBURGH, *February* 12, 1788.

Some things in your late letters hurt me—not that *you say them*, but that *you mistake me*. Religion, my honoured Madam, has not only been all my life my chief dependance, but my dearest enjoyment. I have, indeed, been the luckless victim of wayward follies; but, alas! I have ever been "more fool than knave." A mathematician without religion is a probable character; an irreligious poet is a monster.

R. B.

LXXIV.—TO THE REV. JOHN SKINNER.
EDINBURGH, 14*th February* 1788.

Reverend and Dear Sir,—I have been a cripple now near three months, though I am getting vastly better, and have been very much hurried beside, or else I would have wrote you sooner. I must beg your pardon for the epistle you sent me appearing in the Magazine. I had given a copy or two to some of my intimate friends, but did not know of the printing of it till the publication of the Magazine. However, as it does great honour to us both, you will forgive it.

The second volume of the songs I mentioned to you in my last is published to-day. I send you a copy, which I beg you will accept as a mark of the veneration I have long had, and shall ever have, for your character, and of the claim I make to your continued acquaintance. Your songs appear in the third volume, with your name in the index; as I assure you, Sir, I have heard your "Tullochgorum," particularly among our west-country folks, given to many different names, and most commonly to the immortal author of "The Minstrel," who, indeed, never wrote any thing superior to "Gie's a sang, Montgomery cried." Your brother[58] has promised me your verses to the Marquis of Huntley's reel, which certainly deserve a place in the collection. My kind host, Mr. Cruikshank, of the High School here, and said to be one of the best Latins in this age, begs me to make you his grateful acknowledgments for the entertainment he has got in a Latin publication of yours, that I borrowed for him from your acquaintance and much-respected friend in this place, the Rev. Dr. Webster. Mr. Cruikshank maintains that you write the best Latin since Buchanan. I leave Edinburgh to-morrow, but shall return in three weeks. Your song you mentioned in your last, to the tune of "Dumbarton Drums," and the other, which you say was done by a brother in trade of mine, a ploughman, I shall thank you for a copy of each. I am ever, Reverend Sir, with the most respectful esteem and sincere veneration, yours, R. B.

[58] Half-brother, James, a writer to the Signet.

LXXV.—TO MRS. ROSE, OF KILRAVOCK.

EDINBURGH, *February* 17*th*, 1788.

MADAM,—You are much indebted to some indispensable business I have had on my hands, otherwise my gratitude threatened such a return for your obliging favour, as would have tired your patience. It but poorly expresses my feelings to say, that I am sensible of your kindness: it may be said of hearts such as yours is, and such, I hope, mine is, much more justly than Addison applies it,—

Some souls by instinct to each other turn.

There was something in my reception at Kilravock so different from the cold, obsequious, dancing-school bow of politeness, that it almost got into my head that friendship had occupied her ground without the intermediate march of acquaintance. I wish I could transcribe, or rather transfuse into language, the glow of my heart when I read your letter. My ready fancy, with colours more mellow than life itself, painted the beautifully wild scenery of Kilravock—the venerable grandeur of the castle—the spreading woods—the winding river, gladly leaving his unsightly, heathy source, and lingering with apparent delight as he passes the fairy walk at the bottom of the garden;—your late distressful anxieties—your present enjoyments—your dear little angel, the pride of your hopes;—my aged friend, venerable in worth and years, whose loyalty and other virtues will strongly entitle her to the support of the Almighty Spirit here, and His peculiar favour in a happier state of existence. You cannot imagine, Madam, how much such feelings delight me; they are my dearest proofs of my own immortality. Should I never revisit the north, as probably I never will, nor again see your hospitable mansion, were I, some twenty years hence, to see your little fellow's name making a proper figure in a newspaper paragraph, my heart would bound with pleasure.

I am assisting a friend in a collection of Scottish songs, set to their proper tunes; every air worth preserving is to be included; among others I have given "Morag," and some few Highland airs which pleased me most, a dress which will be more generally known, though far, far inferior in real merit. As a small mark of my grateful esteem, I beg leave to present you with a copy of the work, as far as it is printed; the Man of Feeling, that first of men, has promised to transmit it by the first opportunity.

I beg to be remembered most respectfully to my venerable friend, and to your little Highland chieftain. When you see the "two fair spirits of the hill," at Kildrummie, tell them that I have done myself the honour of setting myself down as one of their admirers for at least twenty years to come, consequently they must look upon me as an acquaintance for the same period; but, as the Apostle Paul says, "this I ask of grace, not of debt."—I have the honour to be, Madam, etc., ROBERT BURNS.

LXXVI-To RICHARD BROWN, GREENOCK.

MOSSGIEL, 24*th February* 1788.

MY DEAR SIR,—I cannot get the proper direction for my friend in Jamaica, but the following will do:—To Mr, Jo. Hutchinson, at Jo. Brownrigg's, Esq., care of Mr. Benjamin Henriquez, merchant, Orange Street, Kingston. I arrived here, at my brother's, only yesterday, after fighting my way through Paisley and Kilmarnock, against those old powerful foes of mine, the devil, the world, and the flesh—so terrible in the fields of dissipation. I have met with few incidents in my life which gave me so much pleasure as meeting you in Glasgow. There is a time of life beyond which we cannot form a tie worth the name of friendship, "O youth! enchanting stage, profusely blest." Life is a fairy scene: almost all that deserves the name of enjoyment or pleasure is only a charming delusion; and in comes repining age, in all the gravity of hoary wisdom, and wretchedly chases away the bewitching phantom. When I think of life, I resolve to keep a strict look-out in the course of economy, for the sake of worldly convenience and independence of mind; to cultivate intimacy with a few of the companions of youth, that they may be the friends of age; never to refuse my liquorish humour a handful of the sweetmeats of life, when they come not too dear; and, for futurity,—

The present moment is our ain,
The neist we never saw!

How like you my philosophy? Give my best compliments to Mrs. B., and believe me to be, my dear Sir, yours most truly, ROBERT BURNS.

LXXVII.—To MR. WILLIAM CRUIKSHANK.[59]

MAUCHLINE, *March 3rd*, 1788.

My dear Sir,—Apologies for not writing are frequently like apologies for not singing—the apology better than the song. I have fought my way severely through the savage hospitality of this country, the object of all hosts being to send every guest drunk to bed if they can.

I executed your commission in Glasgow, and I hope the cocoa came safe. 'Twas the same price and the very same kind as your former parcel, for the gentleman recollected your buying there perfectly well.

I Should return my thanks for your hospitality (I leave a blank for the epithet, as I know none can do it justice) to a poor, wayfaring bard, who was spent and almost overpowered fighting with prosaic wickedness in high places; but I am afraid lest you should burn the letter whenever you come to the passage, so I pass over it in silence. I am just returned from visiting Mr. Miller's farm. The friend whom I told you I would take with me was highly pleased with the farm; and as he is, without exception, the most intelligent farmer in the country, he has staggered me a good deal. I have the two plans of life before me; I shall balance them to the best of my judgment; and fix on the most eligible. I have written Mr. Miller, and shall wait on him when I come to town, which shall be the beginning or middle of next week: I would be in sooner, but my unlucky knee is rather worse, and I fear for some time will scarcely stand the fatigue of my Excise instructions. I only mention these ideas to you, and, indeed, except Mr. Ainslie, whom I intend writing to tomorrow, I will not write at all to Edinburgh till I return to it. I would send my compliments to Mr. Nicol, but he would be hurt if he knew I wrote to anybody and not to him; so I shall only beg my best, kindest, kindest compliments to my worthy hostess, and the sweet little rose-bud.

So soon as I am settled in the routine of life, either as an Excise-officer, or as a farmer, I propose myself great pleasure from a regular correspondence with the only man almost I ever saw, who joined the most attentive prudence with the warmest generosity.

I am much interested for that best of men, Mr. Wood; I hope he is in better health and spirits than when I saw him last.—I am ever, my dearest friend, your obliged, humble servant, R. B.

[59] One of the masters of the High School of Edinburgh.

LXXVIII.—To MR. ROBERT AINSLIE.

MAUCHLINE, *3rd March* 1788.

MY DEAR FRIEND,—I am just returned from Mr. Miller's farm. My old friend whom I took with me was highly pleased with the bargain, and advised me to accept of it. He is the most intelligent sensible farmer in the county, and his advice has staggered me a good deal. I have the two plans before me; I shall endeavour to balance them to the best of my judgment, and fix on the most eligible. On the whole, if I find Mr. Miller in the same favourable disposition as when I saw him last, I shall, in all probability, turn farmer.

I have been through sore tribulation and under much buffeting of the wicked one, since I came to this country. Jean I found banished, forlorn, destitute, and friendless; I have reconciled her to her fate, and I have reconciled her to her mother.... I swore her privately and solemnly never to attempt any claim on me as a husband, even though anybody should persuade her she had such a claim....

I shall be in Edinburgh middle of next week. My farming ideas I shall keep private till I see. I got a letter from Clarinda yesterday, and she tells me she has got no letter of mine but one. Tell her that I wrote to her from Glasgow, from Kilmarnock, from Mauchline, and yesterday from Cumnock as I returned from Dumfries. Indeed she is the only person in

Edinburgh I have written to till this day. How are your soul and body putting up?—a little like man and wife I suppose.—Your faithful friend,

ROBERT BURNS.

LXXIX.—To MR. RICHARD BROWN.

MAUCHLINE, *7th March* 1788.

I have been out of the country, my dear friend, and have not had an opportunity of writing till now, when, I am afraid, you will be gone out of the country too. I have been looking at farms, and, after all, perhaps I may settle in the character of a farmer. I have got so vicious a bent to idleness, and have ever been so little a man of business, that it will take no ordinary effort to bring my mind properly into the routine: but you will say a "great effort is worthy of you." I say so myself; and butter up my vanity with all the stimulating compliments I can think of. Men of grave, geometrical minds, the sons of "which was to be demonstrated," may cry up reason as much as they please; but I have always found an honest passion, or native instinct, the truest auxiliary in the warfare of this world. Reason almost always comes to me like an unlucky wife to a poor devil of a husband, just in sufficient time to add her reproaches to his other grievances.

I am gratified with your kind inquiries after Jean; as, after all, I may say with Othello—
Excellent wretch!
Perdition catch my soul, but I do love thee!

I go for Edinburgh on Monday.—Yours,

ROBERT BURNS.

LXXX.—TO MR. ROBERT MUIR.

MOSSGIEL, *7th March* 1788.

DEAR SIR,—I have partly changed my ideas, my dear friend, since I saw you. I took old Glenconner with me to Mr. Miller's farm, and he was so pleased with it, that I have wrote an offer to Mr. Miller, which, if he accepts, I shall sit down a plain farmer, the happiest of lives when a man can live by it. In this case I shall not stay in Edinburgh above a week. I set out on Monday, and would have come by Kilmarnock; but there are several small sums owing me for my first edition about Galston and Newmilns, and I shall set off so early as to despatch my business and reach Glasgow by night. When I return, I shall devote a forenoon or two to make some kind of acknowledgment for all the kindness I owe your friendship. Now that I hope to settle with some credit and comfort at home, there was not any friendship or friendly correspondence that promised me more pleasure than yours; I hope I will not be disappointed. I trust the spring will renew your shattered frame, and make your friends happy. You and I have often agreed that life is no great blessing on the whole. The close of life, indeed, to a reasoning age, is
Dark as was chaos, ere the infant sun
Was roll'd together, or had tried his beams
Athwart the gloom profound.

But an honest man has nothing to fear. If we lie down in the grave, the whole man a piece of broken machinery, to moulder with the clods of the valley, be it so; at least there is an end of pain, care, woes, and wants. If that part of us called mind does survive the apparent destruction of the man—away with old-wife prejudices and tales. Every age and every nation has had a different set of stories; and as the many are always weak, of consequence they have often, perhaps always, been deceived. A man conscious of having acted an honest part among his fellow-creatures—even granting that he may have been the sport at times of passions and instincts—he goes to a great unknown Being, who could have no other end in giving him existence but to make him happy, who gave him those passions and instincts, and well knows their force.

These, my worthy friend, are my ideas; and I know they are not far different from yours. It becomes a man of sense to think for himself, particularly in a case where all men are equally interested, and where, indeed, all men are equally in the dark.

Adieu, my dear Sir; God send us a cheerful meeting!
R. B.

LXXXI—To MRS. DUNLOP.

MOSSGIEL, 7*th March* 1788.

MADAM,—The last paragraph in yours of the 30th February affected me most; so I shall begin my answer where you ended your letter. That I am often a sinner with any little wit I have, I do confess; but I have taxed my recollection to no purpose to find out when it was employed against you. I hate an ungenerous sarcasm a great deal worse than I do the devil—at least as Milton describes him; and though I may be rascally enough to be sometimes guilty of it myself, I cannot endure it in others. You, my honoured friend, who cannot appear in any light but you are sure of being respectable—you can afford to pass by an occasion to display your wit, because you may depend for fame on your sense; or, if you choose to be silent, you know you can rely on the gratitude of many, and the esteem of all; but, God help us, who are wits or witlings by profession, if we stand not for fame there, we sink unsupported!

I am highly flattered by the news you tell me of Coila. I may say to the fair painter[60] who does me so much honour, as Dr. Beattie says to Ross, the poet of his muse Scota, from which, by the by, I took the idea of Coila: ('tis a poem of Beattie's in the Scottish dialect, which, perhaps, you have never seen):—

Ye shak your head, but o' my fegs,

Ye've set auld Scota on her legs;

Lang had she lien wi' beffs and flegs,

Bumbaz'd and dizzie,

Her fiddle wanted strings and pegs,

Wae's me, poor hizzie.

R.B.

[60] One of Mrs. Dunlop's daughters was painting a sketch from the "Coila of the Vision".

LXXXII—TO MR. WM. NICOL (PERHAPS).

MAUCHLINE, 7*th March* 1788.

MY DEAR SIR,—My life, since I saw you last, has been one continued hurry; that savage hospitality which knocks a man down with strong liquors, is the devil. I have a sore warfare in this world; the devil, the world, and the flesh, are three formidable foes. The first I generally try to fly from; the second, alas! generally flies from me; but the third is my plague, worse than the ten plagues of Egypt.

I have been looking over several farms in this country; one in particular, in Nithsdale, pleased me so well, that if my offer to the proprietor is accepted, I shall commence farmer at Whit-Sunday. If farming do not appear eligible, I shall have recourse to any other shift; but this to a friend.

I set out for Edinburgh on Monday morning; how long I stay there is uncertain, but you will know so soon as I can inform you myself. However I determine, poesy must be laid aside for some time; my mind has been vitiated with idleness, and it will take a good deal of effort to habituate it to the routine of business.—I am, my dear Sir, yours sincerely, R. B.

LXXXIII.—TO MISS CHALMERS.

EDINBURGH, *March* 14*th*, 1788.

I know, my ever dear friend, that you will be pleased with the news when I tell you I have at last taken a lease of a farm. Yesternight I completed a bargain with Mr. Miller, of Dalswinton, for the farm of Ellisland, on the banks of the Nith, between five and six miles above Dumfries. I begin at Whit-Sunday to build a house, drive lime, etc., and Heaven be my help! for it will take a strong effort to bring my mind into the routine of business. I have discharged all the army of my former pursuits, fancies, and pleasures—a motley host! and have literally and strictly retained only the ideas of a few friends, which I have incorporated into a life-guard. I trust in Dr. Johnson's observation, "Where much is attempted, something is done." Firmness, both in sufferance and exertion, is a character I would wish to be thought to possess: and have always despised the whining yelp of complaint, and the cowardly, feeble resolve.

Poor Miss K.[61] is ailing a good deal this winter, and begged me to remember her to you the first time I wrote to you. Surely woman, amiable woman, is often made in vain. Too delicately formed for the rougher pursuits of ambition; too noble for the dirt of avarice, and even too gentle for the rage of pleasure; formed, indeed, for, and highly susceptible of enjoyment and rapture; but that enjoyment, alas! almost wholly at the mercy of the caprice, malevolence, stupidity, or wickedness of an animal at all times comparatively unfeeling, and often brutal. R.B.

[61] Miss Kennedy, sister of Gavin Hamilton. She lived nearly half a century after this.

THE CLARINDA LETTERS.
NOTE PREFATORY TO THE LETTERS TO CLARINDA

We have now arrived, in the history of Burns, as his general correspondence reveals it, at the middle of March 1788. Before the end of the month he had broken off from Clarinda, and shortly afterwards he married Jean Armour. The correspondence with Clarinda began in the last month of 1787, and ran its course in three months. It is now necessary to go back to the commencement of this correspondence, and to follow it down to its first conclusion at the point to which his general correspondence has brought us. It has been thought preferable to take it by itself.

Clarinda's maiden name was Agnes Craig. She was the daughter of Mr. Andrew Craig, who had been a surgeon in Glasgow. Lord Craig of the Court of Session was her cousin. She was born in the same year as Burns, but three months later. At the age of seventeen she was married to Mr. James M'Lehose, a law agent in Glasgow. Incompatibility of temper resulted in a separation of the unhappy pair five years after their marriage. The lady went home to her father, and on his death in 1782 removed to Edinburgh, where she lived independently on a small annuity. Her two sons lived with her. Her husband meanwhile went out to the West Indies to push his fortune.

LETTERS TO CLARINDA.

I.

Thursday Evening [*Dec. 6th*, 1787].

MADAM,—I had set no small store by my tea-drinking tonight, and have not often been so disappointed. Saturday evening I shall embrace the opportunity with the greatest pleasure. I leave this town this day se'ennight, and, probably, for a couple of twelvemonths; but must ever regret that I so lately got an acquaintance I shall ever highly esteem, and in whose welfare I shall ever be warmly interested.

Our worthy common friend, in her usual pleasant way, rallied me a good deal on my new acquaintance, and in the humour of her ideas I wrote some lines, which I inclose you, as I think they have a good deal of poetic merit: and Miss Nimmo tells me you are not only a critic, but a poetess. Fiction, you know, is the native region of poetry; and I hope you will pardon my vanity in sending you the bagatelle as a tolerably off-hand *jeu-d'esprit*. I have several poetic trifles, which I shall gladly leave with Miss Nimmo, or you, if they were worth house room; as there are scarcely two people on earth by whom it would mortify me more to be forgotten, though at the distance of ninescore miles.—I am, Madam, with the highest respect, your very humble servant,

ROBERT BURNS.

II.

Saturday Evening, Dec. 8th, 1787.

I can say with truth, Madam, that I never met with a person in my life whom I more anxiously wished to meet again than yourself. To-night I was to have had that very great pleasure; I was intoxicated with the idea, but an unlucky fall from a coach has so bruised one of my knees, that I can't stir my leg; so if I don't see you again, I shall not rest in my grave for chagrin. I was vexed to the soul I had not seen you sooner; I determined to cultivate your friendship with the enthusiasm of religion; but thus has Fortune ever served me. I cannot bear the idea of leaving Edinburgh without seeing you. I know not how to account for it—I am strangely taken with some people, nor am I often mistaken. You are a stranger to me; but I am an odd being: some yet unnamed feelings, things, not principles, but better than whims, carry me farther than boasted reason ever did a philosopher. Farewell! every happiness be yours! ROBERT BURNS.

III.

Dec. 12, 1787.

I stretch a point indeed, my dearest Madam, when I answer your card on the rack of my present agony. Your friendship, Madam! By heavens, I was never proud before. Your lines, I maintain it, are poetry, and good poetry; mine were indeed partly fiction and partly a friendship, which, had I been so blest as to have met with you in time, might have led me—god of love only knows where. Time is too short for ceremonies. I swear solemnly, in all the tenor of my former oath, to remember you in all the pride and warmth of friendship until I cease to be! To-morrow, and every day till I see you, you shall hear from me. Farewell! May you enjoy a better night's repose than I am likely to have. R. B.

IV.

Thursday, Dec. 20, 1787.

Your last, my dear Madam, had the effect on me that Job's situation had on his friends when they sat down seven days and seven nights astonished and spake not a word. "Pay my addresses to a married woman!" I started as if I had seen the ghost of him I had injured. I recollected my expressions; some of them were indeed in the law phrase "habit and repute," which is being half guilty. I cannot possibly say, Madam, whether my heart might not have gone astray a little; but I can declare upon the honour of a poet that the vagrant has wandered unknown to me. I have a pretty handsome troop of follies of my own, and, like some other people's, they are but undisciplined blackguards; but the luckless rascals have something like honour in them—they would not do a dishonest thing.

To meet with an unfortunate woman, amiable and young, deserted and widowed by those who were bound by every tie of duty, nature, and gratitude to protect, comfort and cherish her; add to all, when she is perhaps one of the first of lovely forms and noble minds—the mind, too, that hits one's taste as the joys of Heaven do a saint—should a faint idea, the natural child of imagination, thoughtfully peep over the fence—were you, my friend, to sit in judgment, and the poor, airy straggler brought before you, trembling, self-condemned, with artless eyes, brimful of contrition, looking wistfully on its judge—you could not, my dear Madam, condemn the hapless wretch to death without benefit of clergy? I won't tell you what reply my heart made to your raillery of seven years, but I will give you what a brother of my trade says on the same allusion:—

The patriarch to gain a wife,
Chaste, beautiful, and young,
Served fourteen years a painful life,
And never thought it long.

O were you to reward such cares,
And life so long would stay,
Not fourteen but four hundred years
Would seem but as a day.[62]

I have written you this scrawl because I have nothing else to do, and you may sit down and find fault with it, if you have no better way of consuming your time. But finding fault with the vagaries of a poet's fancy is much such another business as Xerxes chastising the waves of Hellespont.

My limb now allows me to sit in some peace: to walk I have yet no prospect of, as I can't mark it to the ground.

I have just now looked over what I have written, and it is such a chaos of nonsense that I daresay you will throw it into the fire and call me an idle, stupid fellow; but, whatever you may think of my brains, believe me to be, with the most sacred respect and heart-felt esteem, my dear Madam, your humble Servant, ROBT. BURNS.
[62] Tom D'Urfey's Songs.

V.

Friday Evening, 28*th December* 1787.

I beg your pardon, my dear "Clarinda," for the fragment scrawl I sent you yesterday. I really do not know what I wrote. A gentleman, for whose character, abilities, and critical knowledge I have the highest veneration, called in just as I had begun the second sentence, and I would not make the porter wait. I read to my much-respected friend several of my own bagatelles, and, among others, your lines, which I had copied out. He began some criticisms on them as on the other pieces, when I informed him they were the work of a young lady in this town, which, I assure you, made him stare. My learned friend seriously protested that he did not believe any young woman in Edinburgh was capable of such lines; and if you know anything of Professor Gregory, you will neither doubt of his abilities nor his sincerity. I do love you, if possible, still better for having so fine a taste and turn for poesy. I have again gone wrong in my usual unguarded way, but you may erase the word, and put esteem, respect, or any other tame Dutch expression you please in its place. I believe there is no holding converse, or carrying on correspondence, with an amiable woman, much less a *gloriously amiable fine woman,* without some mixture of that delicious passion, whose most devoted slave I have more than once had the honour of being. But why be hurt or offended on that account? Can no honest man have a prepossession for a fine woman, but he must run his head against an intrigue? Take a little of the tender witchcraft of love, and add to it the generous, the honourable sentiments of manly friendship, and I know but *one* more delightful morsel, which few, few in any rank ever taste. Such a composition is like adding cream to strawberries; it not only gives the fruit a more elegant richness, but has a deliciousness of its own.

I inclose you a few lines I composed on a late melancholy occasion. I will not give above five or six copies of it in all, and I should be hurt if any friend should give any copies without my consent.

You cannot imagine, Clarinda (I like the idea of Arcadian names in a commerce of this kind), how much store I have set by the hopes of your future friendship. I do not know if you have a just idea of my character, but I wish you to see me as *I am.* I am, as most people of my trade are, a strange Will-o'-Wisp being: the victim, too frequently, of much imprudence and many follies. My great constituent elements are *pride* and *passion.* The first I have endeavoured to humanise into integrity and honour; the last makes me a devotee to the warmest degree of enthusiasm, in love, religion, or friendship—either of them, or all together, as I happen to be inspired. 'Tis true, I never saw you but once; but how much acquaintance did I form with you in that once? Do not think I flatter you, or have a design upon you, Clarinda; I have too much pride for the one, and too little cold contrivance for the other; but of all God's creatures I ever could approach in the beaten way of my acquaintance, you struck me with the deepest, the strongest, the most permanent impression. I say the most permanent, because I know myself well, and how far I can promise either on my prepossessions or powers. Why are you unhappy? And why are so many of our fellow-creatures, unworthy to belong to the same species with you, blest with all they can wish? You have a hand all benevolent to give-why were you denied the pleasure? You have a heart formed—gloriously formed—for all the most refined luxuries of love:-why was that heart ever wrung? O Clarinda! shall we not meet in a state, some yet unknown state of being, where the lavish hand of plenty shall minister to the highest wish of benevolence; and where the chill north-wind of prudence shall never blow over the flowery fields of enjoyment? If we do not, man was made in vain! I deserved most of the unhappy hours that have lingered over my head; they were the wages of my labour: but what unprovoked demon, malignant as hell, stole upon the confidence of unmistrusting busy Fate, and dashed your cup of life with undeserved sorrow?

Let me know how long your stay will be out of town; I shall count the hours till you inform me of your return. Cursed *etiquette* forbids your seeing me just now; and so soon as I can walk I must bid Edinburgh adieu. Lord! why was I born to see misery which I cannot relieve, and to meet with friends whom I cannot enjoy? I look back with the pang of unavailing avarice on my loss in not knowing you sooner: all last winter, these three months past, what luxury of intercourse have I not lost! Perhaps, though,'twas better for my peace. You see I am either above, or incapable of dissimulation. I believe it is want of that particular genius. I despise design, because I want either coolness or wisdom to be capable of it. I am interrupted. Adieu! my dear Clarinda!
SYLVANDER.

VI.

Thursday, Jan. 3, 1788.

You are right, my dear Clarinda: a friendly correspondence goes for nothing, except one writes his or her undisguised sentiments. Yours please me for their instrinsic merit, as well as because they are *yours*, which I assure you, is to me a high recommendation. Your religious sentiments, Madam, I revere. If you have, on some suspicious evidence, from some lying oracle, learned that I despise or ridicule so sacredly important a matter as real religion, you have, my Clarinda, much misconstrued your friend. "I am not mad, most noble Festus!" Have you ever met a perfect character? Do we not sometimes rather exchange faults, than get rid of them? For instance, I am perhaps tired with, and shocked at a life too much the prey of giddy inconsistencies and thoughtless follies; by degrees I grow sober, prudent, and statedly pious—I say statedly, because the most unaffected devotion is not at all inconsistent with my first character—I join the world in congratulating myself on the happy change. But let me pry more narrowly into this affair. Have I, at bottom, any thing of a sacred pride in these endowments and emendations? Have I nothing of a presbyterian sourness, an hypocritical severity, when I survey my less regular neighbours? In a word, have I missed all those nameless and numberless modifications of indistinct selfishness, which are so near our own eyes, that we can scarcely bring them within the sphere of our vision, and which the known spotless cambric of our character hides from the ordinary observer?

My definition of worth is short; truth and humanity respecting our fellow-creatures; reverence and humility in the presence of that Being, my Creator and Preserver, and who, I have every reason to believe, will one day be my Judge. The first part of my definition is the creature of unbiassed instinct; the last is the child of after reflection. Where I found these two essentials I would gently note and slightly mention any attendant flaws—flaws, the marks, the consequences of human nature.

I can easily enter into the sublime pleasures that your strong imagination and keen sensibility must derive from religion, particularly if a little in the shade of misfortune; but I own I cannot, without a marked grudge, see Heaven totally engross so amiable, so charming a woman, as my friend Clarinda; and should be very well pleased at *a circumstance* that would put it in the power of somebody (happy somebody!) to divide her attention, with all the delicacy and tenderness of an earthly attachment.

You will not easily persuade me that you have not a grammatical knowledge of the English language. So far from being inaccurate, you are elegant beyond any woman of my acquaintance, except one,—whom I wish you knew.

Your last verses to me have so delighted me, that I have got an excellent old Scots air that suits the measure, and you shall see them in print in the Scots *Musical Museum*, a work publishing by a friend of mine in this town. I want four stanzas, you gave me but three, and one of them alluded to an expression in my former letter; so I have taken your two first verses, with a slight alteration in the second, and have added a third, but you must help me to a fourth. Here they are; the latter half of the first stanza would have been worthy of Sappho; I am in raptures with it.

Talk not of Love, it gives me pain,
For Love has been my foe:
He bound me with an iron chain,
And sunk me deep in woe.

But Friendship's pure and lasting joys
My heart was formed to prove:
There welcome, win and wear the prize,
But never talk of Love.

Your friendship much can make me blest,
O why that bliss destroy!
[only]
Why urge the odious one request,
[will]
You know I must deny.

The alteration in the second stanza is no improvement, but there was a slight inaccuracy in your rhyme. The third I only offer to your choice, and have left two words for your determination. The air is "The banks of Spey," and is most beautiful.

To-morrow evening I intend taking a chair, and paying a visit at Park Place to a much-valued old friend.[63] If I could be sure of finding you at home (and I will send one of the chairmen to call), I would spend from five to six o'clock with you, as I go past. I cannot do more at this time, as I have something on my hand that hurries me much. I propose giving you the first call, my old friend the second, and Miss Nimmo as I return home. Do not break any engagement for me, as I will spend another evening with you at any rate before I leave town.

Do not tell me that you are pleased, when your friends inform you of your faults. I am ignorant what they are; but I am sure they must be such evanescent trifles, compared with your personal and mental accomplishments, that I would despise the ungenerous narrow soul, who would notice any shadow of imperfections you may seem to have, any other way than in the most delicate agreeable raillery. Coarse minds are not aware how much they injure the keenly feeling tie of bosom friendship, when, in their foolish officiousness, they mention what nobody cares for recollecting. People of nice sensibility, and generous minds, have a certain intrinsic dignity, that fires at being trifled with, or lowered, or even too nearly approached.

You need make no apology for long letters; I am even with you. Many happy new years to you, charming Clarinda! I can't dissemble, were it to shun perdition. He who sees you as I have done, and does not love you, deserves to be damn'd for his stupidity! He who loves you, and would injure you, deserves to be doubly damn'd for his villany! Adieu.

SYLVANDER.

P.S. What would you think of this for a fourth stanza?

Your thought, if love must harbour there,
Conceal it in that thought,
Nor cause me from my bosom tear
The very friend I sought.

[63] Probably Mr. Nicol, who lived in Buccleuch Pend, a short distance from Clarinda's residence.

VII.

Saturday Noon [5th January].

Some days, some nights, nay, some *hours*, like the "ten righteous persons in Sodom," save the rest of the vapid, tiresome, miserable months and years of life. One of these hours my dear Clarinda blest me with yesternight.

One well-spent hour,
In such a tender circumstance for friends,
Is better than an age of common time!
THOMSON.

My favourite feature in Milton's Satan is his manly fortitude in supporting what cannot be remedied—in short, the wild broken fragments of a noble exalted mind in ruins. I meant no more by saying he was a favourite hero of mine.

I mentioned to you my letter to Dr. Moore, giving an account of my life: it is truth, every word of it; and will give you a just idea of the man whom you have honoured with your friendship. I am afraid you will hardly be able to make sense of so torn a piece. Your verses I shall muse on, deliciously, as I gaze on your image in my mind's eye, in my heart's core: they will be in time enough for a week to come. I am truly happy your headache is better. O, how can pain or evil be so daringly unfeeling, cruelly savage, as to wound so noble a mind, so lovely a form!

My little fellow is all my namesake. Write me soon. My every, strongest good wishes attend you, Clarinda!

SYLVANDER.

I know not what I have written—I am pestered with people around me.

VIII.

Jan. 8, 1788, Tuesday Night.

I am delighted, charming Clarinda, with your honest enthusiasm for religion. Those of either sex, but particularly the female, who are lukewarm in that most important of all things, "O my soul, come not thou into their secrets!" I feel myself deeply interested in your good opinion, and will lay before you the outlines of my belief. He who is our Author and Preserver, and will one day be our Judge, must be (not for his sake in the way of duty, but from the native impulse of our hearts), the object of our reverential awe and grateful adoration: He is Almighty and all-bounteous, we are weak and dependent; hence prayer and every other sort of devotion. "He is not willing that any should perish, but that all should come to everlasting life;" consequently it must be in every one's power to embrace his offer of "everlasting life;" otherwise he could not, in justice, condemn those who did not. A mind pervaded, actuated, and governed by purity, truth, and charity, though it does not merit heaven, yet is an absolute necessary prerequisite, without which heaven can neither be obtained nor enjoyed; and, by divine promise, such a mind shall never fail of attaining "everlasting life;" hence the impure, the deceiving, and the uncharitable extrude themselves from eternal bliss, by their unfitness for enjoying it. The Supreme Being has put the immediate administration of all this, for wise and good ends known to himself, into the hands of Jesus Christ, a great personage, whose relation to him we cannot comprehend, but whose relation to us is a guide and Saviour; and who, except for our own obstinacy and misconduct, will bring us all, through various ways, and by various means, to bliss at last.

These are my tenets, my lovely friend; and which I think cannot well be disputed. My creed is pretty nearly expressed in the last clause of Jamie Dean's grace, an honest weaver in Ayrshire,—"Lord, grant that we may lead a gude life; for a gude life maks a gude end, at least it helps weel!"

I am flattered by the entertainment you tell me you have found in my packet. You see me as I have been, you know me as I am, and may guess at what I am likely to be. I too may say, "Talk not of love," etc., for indeed he has "plunged me deep in woe!" Not that I ever saw a woman who pleased unexceptionably, as my Clarinda elegantly says, "in the companion, the friend, and the mistress." *One* indeed I could except—*One*, before passion threw its mists over my discernment, I knew—*the* first of women! Her name is indelibly written in my heart's core—but I dare not look in on it—a degree of agony would be the consequence. Oh! thou perfidious, cruel, mischief-making demon, who presidest over that frantic passion—thou mayest, thou dost poison my peace, but thou shalt not taint my honour. I would not, for a single moment, give an asylum to the most distant imagination, that would shadow the faintest outline of a selfish gratification, at the expense of her whose happiness is twisted with the threads of my existence.—May she be as happy as she deserves! and if my tenderest, faithfullest friendship, can add to her bliss, I shall at least have one solid mine of enjoyment in my bosom! *Don't guess at these ravings!*

I watched at our front window to-day, but was disappointed. It has been a day of disappointments. I am just risen from a two hours' bout after supper, with silly or sordid souls, who could relish nothing in common with me but the Port.—*One!*—Tis now "witching time of night;" and whatever is out of joint in the foregoing scrawl, impute it to enchantments and spells; for I can't look over it, but will seal it up directly, as I don't care for to-morrow's criticisms on it.

You are by this time fast asleep, Clarinda; may good angels attend and guard you as constantly and faithfully as my good wishes do.
Beauty, which, whether waking or asleep,
Shot forth peculiar graces.

John Milton, I wish thy soul better rest than I expect on my own pillow to-night! O for a little of the cart-horse part of human nature! Good night, my dearest Clarinda!
SYLVANDER.

IX
Thursday Noon, 10*th January* 1788.
I am certain I saw you, Clarinda; but you don't look to the proper storey for a poet's lodging—
Where speculation roosted near the sky.

I could almost have thrown myself over for vexation. Why didn't you look higher? It has spoiled my peace for this day. To be so near my charming Clarinda; to miss her look while it was searching for me—I am sure the soul is capable of disease, for mine has convulsed itself into an inflammatory fever.

You have converted me, Clarinda. (I shall love that name while I live: there is heavenly music in it.) Booth and Amelia I know well.[64] Your sentiments on that subject, as they are on every subject, are just and noble. "To be feelingly alive to kindness, and to unkindness," is a charming female character.

What I said in my last letter, the powers of fuddling sociality only know for me. By yours, I understand my good star has been partly in my horizon, when I got wild in my reveries. Had that evil planet, which has almost all my life shed its baleful rays on my devoted head, been, as usual, in my zenith, I had certainly blabbed something that would have pointed out to you the dear object of my tenderest friendship, and, in spite of me, something more. Had that fatal information escaped me, and it was merely chance, or kind stars, that it did not, I had been undone!

You would never have written me, except perhaps *once* more! O, I could curse circumstances, and the coarse tie of human laws, which keeps fast what common sense would loose, and which bars that happiness itself cannot give—happiness which otherwise Love and Honour would warrant! But hold—I shall make no more "hair-breadth 'scapes."

My friendship, Clarinda, is a life-rent business. My likings are both strong and eternal. I told you I had but one male friend: I have but two female. I should have a third, but she is surrounded by the blandishments of flattery and courtship. The name I register in my heart's core is *Peggy Chalmers*. Miss Nimmo can tell you how divine she is. She is worthy of a place in the same bosom with my Clarinda. That is the highest compliment I can pay her.

Farewell, Clarinda! Remember
SYLVANDER.
[64] See Fielding's *Amelia*.

X.
Saturday Morning, 12*th January*.
Your thoughts on religion, Clarinda, shall be welcome. You may perhaps distrust me, when I say 'tis also my favourite topic; but mine is the religion of the bosom. I hate the very idea of a controversial divinity; as I firmly believe, that every honest upright man, of

whatever sect, will be accepted of the Deity. If your verses, as you seem to hint, contain censure, except you want an occasion to break with me, don't send them. I have a little infirmity in my disposition, that where I fondly love, or highly esteem, I cannot bear reproach.

"Reverence thyself" is a sacred maxim, and I wish to cherish it. I think I told you Lord Bolingbroke's saying to Swift—"Adieu, dear Swift, with all thy faults I love thee entirely; make an effort to love me with all mine." A glorious sentiment, and without which there can be no friendship! I do highly, very highly, esteem you indeed, Clarinda—you merit it all! Perhaps, too, I scorn dissimulation! I could fondly love you: judge then what a maddening sting your reproach would be. "O! I have sins to *Heaven* but none to *you!*" With what pleasure I meet you to-day, but I cannot walk to meet the fly. I hope to be able to see you on *foot* about the middle of next week.

I am interrupted—perhaps you are not sorry for it, you will tell me—but I won't anticipate blame. O Clarinda! did you know how dear to me is your look of kindness, your smile of approbation! you would not, either in prose or verse, risk a censorious remark. Curst be the verse, how well soe'er it flow,
That tends to make one worthy man my foe!
SYLVANDER.

XI.

Saturday, Jan. 12, 1788.

You talk of weeping, Clarinda! Some involuntary drops wet your lines as I read them. *Offend me,* my dearest angel! You cannot offend me, you never offended me! If you had ever given me the least shadow of offence so pardon me, God, as I forgive Clarinda! I have read yours again; it has blotted my paper. Though I find your letter has agitated me into a violent headache, I shall take a chair and be with you about eight. A friend is to be with us to tea on my account, which hinders me from coming sooner. Forgive, my dearest Clarinda, my unguarded expressions. For Heaven's sake, forgive me, or I shall never be able to bear my own mind. Your unhappy Sylvander.

XII.

Monday Evening, 11 *o'clock,* 14*th January.*

Why have I not heard from you, Clarinda? To-day I expected it; and before supper when a letter to me was announced, my heart danced with rapture: but behold, 'twas some fool, who had taken it into his head to turn poet, and made me an offering of the first-fruits of his nonsense. "It is not poetry, but prose run mad." Did I ever repeat to you an epigram I made on a Mr. Elphinstone,[65] who has given a translation of Martial, a famous Latin poet? The poetry of Elphinstone can only equal his prose notes. I was sitting in a merchant's shop of my acquaintance, waiting somebody; he put Elphinstone into my hand, and asked my opinion of it; I begged leave to write it on a blank leaf, which I did,—

TO MR. ELPHINSTONE.
O thou, whom poesy abhors!
Whom prose has turned out of doors!
Heardst thou yon groan? proceed no further!
'Twas laurel'd Martial calling murther!

I am determined to see you, if at all possible, on Saturday evening. Next week I must sing—
The night is my departing night,
The morn's the day I maun awa;
There's neither friend nor foe o' mine
But wishes that I were awa!
What I hae done for lack o' wit,
I never, never can reca';

I hope ye're a' my friends as yet,
Gude night, and joy be wi' you a'!

If I could see you sooner, I would be so much the happier; but I would not purchase the *dearest gratification* on earth, if it must be at your expense in worldly censure, far less inward peace!

I shall certainly be ashamed of thus scrawling whole sheets of incoherence. The only *unity* (a sad word with poets and critics!) in my ideas, is CLARINDA. There my heart "reigns and revels."

What art thou, Love? whence are those charms,
That thus thou bear'st an universal rule?
For thee the soldier quits his arms,
The king turns slave, the wise man fool.
In vain we chase thee from the field,
And with cool thoughts resist thy yoke:
Next tide of blood, alas! we yield;
And all those high resolves are broke!

I like to have quotations for every occasion They give one's ideas so pat, and save one the trouble of finding expression adequate to one's feelings. I think it is one of the greatest pleasures attending a poetic genius, that we can give our woes, cares, joys, loves, etc., an embodied form in verse, which, to me, is ever immediate ease. Goldsmith says finely of his Muse—

Thou source of all my bliss and all my woe;
Thou foundst me poor at first, and keep'st me so.

My limb has been so well to-day, that I have gone up and down stairs often without my staff. To-morrow I hope to walk once again on my own legs to dinner. It is only next street.—Adieu. Sylvander.

[65] A native of Edinburgh, and a schoolmaster in London. He was a friend of Samuel Johnson

XIII.
Tuesday Evening, Jan. 15.

That you have faults, my Clarinda, I never doubted; but I knew not where they existed, and Saturday night made me more in the dark than ever. O Clarinda! why will you wound my soul, by hinting that last night must have lessened my opinion of you? True, I was "behind the scenes with you;" but what did I see? A bosom glowing with honour and benevolence; a mind ennobled by genius, informed and refined by education and reflection, and exalted by native religion, genuine as in the climes of heaven: a heart formed for all the glorious meltings of friendship, love, and pity. These I saw—I saw the noblest immortal soul creation ever showed me.

I looked long, my dear Clarinda, for your letter; and am vexed that you are complaining. I have not caught you so far wrong as in your idea, that the commerce you have with *one* friend hurts you, if you cannot tell every tittle of it to *another*. Why have so injurious a suspicion of a good God, Clarinda, as to think that Friendship and Love, on the sacred inviolate principles of Truth, Honour, and Religion! can be anything else than an object of His divine approbation.

I have mentioned in some of my former scrawls, Saturday evening next. Do allow me to wait on you that evening. Oh, my angel! how soon must we part! and when can we meet again! I look forward on the horrid interval with tearful eyes! What have I lost by not knowing you sooner. I fear, I fear my acquaintance with you is too short, to make that *lasting* impression on your heart I could wish.
SYLVANDER.

XIV.

Saturday Morning, 19*th Jan*

There is no time, my Clarinda, when the conscious thrilling chords of Love and Friendship give such delight, as in the pensive hours of what our favourite Thomson calls, "philosophic melancholy." The sportive insects, who bask in the sunshine of prosperity; or the worms that luxuriantly crawl amid their ample wealth of earth, they need no Clarinda: they would despise Sylvander—if they durst. The family of Misfortune, a numerous group of brothers and sisters! they need a resting place to their souls: unnoticed, often condemned by the world—in some degree, perhaps, condemned by themselves, they feel the full enjoyment of ardent love, delicate tender endearments, mutual esteem and mutual reliance.

In this light I have often admired religion. In proportion as we are wrung with grief, or distracted with anxiety, the ideas of a compassionate Deity, an Almighty Protector, are doubly dear.

'*Tis this*, my friend, that streaks our morning bright;

'*Tis this* that gilds the horrors of our night.'

I have been this morning taking a peep through, as Young finely says, "the dark postern of time long elaps'd;" and, you will easily guess,'twas a rueful prospect. What a tissue of thoughtlessness, weakness, and folly! My life reminded me of a ruined temple; what strength, what proportion in some parts! what unsightly gaps, what prostrate ruin in others! I kneeled down before the Father of mercies, and said, "Father, I have sinned against heaven, and in thy sight, and am no more worthy to be called thy son!" I rose, eased and strengthened. I despise the superstition of a fanatic, but I love the religion of a man. "The future," said I to myself, "is still before me;" there let me

on reason build resolve,

That column of true majesty in man!

"I have difficulties many to encounter," said I; "but they are not absolutely insuperable; and where is firmness of mind shown but in exertion? mere declamation is bombast rant." Besides, wherever I am, or in whatever situation I may be—

'Tis nought to me:

Since God is ever present, ever felt,

In the void waste as in the city full;

And where He vital breathes, there must be joy!

Saturday night—half after Ten.

What luxury of bliss I was enjoying this time yesternight! My ever dearest Clarinda, you have stolen away my soul; but you have refined, you have exalted it; you have given it a stronger sense for virtue, and a stronger relish for piety. Clarinda, first of your sex, if ever I am the veriest wretch on earth to forget you, if ever your lovely image is effaced from my soul,

May I be lost, no eye to weep my end;

And find no earth that's base enough to bury me!

What trifling silliness is the childish fondness of the every-day children of the world! 'tis the unmeaning toying of the younglings of the fields and forests; but where Sentiment and Fancy unite their sweets, where Taste and Delicacy refine, where Wit adds the flavour, and Good Sense gives strength and spirit to all, what a delicious draught is the hour of tender endearment! Beauty and Grace, in the arms of Truth and Honour, in all the luxury of mutual love.

Clarinda, have you ever seen the picture realised? Not in all its very richest colouring.

Last night, Clarinda, but for one slight shade, was the glorious picture.

Innocence

Look'd gaily smiling on; while rosy Pleasure

Hid young Desire amid her flowery wreath,

And pour'd her cup luxuriant; mantling high,
The sparkling heavenly vintage, Love and Bliss!

Clarinda, when a poet and poetess of Nature's making, two of Nature's noblest productions! when they drink together of the same cup of Love and Bliss—attempt not, ye coarser stuff of human nature, profanely to measure enjoyment ye never can know! Good night, my dear Clarinda!

SYLVANDER.

XV

Sunday Night, 20*th January.*

The impertinence of fools has joined with a return of an old indisposition, to make me good for nothing to-day. The paper has lain before me all this evening, to write to my dear Clarinda, but—

Fools rush'd on fools, as waves succeed to waves.

I cursed them in my soul; they sacrilegiously disturbed my meditations on her who holds my heart. What a creature is man! A little alarm last night and to-day, that I am mortal, has made such a revolution on my spirits! There is no philosophy, no divinity, comes half so home to the mind. I have no idea of courage that braves heaven. 'Tis the wild ravings of an imaginary hero in bedlam. I can no more, Clarinda; I can scarcely hold up my head; but I am happy you do not know it, you would be so uneasy.

SYLVANDER.

Monday Morning.

I am, my lovely friend, much better this morning on the whole; but I have a horrid languor on my spirits.

Sick of the world, and all its joys,
My soul in pining sadness mourns;
Dark scenes of woe my mind employs,
The past and present in their turns.

Have you ever met with a saying of the great, and like wise good Mr. Locke, author of the famous *Essay on the Human Understanding*? He wrote a letter to a friend, directing it, "not to be delivered till after my decease;" it ended thus—"I know you loved me when living, and will preserve my memory now I am dead. All the use to be made of it is, that this life affords no solid satisfaction, but in the consciousness of having done well, and the hopes of another life. Adieu! I leave my best wishes with you. J. LOCKE."

Clarinda, may I reckon on your friendship for life? I think I may. Thou Almighty Preserver of men! thy friendship, which hitherto I have too much neglected, to secure it shall, all the future days and nights of my life, be my steady care! The idea of my Clarinda follows—

Hide it, my heart, within that close disguise,
Where, mix'd with God's, her lov'd idea lies.

But I fear that inconstancy, the consequent imperfection of human weakness. Shall I meet with a friendship that defies years of absence, and the chances and changes of fortune? Perhaps "such things are;" *one honest* man[65a] I have great hopes from that way: but who, except a romance writer, would think on a *love* that could promise for life, in spite of distance, absence, chance, and change; and that, too, with slender hopes of fruition? For my own part, I can say to myself in both requisitions, "Thou art the man!" I dare, in cool resolve I dare, declare myself that friend, and that lover. If womankind is capable of such things, Clarinda is. I trust that she is; and I feel I shall be miserable if she is not. There is not one virtue which gives worth, or one sentiment which does honour to the sex, that she does not possess superior to any woman I ever saw; her exalted mind, aided a little perhaps by her situation, is, I think, capable of that nobly-romantic love-enthusiasm.

May I see you on Wednesday evening, my dear angel? The next Wednesday again will, I conjecture, be a hated day to us both. I tremble for censorious remark, for your sake, but, in extraordinary cases, may not usual and useful precaution be a little dispensed with? Three evenings, three swift-winged evenings, with pinions of down, are all the past; I dare not calculate the future. I shall call at Miss Nimmo's to-morrow evening;'twill be a farewell call.

I have wrote out my last sheet of paper, so I am reduced to my last half-sheet. What a strange mysterious faculty is that thing called imagination! We have no ideas almost at all of another world; but I have often amused myself with visionary schemes of what happiness might be enjoyed by small alterations—alterations that we can fully enter into, in this present state of existence. For instance, suppose you and I, just as we are at present; the same reasoning powers, sentiments, and even desires; the same fond curiosity for knowledge and remarking observation in our minds; and imagine our bodies free from pain, and the necessary supplies for the wants of nature at all times, and easily, within our reach: imagine further, that we were set free from the laws of gravitation, which bind us to this globe, and could at pleasure fly, without inconvenience, through all the yet unconjectured bounds of creation, what a life of bliss would we lead, in our mutual pursuit of virtue and knowledge, and our mutual enjoyment of friendship and love!

I see you laughing at my fairy fancies, and calling me a voluptuous Mahometan; but I am certain I would be a happy creature, beyond anything we call bliss here below; nay, it would be a paradise congenial to you too. Don't you see us, hand in hand, or rather, my arm about your lovely waist, making our remarks on Sirius, the nearest of the fixed stars; or surveying a comet, flaming innoxious by us, as we just now would mark the passing pomp of a travelling monarch; or in a shady bower of Mercury or Venus, dedicating the hour to love, in mutual converse, relying honour, and revelling endearment, whilst the most exalted strains of poesy and harmony would be the ready spontaneous language of our souls! Devotion is the favourite employment of your heart; so it is of mine: what incentives then to, and powers for reverence, 'gratitude, faith, and hope, in all the fervours of adoration and praise to that Being, whose unsearchable wisdom, power, and goodness, so pervaded, so inspired every sense and feeling! By this time, I daresay, you will be blessing the neglect of the maid that leaves me destitute of paper!

SYLVANDER.

[65a] Alluding to Captain Brown.

XVI.

[*Monday*, 21*st Jan.* 1788.]

... I am a discontented ghost, a perturbed spirit. Clarinda, if ever you forget Sylvander, may you be happy, but he will be miserable. O what a fool I am in love! What an extraordinary prodigal of affection! Why are your sex called the tender sex, when I have never met with one who can repay me in passion? They are either not so rich in love as I am, or they are niggards where I am lavish.

O Thou, whose I am, and whose are all my ways! Thou seest me here, the hapless wreck of tides and tempests in my own bosom: do Thou direct to Thyself that ardent love for which I have so often sought a return in vain from my fellow-creatures! If Thy goodness has yet such a gift in store for me as an equal return of affection from her who, Thou knowest, is dearer to me than life, do Thou bless and hallow our bond of love and friendship; watch over us in all our outgoings and incomings for good: and may the tie that unites our hearts be strong and indissoluble as the thread of man's immortal life!...

I am just going to take your "Blackbird,"[66] the sweetest, I am sure, that ever sung, and prune its wings a little.

SYLVANDER.

[66] Her verses, "To a Blackbird Singing."

XVII.

Thursday Morning, 24th January.

Unlavish Wisdom never works in vain.

I have been tasking my reason, Clarinda, why a woman, who, for native genius, poignant wit, strength of mind, generous sincerity of soul, and the sweetest female tenderness, is without a peer, and whose personal charms have few, very very few parallels, among her sex; why, or how she should fall to the blessed lot of a poor *hairum scairum* poet, whom Fortune had kept for her particular use, to wreak her temper on whenever she was in ill humour. One time I conjectured, that as Fortune is the most capricious jade ever known, she may have taken, not a fit of remorse, but a paroxysm of whim, to raise the poor devil out of the mire, where he had so often and so conveniently served her as a stepping stone, and given him the most glorious boon she ever had in her gift, merely for the maggot's sake, to see how his fool head and his fool heart will bear it. At other times I was vain enough to think, that Nature, who has a great deal to say with Fortune, had given the coquettish goddess some such hint as, "Here is a paragon of female excellence, whose equal, in all my former compositions, I never was lucky enough to hit on, and despair of ever doing so again; you have cast her rather in the shades of life; there is a certain Poet of my making; among your frolics it would not be amiss to attach him to this masterpiece of my hand, to give her that immortality among mankind, which no woman, of any age, ever more deserved, and which few rhymsters of this age are better able to confer."

Evening, 9 o'clock.

I am here, absolutely unfit to finish my letter—pretty hearty after a bowl, which has been constantly plied since dinner till this moment. I have been with Mr. Schetki, the musician, and he has set it [66a]—See Poems. finely.——I have no distinct ideas of anything, but that I have drunk your health twice to-night, and that you are all my soul holds dear in this world.

SYLVANDER.

[66a] "Clarinda, Mistress of my Soul, etc."—See Poems.

XVIII.

[*Friday, Jan. 25.*]

Clarinda, my life, you have wounded my soul. Can I think of your being unhappy, even though it be not described in your pathetic elegance of language, without being miserable? Clarinda, can I bear to be told from you that you "will not see me to-morrow night"—that you "wish the hour of parting were come?" Do not let us impose on ourselves by sounds. If in the moment of tender endearment I perhaps trespassed against the letter of decorum's law I appeal even to you whether I ever sinned in the very least degree against the spirit of her strictest statute. But why, my love, talk to me in such strong terms?—every word of which cuts me to the very soul. You know a hint, the slightest signification of your wish is to me a sacred command. Be reconciled, my angel, to your God, yourself, and me: and I pledge you Sylvander's honour—an oath I daresay you will trust without reserve—that you shall never more have reason to complain of his conduct. Now, my love, do not wound our next meeting with any averted looks or restrained caresses. I have marked the line of conduct, a line I know exactly to your taste, and which I will inviolably keep; but do not you shew the least inclination to make boundaries. Seeming distrust where you know you may confide is a cruel sin against sensibility. "Delicacy, you know, it was, which won me to you at once—take care you do not loosen the dearest, most sacred tie that unites us." Clarinda, I would not have stung *your* soul, I would not have bruised *your* spirit, as that harsh, crucifying *"Take Care"* did mine—no, not to have gained Heaven! Let me again appeal to your dear self, if Sylvander, even when he seemingly half-transgressed the laws of decorum, if he did not shew more chastened trembling, faltering delicacy than the many of the world do in keeping these laws?

O Love and Sensibility, ye have conspired against my peace! I love to madness and I feel to torture! Clarinda, how can I forgive myself that I have ever touched a single chord in your bosom with pain! Would I do it willingly? Would any consideration, any gratification make me do so? Oh, did you love like me, you would not, you could not, deny or put off a meeting with the man who adores you—who would die a thousand deaths before he would injure you; and who must soon bid you a long farewell!

I had proposed bringing my bosom friend, Mr. Ainslie, to-morrow evening at his strong request to see you, as he has only time to stay with us about ten minutes for an engagement. But I shall hear from you—this afternoon, for mercy's sake! for till I hear from you I am wretched. O Clarinda, the tie that binds me to thee is intwisted, incorporated with my dearest threads of life!

SYLVANDER.

XIX.

[Sat., 26 Jan.]

I was on the way, *my Love,* to meet you (I never do things by halves), when I got your card. Mr. Ainslie goes out of town to-morrow morning, to see a brother of his who is newly arrived from France. I am determined that he and I shall call on you together; so, look you, lest I should never see to-morrow, we will call on you to-night; Mary and you may put off tea till about seven; at which time, in the Galloway phrase, "an the beast be to the fore, and the branks bide hale," expect the humblest of your humble servants, and his dearest friend. We propose staying only half-an-hour, "for ought we ken." I could suffer the lash of misery eleven months in the year, were the twelfth to be composed of hours like yesternight. You are the soul of my enjoyment: all else is of the stuff of stocks and stones.

SYLVANDER.

XX.

Sunday Noon, Jan. 27th.

I have almost given up the excise idea. I have been just now to wait on a great person, Miss——'s friend, ——. Why will great people not only deafen us with the din of their equipage, and dazzle us with their fastidious pomp, but they must also be so very dictatorially wise? I have been questioned like a child about my matters, and blamed and schooled for my inscription on Stirling window. Come Clarinda-Come! curse me Jacob, and come defy me Israel!

Sunday Night.

I have been with Miss Nimmo; she is indeed a good soul, as my Clarinda finely says. She has reconciled me in a good measure to the world with her friendly prattle.

Schetki has sent me the song set to a fine air of his composing. I have called the song "Clarinda." I have carried it about in my pocket and hummed it over all day.

Monday Morning.

If my prayers have any weight in heaven, this morning looks in on you and finds you in the arms of Peace, except where it is charmingly interrupted by the ardours of devotion. I find so much serenity of soul, so much positive pleasure, so much fearless daring toward the world when I warm in devotion, or feel the glorious sensation of a consciousness of Almighty friendship, that I am sure I shall soon be an honest enthusiast.

How are Thy Servants blest, O Lord,
How sure is their defence!

I am, my dear madam, yours, SYLVANDER.

XXI.

Tuesday Morning, 29th January.

I cannot go out to-day, my dearest love, without sending you half a line, by way of a sin-offering; but, believe me, 'twas the sin of ignorance. Could you think that I *intended* to hurt you by any thing I said yesternight? Nature has been too kind to you for your happiness, your delicacy, your sensibility. O why should such glorious qualifications be the fruitful source of woe! You have "murdered sleep" to me last night. I went to bed, impressed with an idea that you were unhappy; and every start I closed my eyes, busy Fancy painted you in such scenes of romantic misery, that I would almost be persuaded you were not well this morning.

If I unweeting have offended,
Impute it not.
But while we live
But one short hour perhaps, between us two,
Let there be peace.

If Mary is not gone by this reaches you, give her my best compliments. She is a charming girl, and highly worthy of the noblest love.

I send you a poem to read, till I call on you this night, which will be about nine. I wish I could procure some potent spell, some fairy charm, that would protect from injury, or restore to rest that bosom-chord, "tremblingly alive all o'er," on which hangs your peace of mind. I thought, vainly, I fear, thought that the devotion of love—love strong as even you can feel—love guarded, invulnerably guarded, by all the purity of virtue, and all the pride of honour; I thought such a love would make you happy—shall I be mistaken? I can no more for hurry.

SYLVANDER.

XXII.

Sunday Morning, 3rd February.

I have just been before the throne of my God, Clarinda; according to my association of ideas, my sentiments of love and friendship, I next devote myself to you. Yesternight I was happy—happiness "that the world cannot give." I kindle at the recollection; but it is a flame where innocence looks smiling on, and honour stands by, a sacred guard. Your heart, your fondest wishes, your dearest thoughts, these are yours to bestow; your person is unapproachable by the laws of your country; and he loves not as I do, who would make you miserable.

You are an angel, Clarinda; you are surely no mortal that "the earth owns." To kiss your hand, to live on your smile, is to me far more exquisite bliss than the dearest favours that the fairest of the sex, yourself excepted, can bestow.

Sunday Evening.

You are the constant companion of my thoughts. How wretched is the condition of one who is haunted with conscious guilt, and trembling under the idea of dreaded vengeance! and what a placid calm, what a charming secret enjoyment it gives, to bosom the kind feelings of friendship and the fond throes of love! Out upon the tempest of anger, the acrimonious gall of fretful impatience, the sullen frost of louring resentment, or the corroding poison of withered envy! They eat up the immortal part of man! If they spent their fury only on the unfortunate objects of them, it would be something in their favour; but these miserable passions, like traitor Iscariot, betray their lord and master.

Thou Almighty Author of peace, and goodness, and love! do thou give me the social heart that kindly tastes of every man's cup! Is it a draught of joy?—warm and open my heart to share it with cordial unenvying rejoicing! Is it the bitter potion of sorrow?—melt my heart with sincerely sympathetic woe! Above all, do thou give me the manly mind that resolutely exemplifies, in life and manners, those sentiments which I would wish to be thought to possess! The friend of my soul—there may I never deviate from the firmest fidelity and most active kindness! Clarinda, the dear object of my fondest love; there may the most sacred inviolate honour, the most faithful kindling constancy, ever watch and animate my every thought and imagination!

Did you ever meet with the following lines spoken of Religion, your darling topic?—
'Tis this, my friend, that streaks our morning bright;
'Tis this that gilds the horrors of our night;
When wealth forsakes us, and when friends are few,
When friends are faithless, or when foes pursue;
'Tis this that wards the blow, or stills the smart,
Disarms affliction, or repels its dart:

Within the breast bids purest rapture rise,
Bids smiling Conscience spread her cloudless skies.[67]

I met with these verses very early in life, and was so delighted with them that I have them by me, copied at school.

Good night and sound rest, my dearest Clarinda!
SYLVANDER.

[67] From Hervey's *Meditations*.

XXIII.

Thursday Night, Feb. 7, 1788.

It is perhaps rather wrong to speak highly to a friend of his letter; it is apt to lay one under a little restraint in their future letters, and restraint is the death of a friendly epistle. But there is one passage in your last charming letter, Thomson or Shenstone never exceeded nor often came up to. I shall certainly steal it, and set it in some future poetic production, and get immortal fame by it. 'Tis when you bid the Scenes of Nature remind me of Clarinda. Can I forget you, Clarinda? I would detest myself as a tasteless, unfeeling, insipid, infamous blockhead! I have loved women of ordinary merit whom I could have loved for ever. You are the first, the only unexceptionable individual of the beauteous sex that I ever met with: and never woman more entirely possessed my soul. I know myself, and how far I can depend on passions, well. It has been my peculiar study.

I thank you for going to Myers.[68] Urge him, for necessity calls, to have it done by the middle of next week, Wednesday at latest. I want it for a breast-pin, to wear next my heart. I propose to keep sacred set times, to wander in the woods and wilds for meditation on you. Then, and only then, your lovely image shall be produced to the day, with a reverence akin to devotion....

To-morrow night shall not be the last. Good-night! I am perfectly stupid, as I supped late yesternight.
SYLVANDER.

[68] Miniature painter.

XXIV.

Wednesday, 13th February.

My ever dearest Clarinda,—I make a numerous dinner party wait me, while I read yours and write this. Do not require that I should cease to love you, to adore you in my soul—'tis to me impossible—your peace and happiness are to me dearer than my soul: name the terms on which you wish to see me, to correspond with me, and you have them—I must love, pine, mourn, and adore in secret—this you must not deny me; you will ever be to me
Dear as the light that visits these sad eyes,
Dear as the ruddy drops that warm my heart!

I have not patience to read the puritanic scrawl. Damn'd sophistry! Ye heavens! thou God of nature! thou Redeemer of mankind! ye look down with approving eyes on a passion inspired by the purest flame, and guarded by truth, delicacy, and honour; but the half-inch soul of an unfeeling, cold-blooded, pitiful presbyterian bigot,[69] cannot forgive anything above his dungeon bosom and foggy head.

Farewell; I'll be with you to-morrow evening—and be at rest in your mind—I will be yours in the way you think most to your happiness! I dare not proceed—I love, and will love you, and will with joyous confidence approach the throne of the Almighty Judge of men, with your dear idea, and will despise the scum of sentiment, and the mist of sophistry.
SYLVANDER.

[69] Rev. Mr. Kemp, Clarinda's spiritual adviser.

XXV.

Wednesday Midnight [Feb. 13].

72

MADAM,-After a wretched day I am preparing for a sleepless night. I am going to address myself to the Almighty Witness of my actions, some time, perhaps very soon, my Almighty Judge. I am not going to be the advocate of passion: be Thou my inspirer and testimony, O God, as I plead the cause of truth!

I have read over your friend's[70] haughty dictatorial letter: you are answerable only to your God in such a matter. Who gave any fellow-creature of yours (one incapable of being your judge because not your peer) a right to catechise, scold, undervalue, abuse, and insult—wantonly and inhumanly to insult you thus? I do not even *wish* to deceive you, Madam. The Searcher of hearts is my witness how dear you are to me; but though it were possible you could be still dearer to me, I would not even kiss your hand at the expense of your conscience. Away with declamation! let us appeal to the bar of commonsense. It is not mouthing everything sacred; it is not vague ranting assertions; it is not assuming, haughtily and insultingly, the dictatorial language of a Roman pontiff, that must dissolve a union like ours. Tell me, Madam—Are you under the least shadow of an obligation to bestow your love, tenderness, caresses, affections, heart and soul, on Mr. M'Lehose, the man who has repeatedly, habitually, and barbarously broken through every tie of duty, nature, and gratitude to you? The laws of your country, indeed, for the most useful reasons of policy and sound government, have made your person inviolate; but, are your heart and affections bound to one who gives not the least return of either to you? You cannot do it: it is not in the nature of things: the common feelings of humanity forbid it. Have you then a heart and affections which are no man's right? You have. It would be absurd to suppose the contrary. Tell me then, in the name of common-sense, can it be wrong, is such a supposition compatible with the plainest ideas of right and wrong, that it is improper to bestow the heart and these affections on another—while that bestowing is not in the smallest degree hurtful to your duty to God, to your children, to yourself, or to society at large?

This is the great test; the consequences: let us see them. In a widowed, forlorn, lonely condition, with a bosom glowing with love and tenderness, yet so delicately situated that you cannot indulge these nobler feelings.... [*cetera desunt.*]

[70] Rev. Mr. Kemp.

XXVI.

Thurs., 14 Feb.

"I am distressed for thee, my brother Jonathan!" I have suffered, Clarinda, from your letter. My soul was in arms at the sad perusal; I dreaded that I had acted wrong. If I have robbed you of a friend,[71] God forgive me!

But, Clarinda, be comforted: let me raise the tone of our feelings a little higher and bolder. A fellow-creature who leaves us, who spurns us without a just cause, though once our bosom friend—up with a little honest pride—let them go! How shall I comfort you, who am the cause of the injury? Can I wish that I had never seen you, that we had never met? No! I never will. But have I thrown you friendless? There is almost distraction in that thought.

Father of mercies! against Thee often have I sinned: through Thy grace I will endeavour to do so no more! She who, Thou knowest, is dearer to me than myself, pour Thou the balm of peace into her past wounds, and hedge her about with Thy peculiar care, all her future days and nights. Strengthen her tender noble mind, firmly to suffer, and magnanimously to bear! Make me worthy of that friendship she honours me with. May my attachment to her be pure as devotion, and lasting as immortal life! O Almighty Goodness, hear me! Be to her at all times, particularly in the hour of distress or trial, a Friend and Comforter, a Guide and Guard.

How are Thy servants blest, O Lord,
How sure is their defence!
Eternal Wisdom is their guide,
Their help, Omnipotence!

Forgive me, Clarinda, the injury I have done you! Tonight I shall be with you; as indeed I shall be ill at ease till I see you.

SYLVANDER.

[71] Her minister.

XXVII.

Thursday, 14th Feb., Two o'clock.

I just now received your first letter of yesterday, by the careless negligence of the penny-post. Clarinda, matters are grown very serious with us; then seriously hear me, and hear me, Heaven—I met you, my dear Nancy, by far the first of womankind, at least to me; I esteemed, I loved you at first sight; the longer I am acquainted with you the more innate amiableness and worth I discover in you. You have suffered a loss, I confess, for my sake: but if the firmest, steadiest, warmest friendship; if every endeavour to be worthy of your friendship; if a love, strong as the ties of nature, and holy as the duties of religion—if all these can make anything like a compensation for the evil I have occasioned you, if they be worth your acceptance, or can in the least add to your enjoyment—so help Sylvander, ye Powers above, in his hour of need, as he freely gives these all to Clarinda!

I esteem you, I love you as a friend; I admire you, I love you as a woman, beyond any one in all the circle of creation; I know I shall continue to esteem you, to love you, to pray for you, nay, to pray for myself for your sake.

Expect me at eight. And believe me to be ever, my dearest Madam, yours most entirely, SYLVANDER.

XXVIII.

February 15th, 1788.

When matters, my love, are desperate, we must put on a desperate face—
On reason build resolve,
That column of true majesty in man.

Or, as the same author finely says in another place—

Let thy soul spring up,
And lay strong hold for help on Him that made thee.

I am yours, Clarinda, for life. Never be discouraged at all this. Look forward; in a few weeks I shall be somewhere or other out of the possibility of seeing you: till then I shall write you often, but visit you seldom. Your fame, your welfare, your happiness are dearer to me than any gratification whatever. Be comforted, my love! the present moment is the worst; the lenient hand of Time is daily and hourly either lightening the burden, or making us insensible to the weight. None of these friends, I mean Mr.—— and the other gentleman, can hurt your worldly support; and for their friendship, in a little time you will learn to be easy, and, by and by, to be happy without it. A decent means of livelihood in the world, an approving God, a peaceful conscience, and one firm, trusty friend—can anybody that has these be said to be unhappy? These are yours.

To-morrow evening I shall be with you about eight; probably for the last time till I return to Edinburgh. In the meantime, should any of these two unlucky friends question you respecting me, whether I am the man, I do not think they are entitled to any information. As to their jealousy and spying, I despise them. —Adieu, my dearest Madam!

SYLVANDER.

XXIX.

GLASGOW, *Monday Evening, 9 o'clock, 18th Feb. 1788.*

The attraction of love, I find, is in an inverse proportion to the attraction of the Newtonian philosophy. In the system of Sir Isaac, the nearer objects are to one another, the stronger is the attractive force; in my system, every mile-stone that marked my progress from

Clarinda, awakened a keener pang of attachment to her. How do you feel, my love? Is your heart ill at ease? I fear it.—God forbid that these persecutors should harass that peace, which is more precious to me than my own. Be assured I shall ever think of you, muse on you, and, in my moments of devotion, pray for you. The hour that you are not in all my thoughts— "be that hour darkness! let the shadows of death cover it! let it not be numbered in the hours of the day!"

When I forget the darling theme,
Be my tongue mute! my fancy paint no more!
And, dead to joy, forget, my heart, to beat!

I have just met with my old friend, the ship captain;[72] guess my pleasure—to meet you could alone have given me more. My brother William, too, the young saddler, has come to Glasgow to meet me; and here are we three spending the evening.

I arrived here too late to write by post; but I'll wrap half a dozen sheets of blank paper together, and send it by the fly, under the name of a parcel. You shall hear from me next post town. I would write you a long letter, but for the present circumstance of my friend.

Adieu, my Clarinda! I am just going to propose your health by way of grace-drink. SYLVANDER.

[72] Richard Brown, whom he first knew at Irvine.

XXX.

CUMNOCK, *2nd March* 1788.

I hope, and am certain, that my generous Clarinda[73] will not think my silence, for now a long week, has been in any decree owing to my forgetfulness. I have been tossed about through the country ever since I wrote you; and am here, returning from Dumfries-shire, at an inn, the post office of the place, with just so long time as my horse eats his corn, to write you. I have been hurried with business and dissipation almost equal to the insidious decree of the Persian monarch's mandate, when he forbade asking petition of God or man for forty days. Had the venerable prophet been as throng as I, he had not broken the decree, at least not thrice a day.

I am thinking my farming scheme will yet hold. A worthy intelligent farmer, my father's friend and my own, has been with me on the spot: he thinks the bargain practicable. I am myself, on a more serious review of the lands, much better pleased with them. I won't mention this in writing to any body but you and Ainslie. Don't accuse me of being fickle: I have the two plans of life before me, and I wish to adopt the one most likely to procure me independence. I shall be in Edinburgh next week. I long to see you: your image is omnipresent to me; nay, I am convinced I would soon idolatrise it most seriously; so much do absence and memory improve the medium through which one sees the much-loved object. To-night, at the sacred hour of eight, I expect to meet you—at the Throne of Grace. I hope, as I go home tonight, to find a letter from you at the post office in Mauchline. I have just once seen that dear hand since I left Edinburgh—a letter indeed which much affected me. Tell me, first of womankind! will my warmest attachment, my sincerest friendship, my correspondence, will they be any compensation for the sacrifices you make for my sake! If they will, they are yours. If I settle on the farm I propose, I am just a day and a half's ride from Edinburgh. We will meet—don't you say, "perhaps too often!"

Farewell, my fair, my charming Poetess! May all good things ever attend you! I am ever, my dearest Madam, yours, SYLVANDER.

[73] The letter about the 23rd of February seems to be wanting.

XXXI.

MAUCHLINE, 6 *Mar.*

I own myself guilty, Clarinda; I should have written you last week; but when you recollect, my dearest Madam, that yours of this night's post is only the third I have got from you, and that this is the fifth or sixth I have sent to you, you will not reproach me, with a good grace, for unkindness. I have always some kind of idea, not to sit down to write a letter except I have time and possession of my faculties, so as to do some justice to my letter; which at present is rarely my situation. For instance, yesterday I dined at a friend's at some distance; the savage hospitality of this country spent me the most part of the night over the nauseous potion in the bowl: this day—sick—headache—low spirits—miserable—fasting, except for a draught of water or small beer: now eight o'clock at night—only able to crawl ten minutes walk into Mauchline to wait the post, in the pleasurable hope of hearing from the mistress of my soul.

But, truce with all this! When I sit down to write to you, all is harmony and peace. A hundred times a day do I figure you, before your taper, your book, or work laid aside, as I get within the room. How happy have I been! and how little of that scantling portion of time, called the life of man, is sacred to happiness! much less transport!

I could moralise to-night like a death's head.

O what is life, that thoughtless wish of all!

A drop of honey in a draught of gall.

Nothing astonishes me more, when a little sickness clogs the wheels of life, than the thoughtless career we run in the hour of health. "None saith, where is God, my Maker, that giveth songs in the night; who teacheth us more knowledge than the beasts of the field, and more understanding than the fowls of the air."

Give me, my Maker, to remember thee! Give me to act up to the dignity of my nature! Give me to feel "another's woe;" and continue with me that dear-loved friend that feels with mine!

The dignified and dignifying consciousness of an honest man, and the well-grounded trust in approving Heaven, are two most substantial foundations of happiness.

SYLVANDER.

XXXII

.MOSSGIEL, *7th March* 1788.

Clarinda, I have been so stung with your reproach for unkindness, a sin so unlike me, a sin I detest more than a breach of the whole Decalogue, fifth, sixth, seventh and ninth articles excepted, that I believe I shall not rest in my grave about it, if I die before I see you. You have often allowed me the head to judge, and the heart to feel, the influence of female excellence.

Was it not blasphemy, then, against your own charms, and against my feelings, to suppose that a short fortnight could abate my passion? You, my love, may have your cares and anxieties to disturb you, but they are the usual recurrences of life; your future views are fixed, and your mind in a settled routine. Could not you, my ever dearest Madam, make a little allowance for a man, after long absence, paying a short visit to a country full of friends, relations, and early intimates? Cannot you guess, my Clarinda, what thoughts, what cares, what anxious forebodings, hopes and fears, must crowd the breast of the man of keen sensibility, when no less is on the tapis than his aim, his employment, his very existence, through future life!

Now that, not my apology, but my defence is made, I feel my soul respire more easily. I know you will go along with me in my justification—would to Heaven you could in my adoption too! I mean an adoption beneath the stars—an adoption where I might revel in the immediate beams of

Her, the bright sun of all her sex.

I would not have you, my dear Madam, so much hurt at Miss Nimmo's coldness. 'Tis placing yourself below her, an honour she by no means deserves. We ought, when we wish to be economists in happiness—we ought, in the first place, to fix the standard of our own character; and when, on full examination, we know where we stand, and how much ground we occupy, let us contend for it as property; and those who seem to doubt, or deny us what is justly ours, let us either pity their prejudices, or despise their judgment. I know, my dear, you will say this is self-conceit; but I call it self-knowledge. The one is theoverweening opinion of a fool, who fancies himself to be what he wishes himself to be thought; the other is the honest justice that a man of sense, who has thoroughly examined the subject, owes to himself. Without this standard, this column in our own mind, we are perpetually at the mercy of the petulance, the mistakes, the prejudices, nay, the very weakness and wickedness of our fellow-creatures.

I urge this, my dear, both to confirm myself in the doctrine, which, I assure you, I sometimes need; and because I know that this causes you often much disquiet. To return to Miss Nimmo: she is most certainly a worthy soul, and equalled by very, very few, in goodness of heart. But can she boast more goodness of heart than Clarinda? Not even prejudice will dare to say so. For penetration and discernment, Clarinda sees far beyond her: to wit, Miss Nimmo dare make no pretence; to Clarinda's wit, scarcely any of her sex dare make pretence. Personal charms, it would be ridiculous to run the parallel. And for conduct in life, Miss Nimmo was never called out, either much to do or to suffer; Clarinda has been both; and has performed her part, where Miss Nimmo would have sunk at the bare idea.

Away, then, with these disquietudes! Let us pray with the honest weaver of Kilbarchan—"Lord, send us a gude conceit o' oursel!" Or, in the words of the auld sang,

Who does me disdain, I can scorn them again,

And I'll never mind any such foes.

There is an error in the commerce of intimacy[74] ...

way of exchange, have not an equivalent to give us; and, what is still worse, have no idea of the value of our goods. Happy is our lot indeed, when we meet with an honest merchant, who is qualified to deal with us on our own terms; but that is a rarity. With almost everybody we must pocket our pearls, less or more, and learn in the old Scotch phrase—"To gie sic like as we get." For this reason one should try to erect a kind of bank or store-house in one's own mind; or, as the Psalmist says, "We should commune with our own hearts, and be still." This is exactly [MS. dilapidated.]

[74] The MS. is so worn as to be indecipherable.

XXXIII.

EDINBURGH, 18*th March* 1788.

I am just hurrying away to wait on the great man, Clarinda; but I have more respect on my own peace and happiness than to set out without waiting on you; for my imagination, like a child's favourite bird, will fondly flutter along with this scrawl till it perch on your bosom I thank you for all the happiness of yesterday—the walk delightful, the evening rapture. Do not be uneasy today, Clarinda. I am in rather better spirits today, though I had but an indifferent night. Care, anxiety, sat on my spirits. All the cheerfulness of this morning is the fruit of some serious, important ideas that lie, in their realities, beyond the dark and narrow house. The Father of mercies be with you, Clarinda. Every good thing attend you!

SYLVANDER.

XXXIV.

Friday 9 [*p.m.*, 21*st March* 1788].

I am just now come in, and have read your letters. The first thing I did was to thank the Divine Disposer of events that he has had such happiness in store for me as the connexion I have with you. Life, my Clarinda, is a weary, barren path; and woe be to him or her that ventures on it alone! For me, I have my dearest partner of my soul. Clarinda and I will make out our pilgrimage together. Wherever I am, I shall constantly let her know how I go on, what I observe in the world around me, and what adventures I meet with. Would it please you, my love, to get every week, or every fortnight at least, a packet of two or three sheets of remarks, nonsense, news, rhymes and old songs? Will you open with satisfaction and delight a letter from a man who loves you, who has loved you, and who will love you to death, through death, and for ever? O Clarinda! what do I owe to heaven for blessing me with such a piece of exalted excellence as you! I call over your idea, as a miser counts over his treasure. Tell me, were you studious to please me last night? I am sure you did it to transport.

How rich am I who have such a treasure as you! You know me; you know how to make me happy, and you do it most effectually. God bless you with "long life, long youth, long pleasure, and a friend!" Tomorrow night, according to your own direction, I shall watch the window—'tis the star that guides me to Paradise. The great relish to all is that honour, that innocence, that Religion are the witnesses and guarantees of our affection, Adieu, Clarinda! I am going to remember you in my prayers.

SYLVANDER.

GENERAL CORRESPONDENCE.
LETTERS

(General Correspondence Resumed.)

LXXXIV.—To MR. GAVIN HAMILTON.
[*April* 1788] MOSSGIEL, *Friday Morning.*

The language of refusal is to me the most difficult language on earth, and you are the man in the world, excepting one of Right Hon. designation, to whom it gives me the greatest pain to hold such language. My brother has already got money,[75] and shall want nothing in my power to enable him to fulfil his engagement with you; but to be security on so large a scale, even for a brother, is what I dare not do, except I were in such circumstances of life as that the worst that might happen could not greatly injure me.

I never wrote a letter which gave me so much pain in my life, as I know the unhappy consequences:—I shall incur the displeasure of a gentleman for whom I have the highest respect and to whom I am deeply obliged.—I am etc.

ROBERT BURNS.

[75] Altogether £180. Gilbert is meant, and the business referred to was renewal of lease of Mossgiel, the poet to be cautioner.

LXXXV.—To MR. WILLIAM DUNBAR, W.S., EDINBURGH.
MAUCHLINE, 7*th April* 1788.

I have not delayed so long to write you, my much respected friend, because I thought no further of my promise. I have long since given up that formal kind of correspondence where one sits down irksomely to write a letter, because he is in duty bound to do so.

I have been roving over the country, as the farm[76] I have taken is forty miles from this place, hiring servants and preparing matters; but most of all, I am earnestly busy to bring about a revolution in my own mind. As, till within these eighteen months, I never was the wealthy master of ten guineas, my knowledge of business is to learn. Add to this, my late scenes of idleness and dissipation have enervated my mind to an alarming degree. Skill in the sober science of life is my most serious, and hourly study. I have dropped all conversation and all reading (prose reading) but what tends in some way or other to my serious aim. Except one worthy young fellow[77] I have not a single correspondent in Edinburgh. You have indeed kindly made me an offer of that kind. The world of wits, the *gens comme-il-faut*, which I lately left, and in which I never again will intimately mix—from that port, Sir, I expect your gazette, what the *beaux esprits* are saying, what they are doing, and what they are singing. Any sober intelligence from my sequestered life is all you have to expect from me. I have scarcely made a single distich since I saw you. When I meet with an old Scots air that has any facetious idea in its name, I have a peculiar pleasure in following out that idea for a verse or two.

I trust this will find you in better health than I did the last time I called for you. A few lines from you, directed to me, at Mauchline, were it but to let me know how you are, will settle my mind a good deal. Now, never shun the idea of writing me because, perhaps, you may be out of humour or spirits. I could give you a hundred good consequences attending a

78

dull letter; one, for example, and the remaining ninety-nine some other time—it will always serve to keep in countenance, my much respected Sir, your obliged friend and humble servant, R. B.

[76] Ellisland, near Dumfries.

[77] Robert Ainslie, W.S.

LXXXVI.—To MRS. DUNLOP.

MAUCHLINE, 28*th April* 1788.

MADAM,—Your powers of reprehension must be great indeed, as I assure you they make my heart ache with penitential pangs, even though I was really not guilty. As I commence farming at Whitsunday, you will easily guess I must be pretty busy; but that is not all. As I got the offer of the Excise business without solicitation, and as it costs me only six months' attendance for instructions, to entitle me to a commission—which commission lies by me, and at any future period, on my simple petition, can be resumed—I thought five-and-thirty pounds a-year was no bad *dernier ressort* for a poor poet, if Fortune in her jade tricks should kick him down from the little eminence to which she has lately helped him up.

For this reason, I am at present attending these instructions, to have them completed before Whitsunday. Still, Madam, I prepared with the sincerest pleasure to meet you at the Mount, and came to my brother's on Saturday night, to set out on Sunday; but for some nights preceding I had slept in an apartment, where the force of the winds and rains was only mitigated by being sifted through numberless apertures in the windows, walls, etc. In consequence I was on Sunday, Monday, and part of Tuesday, unable to stir out of bed, with all the miserable effects of a violent cold.

You see, Madam, the truth of the French maxim, *le vrai n'est pas toujours le vrai-semblable;* your last was so full of expostulation, and was something so like the language of an offended friend, that I began to tremble for a correspondence, which I had with grateful pleasure set down as one of the greatest enjoyments of my future life.

Your books have delighted me; Virgil, Dryden, and Tasso were all equally strangers to me; but of this more at large in my next. R. B.

LXXXVII.—To MR. JAMES SMITH, AVON PRINTFIELD, LINLITHGOW.

MAUCHLINE, *April* 28*th*, 1788.

Beware of your Strasburgh, my good Sir! Look on this as the opening of a correspondence, like the opening of a twenty-four gun battery!

There is no understanding a man properly, without knowing something of his previous ideas; that is to say, if the man has any ideas; for I know many who, in the animal-muster, pass for men, that are the scanty masters of only one idea on any given subject, and by far the greatest part of your acquaintances and mine can barely boast of ideas, 1.25—1.5—1.75 (or some such fractional matter); so to let you a little into the secrets of my pericranium, there is, you must know, a certain clean-limbed, handsome, bewitching young hussy of your acquaintance, to whom I have lately and privately given a matrimonial title to my corpus.

Bode a robe and wear it,
Bode a pock and bear it,

says the wise old Scots adage! I hate to presage ill-luck; and as my girl has been doubly kinder to me than even the best of women usually are to their partners of our sex, in similar circumstances, I reckon on twelve times a brace of children against I celebrate my twelfth wedding-day: these twenty-four will give me twenty-four gossipings, twenty-four christenings (I mean one equal to two), and I hope, by the blessing of the God of my fathers, to make them twenty-four dutiful children to their parents, twenty-four useful members of society, and twenty-four approved servants of their God....

"Light's heartsome," quo' the wife when she was stealing sheep. You see what a lamp I have hung up to lighten your paths, when you are idle enough to explore the combinations and relations of my ideas. 'Tis now as plain as a pike-staff, why a twenty-four gun battery was a metaphor I could readily employ.

Now for business. I intend to present Mrs. Burns with a printed shawl, an article of which I dare say you have variety: 'tis my first present to her since I have irrevocably called her mine, and I have a kind of whimsical wish to get her the first said present from an old and much-valued friend of hers and mine, a trusty Trojan, on whose friendship I count myself possessed of as a life-rent lease.

Look on this letter as a "beginning of sorrows;" I will write you till your eyes ache reading nonsense.

Mrs. Burns ('tis only her private designation) begs her best compliments to you. R. B.

LXXXVIII—To PROFESSOR DUGALD STEWART.
MAUCHLINE, 3rd May 1788.

SIR,—I enclose you one or two more of my bagatelles. If the fervent wishes of honest gratitude have any influence with that great unknown Being who frames the chain of causes and events, prosperity and happiness will attend your visit to the Continent, and return you safe to your native shore.

Wherever I am, allow me, Sir, to claim it as my privilege to acquaint you with my progress in my trade of rhymes; as I am sure I could say it with truth, that, next to my little fame, and the having it in my power to make life more comfortable to those whom nature has made dear to me, I shall ever regard your countenance, your patronage, your friendly good offices, as the most valued consequence of my late success in life. R. B.

LXXXIX.—To MRS. DUNLOP.
MAUCHLINE, 4th May 1788.

MADAM,—Dryden's Virgil has delighted me. I do not know whether the critics will agree with me, but the Georgics are to me by far the best of Virgil. It is indeed a species of writing entirely new to me, and has filled my head with a thousand fancies of emulation; but, alas! when I read the Georgics, and then survey my own powers, 'tis like the idea of a Shetland pony, drawn up by the side of a thorough-bred hunter, to start for the plate. I own I am disappointed in the AEneid. Faultless correctness may please, and does highly please, the lettered critic; but to that awful character T have not the most distant pretensions. I do not know whether I do not hazard my pretensions to be a critic of any kind, when I say that I think Virgil, in many instances, a servile copier of Homer. If I had the Odyssey by me, I could parallel many passages where Virgil has evidently copied, but by no means improved, Homer. Nor can I think there is anything of this owing to the translators; for, from everything I have seen of Dryden, I think him, in genius and fluency of language, Pope's master. I have not perused Tasso enough to form an opinion: in some future letter you shall have my ideas of him; though I am conscious my criticisms must be very inaccurate and imperfect, as there I have ever felt and lamented my want of learning most. R. B.

XC.—To MR. SAMUEL BROWN, KIRKOSWALD.
MOSSGIEL, 4th May 1788.

DEAR UNCLE,—This, I hope, will find you and your conjugal yoke-fellow in your good old way. I am impatient to know if the Ailsa[78] fowling be commenced for this season yet, as I want three or four stones of feathers, and I hope you will bespeak them for me. It would be a vain attempt for me to enumerate the various transactions I have been engaged in since I saw you last; but this know—I engaged in a smuggling trade, and no poor man ever experienced better returns, two for one: but as freight and delivery have turned out so dear, I am thinking of taking out a license and beginning in fair trade. I have taken a farm, on the borders of the Nith, and in imitation of the old patriarchs, get men-servants and maid-servants, and flocks and herds, and beget sons and daughters.—Your obedient nephew,
ROBERT BURNS.

[78] A well-known rock in the Firth of Clyde, frequented by innumerable sea-fowl.

XCI.—To MR. JAMES JOHNSON, ENGRAVER, EDINBURGH.

MAUCHLINE, 25*th May* 1788.

MY DEAR SIR,—I am really uneasy about that money which Mr. Creech owes me per note in your hand, and I want it much at present, as I am engaging in business pretty deeply both for myself and my brother. A hundred guineas can be but a trifling affair to him, and 'tis a matter of most serious importance to me.[79] To-morrow I begin my operations as a farmer, and so God speed the plough!

I am so enamoured of a certain girl.... To be serious, I found I had a long and much-loved fellow-creature's happiness or misery in my hands; and though pride and seeming justice were murderous king's advocates on the one side, yet humanity, generosity, and forgiveness were such powerful, such irresistible counsel on the other, that a jury of all endearments and new attachments brought in a unanimous verdict of *not guilty*. And the panel, be it known unto all whom it concerns, is installed and instated into all the rights, privileges, etc., that belong to the name, title, and designation of wife.

[79] Creech paid the amount five days after the date of this letter.

XCII.—To MR. ROBERT AINSLIE.

MAUCHLINE, *May 26th*, 1788.

MY DEAR FRIEND,—I am two kind letters in your debt; but I have been from home, and horridly busy, buying and preparing for my farming business, over and above the plague of my Excise instructions, which this week will finish.

As I flatter my wishes that I foresee many future years' correspondence between us, 'tis foolish to talk of excusing dull epistles! a dull letter may be a very kind one. I have the pleasure to tell you that I have been extremely fortunate in all my buyings and bargainings hitherto, Mrs. Burns not excepted; which title I now avow to the world. I am truly pleased with this last affair. It has indeed added to my anxieties for futurity, but it has given a stability to my mind and resolutions unknown before; and the poor girl has the most sacred enthusiasm of attachment to me, and has not a wish but to gratify my every idea of her deportment. I am interrupted. Farewell! my dear Sir. R. B.

XCIII.—To MRS. DUNLOP.

27*th May* 1788.

MADAM,—I have been torturing my philosophy to no purpose to account for that kind partiality of yours, which has followed me, in my return to the shade of life, with assiduous benevolence. Often did I regret, in the fleeting hours of my late will-o'-wisp appearance, that "here I had no continuing city;" and, but for the consolation of a few solid guineas, could almost lament the time that a momentary acquaintance with wealth and splendour put me so much out of conceit with the sworn companions of my road through life—insignificance and poverty.

There are few circumstances relating to the unequal distribution of the good things of this life that give me more vexation (I mean in what I see around me) than the importance the opulent bestow on their trifling family affairs, compared with the very same things on the contracted scale of a cottage. Last afternoon I had the honour to spend an hour or two at a good woman's fireside, where the planks that composed the floor were decorated with a splendid carpet, and the gay table sparkled with silver and china. 'Tis now about term-day, and there has been a revolution among those creatures who, though in appearance partakers, and equally noble partakers, of the same nature with Madame, are from time to time—their nerves, their sinews, their health, strength, wisdom, experience, genius, time, nay, a good part of their very thoughts—sold for months and years, not only to the necessities, the conveniences, but the caprices of the important few. We talked of the insignificant creatures; nay, notwithstanding their general stupidity and rascality, did some of the poor devils the honour to commend them. But light be the turf upon his breast who taught "Reverence thyself!" We looked down on the unpolished wretches, their impertinent wives, and clouterly brats, as the lordly bull does on the little dirty ant-hill, whose puny inhabitants he crushes in the carelessness of his ramble, or tosses in the air in the wantonness of his pride.

R. B.

XCIV.—TO MRS. DUNLOP, AT MR. DUNLOP'S, HADDINGTON.

ELLISLAND, 13*th June* 1788.

Where'er I roam, whatever realms I see,
My heart, untravell'd, fondly turns to thee;
Still to my friend it turns with ceaseless pain,
And drags, at each remove, a lengthen'd chain.
GOLDSMITH.

This is the second day, my honoured friend, that I have been on my farm. A solitary inmate of an old smoky spence; far from every object I love, or by whom I am beloved; nor any acquaintance older than yesterday, except Jenny Geddes, the old mare I ride on; while uncouth cares and novel plans hourly insult my awkward ignorance and bashful inexperience. There is a foggy atmosphere native to my soul in the hour of care; consequently the dreary objects seem larger than the life. Extreme sensibility, irritated and prejudiced on the gloomy side by a series of misfortunes and disappointments, at that period of my existence when the soul is laying in her cargo of ideas for the voyage of life, is, I believe, the principal cause of this unhappy frame of mind.

The valiant, in himself, what can he suffer?
Or what need he regard his *single* woes?

Your surmise, Madam, is just: I am indeed a husband.

I found a once much-loved and still much-loved female, literally and truly cast out to the mercy of the naked elements—but there is no sporting with a fellow-creature's happiness or misery.... The most placid good-nature and sweetness of disposition; a warm heart, gratefully devoted with all its powers to love me; vigorous health and sprightly cheerfulness, set off to the best advantage by a more than common handsome figure—these, I think, in a woman may make a good wife though she should never have read a page but the Scriptures of the Old and New Testaments, nor have danced in a brighter assembly than a penny pay wedding.

R. B.

XCV.-TO MR. ROBERT AINSLIE.

ELLISLAND, *June 14th*, 1788.

This is now the third day, my dearest Sir, that I have sojourned in these regions; and during these three days you have occupied more of my thoughts than in three weeks preceding: in Ayrshire I have several variations of friendship's compass, here it points invariably to the pole. My farm gives me a good many uncouth cares and anxieties, but I hate the language of complaint. Job, or some one of his friends, says well—"Why should a living man complain?"

I have lately been much mortified with contemplating an unlucky imperfection in the very framing and construction of my soul; namely, a blundering inaccuracy of her olfactory organs in hitting the scent of craft or design in my fellow-creatures. I do not mean any compliment to my ingenuousness, or to hint that the defect is in consequence of the unsuspicious simplicity of conscious truth and honour: I take it to be, in some way or other, an imperfection in the mental sight; or, metaphor apart, some modification of dulness. In two or three instances lately, I have been most shamefully out.

I have all along, hitherto, in the warfare of life, been bred to arms among the light horse—the piquet-guards of fancy; a kind of hussars and Highlanders of the brain; but I am firmly resolved to sell out of these giddy battalions, who have no ideas of a battle but fighting the foe, or of a siege but storming the town. Cost what it will, I am determined to buy in among the grave squadrons of heavy-armed thought, or the artillery corps of plodding contrivance.

What books are you reading, or what is the subject of your thoughts, besides the great studies of your profession? You said something about religion in your last. I don't exactly remember what it was, as the letter is in Ayrshire; but I thought it not only prettily said, but nobly thought. You will make a noble fellow if once you were married. I make no reservation of your being well-married; you have so much sense, and knowledge of human nature, that though you may not realise perhaps the ideas of romance, yet you will never be ill-married.

Were it not for the terrors of my ticklish situation respecting provision for a family of children, I am decidedly of opinion that the step I have taken is vastly for my happiness.[80] As it is, I look to the Excise scheme as a certainty of maintenance; a maintenance!—luxury to what either Mrs. Burns or I were born to. Adieu.

R. B.

[80] This alludes to his marriage.

XCVI.-TO MR. ROBERT AINSLIE.

ELLISLAND, *30th June* 1788.

MY DEAR SIR,—I just now received your brief epistle; and, to take vengeance on your laziness, I have, you see, taken a long sheet of writing-paper, and have begun at the top of the page, intending to scribble on to the very last corner.

I am vexed at that affair of the ..., but dare not enlarge on the subject until you send me your direction, as I suppose that will be altered on your late master and friend's death.[81] I am concerned for the old fellow's exit, only as I fear it may be to your disadvantage in any respect—for an old man's dying, except he have been a very benevolent character, or in some particular situation of life that the welfare of the poor or the helpless depended on him, I think it an event of the most trifling moment to the world. Man is naturally a kind, benevolent animal, but he is dropped into such a needy situation here in this vexatious world, and has such a hungry, growling, multiplying pack of necessities, appetites, passions, and desires about him, ready to devour him for want of other food, that in fact he must lay aside his cares for others that he may look properly to himself. You have been imposed upon in paying Mr. Miers for the profile of a Mr. H. I did not mention it in my letter to you, nor did I ever give Mr. Miers any such order. I have no objection to lose the money, but I will not have any such profile in my possession.

I desired the carrier to pay you, but as I mentioned only 15s. to him, I will rather inclose you a guinea-note. I have it not, indeed, to spare here, as I am only a sojourner in a strange land in this place; but in a day or two I return to Mauchline, and there I have the bank-notes through the house like salt permits.

There is a great degree of folly in talking unnecessarily of one's private affairs. I have just now been interrupted by one of my new neighbours, who has made himself absolutely contemptible in my eyes, by his silly, garrulous pruriency. I know it has been a fault of my own, too; but from this moment I abjure it as I would the service of hell! Your poets, spendthrifts, and other fools of that kidney, pretend, forsooth, to crack their jokes on prudence; but'tis a squalid vagabond glorying in his rags. Still, imprudence respecting money matters is much more pardonable than imprudence respecting character, I have no objection to prefer prodigality to avarice, in some few instances; but I appeal to your observation if you have not met, and often met, with the same disingenuousness, the same hollow-hearted insincerity, and disintegritive depravity of principle, in the hackneyed victims of profusion, as in the unfeeling children of parsimony. I have every possible reverence for the much talked-of world beyond the grave, and I wish that which piety believes, and virtue deserves, may be all matter of fact. But in things belonging to, and terminating in this present scene of existence, man has serious and interesting business on hand. Whether a man shall shake hands with welcome in the distinguished elevation of respect, or shrink from contempt in the abject corner of insignificance: whether he shall wanton under the tropic of plenty, at least enjoy himself in the comfortable latitude of easy convenience, or starve in the arctic circle of dreary poverty; whether he shall rise in the manly consciousness of a self-approving mind, or sink beneath a galling load of regret and remorse—these are alternatives of the last moment.

You see how I preach. You used occasionally to sermonise too; I wish you would, in charity, favour me with a sheet full in your own way. I admire the close of a letter Lord Bolingbroke writes to Dean Swift:—"Adieu, dear Swift! with all thy faults I love thee entirely: make an effort to love me with all mine!" Humble servant, and all that trumpery, is now such a prostituted business, that honest friendship, in her sincere way, must have recourse to her primitive, simple—farewell!

R. B.

[81] Samuel Mitchelson, W.S., with whom young Ainslie served his apprenticeship.

XCVII—TO MRS. DUNLOP.

MAUCHLINE, *July* 10*th*, 1788.

MY MUCH HONOURED FRIEND,—Yours of the 24th June is before me. I found it, as well as another valued friend—my wife, waiting to welcome me to Ayrshire: I met both with the sincerest pleasure.

When I write you, Madam, I do not sit down to answer every paragraph of yours, by echoing every sentiment, like the faithful Commons of Great Britain in Parliament assembled, answering a speech from the best of kings! I express myself in the fulness of my heart, and may, perhaps, be guilty of neglecting some of your kind inquiries; but not from your very odd reason, that I do not read your letters. All your epistles, for several months, have cost me nothing except a swelling throb of gratitude, or a deep-felt sentiment of veneration.

When Mrs. Burns, Madam, first found herself "as women wish to be who love their lords," as I loved her nearly to distraction, we took steps for a private marriage. Her parents got the hint; and not only forbade me her company and their house, but, on my rumoured West Indian voyage, got a warrant to put me in jail, till I should find security in my about-to-be paternal relation. You know my lucky reverse of fortune. On my *éclatant* return to Mauchline, I was made very welcome to visit my girl. The usual consequences began to betray her; and, as I was at that time laid up a cripple in Edinburgh, she was turned, literally turned, out of doors, and I wrote to a friend to shelter her till my return, when our marriage was declared. Her happiness or misery were in my hands, and who could trifle with such a deposit?

To jealousy or infidelity I am an equal stranger. My preservative against the first is the most thorough consciousness of her sentiments of honour and her attachment to me; my antidote against the last is my long and deep-rooted affection for her. I can easily *fancy* a more agreeable companion for my journey of life; but, upon my honour, I have never *seen* the individual instance.

In household matters, of aptness to learn and activity to execute, she is eminently mistress; and during my absence in Nithsdale, she is regularly and constantly apprentice to my mother and sisters in their dairy, and other rural business.

The muses must not be offended when I tell them, the concerns of my wife and family will, in my mind, always take the *pas*; but I assure them their ladyships will ever come next in place.

You are right that a bachelor state would have insured me more friends; but, from a cause you will easily guess, conscious peace in the enjoyment of my own mind, and unmistrusting confidence in approaching my God, would seldom have been of the number.

Circumstanced as I am, I could never have got a female partner for life who could have entered into my favourite studies, relished my favourite authors, etc., without probably entailing on me at the same time expensive living, fantastic caprice, perhaps apish affection, with all the other blessed boarding-school acquirements, which (*pardonnez moi, Madame*) are sometimes to be found among females of the upper ranks, but almost universally pervade the misses of the would-be gentry.[82]

I like your way in your churchyard lucubrations. Thoughts that are the spontaneous result of accidental situations, either respecting health, place, or company, have often a strength, and always an originality, that would in vain be looked for in fancied circumstances, and studied paragraphs. For me, I have often thought of keeping a letter, in progression by me, to send you when the sheet was written out. Now I talk of sheets, I must tell you, my reason for writing to you on paper of this kind is my pruriency of writing to you at large. A page of post is on such a dis-social, narrow-minded scale, that I cannot abide it; and double letters, at least in my miscellaneous reverie manner, are a monstrous tax in a close correspondence. R. B.

[82] In Burns's private memoranda are these words:—"I am more and more pleased with the step I took respecting my Jean. A wife's head is immaterial compared with her heart; and Virtue's (for wisdom, what poet pretends to it?) 'ways are ways of pleasantness, and all her paths are peace.'"

XCVIII.—To MR. PETER HILL, BOOKSELLER, EDINBURGH.

MY DEAR HILL,—I shall say nothing to your mad present—you have so long and often been of important service to me, and I suppose you mean to go on conferring obligations until I shall not be able to lift up my face before you. In the meantime, as Sir Roger de Coverley, because it happened to be a cold day in which he made his will, ordered his servants great-coats for mourning, so, because I have been this week plagued with an indigestion, I have sent you by the carrier a fine old ewe-milk cheese.[83]

Indigestion is the devil: nay, 'tis the devil and all. It besets a man in every one of his senses. I lose my appetite at the sight of successful knavery, and sicken to loathing at the noise and nonsense of self-important folly. When the hollow-hearted wretch takes me by the hand, the feeling spoils my dinner; the proud man's wine so offends my palate that it chokes me in the gullet; and the *pulvilised*, feathered, pert coxcomb, is so disgustful in my nostril that my stomach turns.

If ever you have any of these disagreeable sensations, let me prescribe for you patience, and a bit of my cheese. I know that you are no niggard of your good things among your friends, and some of them are in much need of a slice. There, in my eye, is our friend Smellie; a man positively of the first abilities and greatest strength of mind, as well as one of the best hearts and keenest wits that I have ever met with; when you see him, as, alas! he too is smarting at the pinch of distressful circumstances, aggravated by the sneer of contumelious greatness—a bit of my cheese alone will not cure him, but if you add a tankard of brown stout, and superadd a magnum of bright Oporto, you will see his sorrows vanish like the morning mist before the summer sun.

Candlish, the earliest friend, except my only brother, that I have on earth, and one of the worthiest fellows that ever any man called by the name of friend, if a luncheon of my cheese would help to rid him of some of his superabundant modesty, you would do well to give it him.

David,[84] with his *Courant*, comes, too, across my recollection, and I beg you will help him largely from the said ewe-milk cheese, to enable him to digest those bedaubing paragraphs with which he is eternally larding the lean characters of certain great men in a certain great town. I grant you the periods are very well turned; so, a fresh egg is a very good thing, but when thrown at a man in a pillory, it does not at all improve his figure, not to mention the irreparable loss of the egg.

My facetious friend Dunbar, I would wish also to be a partaker: not to digest his spleen, for that he laughs off, but to digest his last night's wine at the last field-day of the Crochallan corps.[85]

Among our common friends I must not forget one of the dearest of them— Cunningham. The brutality, insolence, and selfishness of a world unworthy of having such a fellow as he is in it, I know sticks in his stomach, and if you can help him to anything that will make him a little easier on that score, it will be very obliging.

As to honest John Sommerville, he is such a contented, happy man, that I know not what can annoy him, except, perhaps, he may not have got the better of a parcel oif modest anecdotes which a certain poet gave him one night at supper, the last time the said poet was in town.

Though I have mentioned so many men of law, I shall have nothing to do with them professedly—the faculty are beyond my prescription. As to their clients, that is another thing; God knows they have much to digest!

The clergy I pass by; their profundity of erudition, and their liberality of sentiment, their total want of pride, and their detestation of hypocrisy, are so proverbially notorious as to place them far, far above either my praise or censure.

I was going to mention a man of worth, whom I have the honour to call friend—the Laird of Craigdarroch; but I have spoken to the landlord of the King's Arms Inn here, to have at the next county meeting a large ewe-milk cheese on the table, for the benefit of the Dumfriesshire Whigs, to enable them to digest the Duke of Queensberry's late political conduct.

I have just this moment an opportunity of a private hand to Edinburgh, as perhaps you would not digest double postage.

R. B.

[83] In return for some valuable books.

[84] Printer of the *Edinburgh Evening Courant*.

[85] A club of boon companions.

XCIX.—To MRS. DUNLOP.

MAUCHLINE, *August 2nd*, 1788.

HONOURED MADAM,—Your kind letter welcomed me, yesternight, to Ayrshire. I am, indeed, seriously angry with you at the quantum of your luckpenny; but, vexed and hurt as I was, I could not help laughing very heartily at the noble lord's apology for the missed napkin.

I would write you from Nithsdale, and give you my direction there, but I have scarce an opportunity of calling at a post-office once in a fortnight. I am six miles from Dumfries, am scarcely ever in it myself, and, as yet, have little acquaintance in the neighbourhood. Besides, I am now very busy on my farm, building a dwelling-house; as at present I am almost an evangelical man in Nithsdale, for I have scarce "where to lay my head."

There are some passages in your last that brought tears in my eyes. "The heart knoweth its own sorrows, and a stranger intermeddleth not therewith." The repository of these "sorrows of the heart" is a kind of *sanctum sanctorum*. and 'tis only a chosen friend, and that, too, at particular, sacred times, who dares enter into them:—
Heaven oft tears the bosom-chords
That nature finest strung.

You will excuse this quotation for the sake of the author. Instead of entering on this subject farther, I shall transcribe you a few lines I wrote in a hermitage, belonging to a gentleman in my Nithsdale neighbourhood. They are almost the only favour the muses have conferred on me in that country.[86]

Since I am in the way of transcribing, the following were the production of yesterday as I jogged through the wild hills of New Cumnock. I intend inserting them, or something like them, in an epistle I am going to write to the gentleman on whose friendship my Excise hopes depend, Mr. Graham of Fintray, one of the worthiest and most accomplished gentlemen, not only of this country, but, I will dare to say it, of this age. The following are just the first crude thoughts "unhousel'd, unanointed, unanneal'd:"[87]—

Here the muse left me. I am astonished at what you tell me of Anthony's writing me. I never received it. Poor fellow ! you vex me much by telling me that he is unfortunate. I shall be in Ayrshire ten days from this date. I have just room for an old Roman FAREWELL.

R. B.

[86] Lines written in Friar's Carse Hermitage.

[87] First Epistle to Robert Graham.

C.—To MRS. DUNLOP.

ELLISLAND, 16*th August* 1788.

I am in a fine disposition, my honoured friend, to send you an elegiac epistle; and want only genius to make it quite Shenstonian:—

Why droops my heart with fancied woes forlorn?
Why sinks my soul beneath each wintry sky?

My increasing cares in this, as yet, strange country—gloomy conjectures in the dark vista of futurity—consciousness of my own inability for the struggle of the world—my broadened mark to misfortune in a wife and children;—I could indulge these reflections, till my humour should ferment into the most acid chagrin, that would corrode the very thread of life.

To counterwork these baneful feelings, I have sat down to write to you; as I declare upon my soul I always find that the most sovereign balm for my wounded spirit.

I was yesterday at Mr. Miller's to dinner, for the first time. My reception was quite to my mind: from the lady of the house quite flattering. She sometimes hits on a couplet or two, *impromptu*. She repeated one or two to the admiration of all present. My suffrage as a professional man was expected: I for once went agonising over the belly of my conscience. Pardon me, ye, my adored household gods, independence of spirit, and integrity of soul! In the course of conversation, *Johnson's Musical Museum*, a collection of Scottish songs with the music, was talked of. We got a song on the harpsichord, beginning

Raving winds around her blowing.

The air was much admired: the lady of the house asked me whose were the words. "Mine, Madam—they are indeed my very best verses;" she took not the smallest notice of them! The old Scottish proverb says well, "King's caff is better than ither folks' corn." I was going to make a New Testament quotation about "casting pearls," but that would be too virulent, for the lady is actually a woman of sense and taste.

After all that has been said on the other side of the question, man is by no means a happy creature. I do not speak of the selected few, favoured by partial heaven, whose souls are tuned to gladness amidst riches and honours, and prudence and wisdom. I speak of the neglected many, whose nerves, whose sinews, whose days are sold to the minions of fortune.

If I thought you had never seen it, I would transcribe for you a stanza of an old Scottish ballad, called "The Life and Age of Man;" beginning thus:—

'Twas in the sixteenth hundred year
Of God and fifty-three
Frae Christ was born, that bought us dear,
As writings testifie.

I had an old grand-uncle, with whom my mother lived a while in her girlish years; the good old man, for such he was, was long blind ere he died, during which time his highest enjoyment was to sit down and cry, while my mother would sing the simple old song of "The Life and Age of Man."

It is this way of thinking; it is these melancholy truths, that make religion so precious to the poor, miserable children of men. If it is a mere phantom, existing only in the heated imagination of enthusiasm,

What truth on earth so precious as the lie?

My idle reasonings sometimes make me a little sceptical, but the necessities of my heart always give the cold philosophisings the lie. Who looks for the heart weaned from earth; the soul affianced to her God; the correspondence fixed with heaven; the pious supplication and devout thanksgiving, constant as the vicissitudes of even and morn; who thinks to meet with these in the court, the palace, in the glare of public life? No; to find them in their precious importance and divine efficacy, we must search among the obscure recesses of disappointment, affliction, poverty, and distress.

I am sure, dear Madam, you are now more than pleased with the length of my letters. I return to Ayrshire middle of next week: and it quickens my pace to think that there will be a letter from you waiting me there. I must be here again very soon for my harvest.

R. B.

CI.—To MR. BEUGO, ENGRAVER, EDINBURGH.

ELLISLAND, *9th Sept.* 1788.

MY DEAR SIR,—There is not in Edinburgh above the number of the graces whose letters would have given so much pleasure as yours of the 3rd instant, which only reached me yesternight.

I am here on my farm, busy with my harvest; but for all that most pleasurable part of life called SOCIAL COMMUNICATION, I am here at the very elbow of existence. The only things that are to be found in this country, in any degree of perfection, are stupidity and canting. Prose they only know in graces, prayers, etc., and the value of these they estimate, as they do their plaiding webs, by the ell! As for the muses, they have as much an idea of a rhinoceros as of a poet. For my old, capricious, but good-natured hussy of a muse,

By banks of Nith I sat and wept
When Coila I thought on,
In midst thereof I hung my harp
The willow trees upon.

I am generally about half my time in Ayrshire with my "darling Jean," and then I, at lucid intervals, throw my horny fist across my becobwebbed lyre, much in the same manner as an old wife throws her hand across the spokes of her spinning-wheel.

I will send you the "Fortunate Shepherdess" as soon as I return to Ayrshire, for there I keep it with other precious treasure. I shall send it by a careful hand, as I would not for anything it should be mislaid or lost. I do not wish to serve you from any benevolence, or other grave Christian virtue; 'tis purely a selfish gratification of my own feelings whenever I think of you.

If your better functions would give you leisure to write me, I should be extremely happy; that is to say, if you neither keep nor look for a regular correspondence. I hate the idea of being obliged to write a letter. I sometimes write a friend twice a week; at other times once a quarter.

I am exceedingly pleased with your fancy in making the author you mention place a map of Iceland, instead of his portrait, before his works; 'twas a glorious idea.

Could you conveniently do me one thing?—whenever you finish any head, I should like to have a proof copy of it. I might tell you a long story about your fine genius; but, as what everybody knows cannot have escaped you, I shall not say one syllable about it.

R. B.

CII.—To MR. ROBERT GRAHAM, OF FINTRAY.

SIR,—When I had the honour of being introduced to you at Athole House, I did not think so soon of asking a favour of you. When Lear, in Shakespeare, asked Old Kent why he wished to be in his service, he answers, "Because you have that in your face which I would fain call master." For some such reason, Sir, do I now solicit your patronage. You know, I dare say, of an application I lately made to your Board to be admitted an officer of the Excise. I have, according to form, been examined by a supervisor, and today I gave in his certificate, with a request for an order for instructions. In this affair, if I succeed, I am afraid I shall but too much need a patronising friend. Propriety of conduct as a man, and fidelity and attention as an officer, I dare engage for; but with anything like business, except manual labour, I am totally unacquainted.

I had intended to have closed my late appearance on the stage of life in the character of a country farmer; but, after discharging some filial and fraternal claims, I find I could only fight for existence in that miserable manner, which I have lived to see throw a venerable parent into the jaws of a jail, whence death, the poor man's last and often best friend, rescued him.

I know, Sir, that to need your goodness, is to have a claim on it; may I, therefore, beg your patronage to forward me in this affair, till I be appointed to a division, where, by the help of rigid economy, I will try to support that independence so dear to my soul, but which has been too often so distant from my situation.

R. B.

CII.—To His WIFE, AT MAUCHLINE.

ELLISLAND, *Friday*, 12*th Sep.* 1788.

MY DEAR LOVE,—I received your kind letter with a pleasure which no letter but one from you could have given me. I dreamed of you the whole night last; but alas! I fear it will be three weeks yet ere I can hope for the happiness of seeing you. My harvest is going on. I have some to cut down still, but I put in two stacks to-day, so I'm as tired as a dog.

You might get one of Gilbert's sweet-milk cheeses, and send it to.... On second thoughts I believe you had best get the half of Gilbert's web of table linen and make it up; though I think it damnable dear, but it is no outlaid money to us, you know. I have just now consulted my old landlady about table linen, and she thinks I may have the best for two shillings a yard; so, after all, let it alone till I return; and some day soon I will be in Dumfries and ask the price there. I expect your new gowns will be very forward or ready to make, against I be home to get the *baiveridge.*[88]

I have written my long-thought-on letter to Mr. Graham, the Commissioner of Excise; and have sent a sheetful of poetry besides.

[88] On her first appearance in public in a new dress a young woman was subject to this tax, if claimed by the young man who happened first to meet her.

CIV.—To Miss CHALMERS, EDINBURGH.

ELLISLAND, NEAR DUMFRIES, *Sept.* 16*th*, 1788.

Where are you? and how are you? and is Lady Mackenzie recovering her health? for I have had but one solitary letter from you. I will not think you have forgot me, Madam and, for my part,

When thee, Jerusalem, I forget,
Skill part from my right hand!

"My heart is not of that rock, nor my soul careless as that sea." I do not make my progress among mankind as a bowl does among its fellows-rolling through the crowd without bearing away any mark or impression, except where they hit in hostile collision.

I am here, driven in with my harvest-folks by bad weather; and as you and your sister once did me the honour of interesting yourselves much *à l' egard de moi*, I sit down to beg the continuation of your goodness. I can truly say that, all the exterior of life apart, I never saw two whose esteem flattered the nobler feelings of my soul—I will not say more, but so much, as Lady Mackenzie and Miss Chalmers. When I think of you—hearts the best, minds the noblest of human kind—unfortunate even in the shades of life—when I think I have met with you, and have lived more of real life with you in eight days than I can do with almost anybody I meet with in eight years—when I think on the improbability of meeting you in this world again—I could sit down and cry like a child! If ever you honoured me with a place in your esteem, I trust I can now plead more desert. I am secure against that crushing grip of iron poverty, which, alas! is less or more fatal to the native worth and purity of, I fear, the noblest souls; and a late important step in my life has kindly taken me out of the way of those ungrateful iniquities, which, however overlooked in fashionable licence, or varnished in fashionable phrase, are indeed but lighter and deeper shades of villainy.

Shortly after my last return to Ayrshire, I married "my Jean." This was not in consequence of the attachment of romance, perhaps; but I had a long and much-loved fellow-creature's happiness or misery in my determination, and I durst not trifle with so important a deposit. Nor have I any cause to repent it. If I have not got polite tattle, modish manners, and fashionable dress, I am not sickened and disgusted with the multiform curse of boarding-school affectation; and I have got the handsomest figure, the sweetest temper, the soundest constitution, and the kindest heart in the county. Mrs. Burns believes, as firmly as her creed, that I am *le plus bel esprit, et le plus honnête homme* in the universe; although she scarcely ever in her life, except the Scriptures of the old and New Testament, and the Psalms of David in metre, spent five minutes together on either prose or verse. I must except also from this last a certain late publication of Scots poems, which she has perused very devoutly; and all the ballads in the country, as she has (O the partial lover! you will cry) the finest "wood note wild" I ever heard. I am the more particular in this lady's character, as I know she will henceforth have the honour of a share in your best wishes. She is still at Mauchline, as I am building my house; for this hovel that I shelter in, while occasionally here, is pervious to every blast that blows, and every shower that falls; and I am only preserved from being chilled to death, by being suffocated with smoke. I do not find my farm that pennyworth I was taught to expect, but I believe, in time, it may be a saving bargain. You will be pleased to hear that I have laid aside the idle*éclat*, and bind every day after my reapers.

To save me from that horrid situation of at any time going down, in a losing bargain of a farm, to misery, I have taken my Excise instructions, and have my commission in my pocket for any emergency of fortune. If I could set all before your view, whatever disrespect you, in common with the world, have for this business, I know you would approve of my idea.

I will make no apology, dear Madam, for this egotistic detail; I know you and your sister will be interested in every circumstance of it. What signify the silly, idle gew-gaws of wealth, or the ideal trumpery of greatness! When fellow-partakers of the same nature fear the same God, have the same benevolence of heart, the same nobleness of soul, the same detestation at everything dishonest, and the same scorn at everything unworthy—if they are not in the dependence of absolute beggary, in the name of common sense, are they not equals? And if the bias, the instinctive bias of their souls run the same way, why may they not be friends?

When I may have an opportunity of sending you this, Heaven only knows. Shenstone says, "When one is confined idle within doors by bad weather, the best antidote against *ennui* is to read the letters of, or write to, one's friends;" in that case then, if the weather continues thus, I may scrawl you half a quire.

I very lately—to wit, since harvest began—wrote a poem, not in imitation, but in the manner of Pope's Moral Epistles. It is only a short essay, just to try the strength of my Muse's pinion in that way. I will send you a copy of it, when once I have heard from you. I have likewise been laying the foundation of some pretty large poetic works; how the superstructure will come on, I leave to that great maker and marrer of projects, time. Johnson's collection of Scots songs is going on in the third volume; and, of consequence, finds me a consumpt for a great deal of idle metre. One of the most tolerable things I have done in that way, is two stanzas I made to an air a musical gentleman of my acquaintance composed for the anniversary of his wedding-day, which happens on the seventh of November. Take it as follows:—

The day returns—my bosom burns—
The blissful day we twa did meet, etc.

I shall give over this letter for shame. If I should be seized with a scribbling fit, before this goes away, I shall make it another letter; and then you may allow your patience a week's respite between the two. I have not room for more than the old, kind, hearty farewell!

To make some amends, *mes chères Mesdames*, for dragging you on to this second sheet; and to relieve a little the tiresomeness of my unstudied and uncorrectible prose, I shall transcribe you some of my late poetic bagatelles; though I have, these eight or ten months, done very little that way. One day, in a hermitage on the banks of Nith, belonging to a gentleman in my neighbourhood, who is so good as give me a key at pleasure, I wrote as follows; supposing myself the sequestered, venerable inhabitant of the lonely mansion.

LINES WRITTEN IN FRIARS-CARSE HERMITAGE.
Thou whom chance may hither lead,
Be thou clad in russet weed, etc.
R. B.

CV.—To MR. MORISON, WRIGHT, MAUCHLINE.
Ellisland, *September* 22*nd* 1788.

MY DEAR SIR,—Necessity obliges me to go into my new house, even before it be plastered. I will inhabit the one end until the other is finished. About three weeks more, I think, will at farthest be my time, beyond which I cannot stay in this present house. If ever you wish to deserve the blessing of him that was ready to perish; if ever you were in a situation that a little kindness would have rescued you from many evils; if ever you hope to find rest in future states of untried being-get these matters of mine ready.[89] My servant will be out in the beginning of next week for the clock. My compliments to Mrs. Morison. —I am, after all my tribulation, Dear Sir, yours,
R. B.

[89] The letter refers to chairs and other articles of furniture which the Poet had ordered.

CVI.—To MRS. DUNLOP, OF DUNLOP.
Mauchline, 27*th Sept.* 1788.

I have received twins, dear Madam, more than once; but scarcely ever with more pleasure than when I received yours of the 12th instant. To make myself understood; I had wrote to Mr. Graham, enclosing my poem addressed to him, and the same post which favoured me with yours brought me an answer from him. It was dated the very day he had received mine; and I am quite at a loss to say whether it was most polite or kind.

Your criticisms, my honoured benefactress, are truly the work of a friend. They are not the blasting depredations of a canker-toothed, caterpillar critic; nor are they the fair statement of cold impartiality, balancing with unfeeling exactitude the *pro* and *con* of an author's merits; they are the judicious observations of animated friendship, selecting the beauties of the piece. I am just arrived from Nithsdale, and will be here a fortnight. I was on horseback this morning by three o'clock; for between my wife and my farm is just forty-six miles. As I jogged on in the dark, I was taken with a poetic fit, as follows:

"Mrs. Ferguson of Craigdarroch's lamentation for the death of her son; an uncommonly promising youth of eighteen or nineteen years of age:—
Fate gave the word—the arrow sped,
And pierced my darling's heart,"(i>etc.)

You will not send me your poetic rambles, but, you see, I am no niggard of mine. I am sure your impromptus give me double pleasure; what falls from your pen can neither be unentertaining in itself, nor indifferent to me.

The one fault you found is just: but I cannot please myself in an emendation.

What a life of solicitude is the life of a parent! You interested me much in your young couple.

I would not take my folio paper for this epistle, and now I repent it. I am so jaded with my dirty long journey, that I was afraid to drawl into the essence of dulness with anything larger than a quarto, and so I must leave out another rhyme of this morning's manufacture.

I will pay the sapientipotent George most cheerfully, to hear from you ere I leave Ayrshire. R. B.

CVII—To MR. PETER HILL.
Mauchline, 1*st October* 1788.

I have been here in this country about three days, and all that time my chief reading has been the "Address to Lochlomond" you were so obliging as to send to me. Were I impanneled one of the author's jury, to determine his criminality respecting the sin of poesy, my verdict should be "Guilty! A poet of nature's making!" It is an excellent method for improvement, and what I believe every poet does, to place some favourite classic author in his walks of study and composition before him as a model. Though your author had not mentioned the name, I could have, at half a glance, guessed his model to be Thomson. Will my brother-poet forgive me if I venture to hint that his imitation of that immortal bard is, in two or three places, rather more servile than such a genius as his required:—*e.g.*

To soothe the maddening passions all to peace.

ADDRESS.

To soothe the throbbing passions into peace.

THOMSON.

 I think the "Address" is in simplicity, harmony, and elegance of versification, fully equal to the "Seasons." Like Thomson, too, he has looked into nature for himself: you meet with no copied description. One particular criticism I made at first reading; in no one instance has he said too much. He never flags in his progress, but, like a true poet of nature's making, kindles in his course. His beginning is simple and modest, as if distrustful of the strength of his passion; only, I do not altogether like—

Truth,

The soul of every song that's nobly great.

 Fiction is the soul of many a song that is nobly great. Perhaps I am wrong: this may be but a prose criticism. Is not the phrase, in line 7, page 6, "Great lake," too much vulgarised by every-day language for so sublime a poem?

Great mass of waters, theme for nobler song,

is perhaps no emendation. His enumeration of a comparison with other lakes is at once harmonious and poetic. Every reader's ideas must sweep the

Winding margin of a hundred miles.

 The perspective that follows mountains blue—the imprisoned billows beating in vain—the wooded isles—the digression on the yew-tree—"Benlomond's lofty, cloud-envelop'd head," etc., are beautiful. A thunder-storm is a subject which has been often tried, yet our poet, in his grand picture, has interjected a circumstance, so far as I know, entirely original in

the gloom

Deep seam'd with frequent streaks of moving fire.

 In his preface to the Storm, "the glens how dark between," is noble highland landscape! The "rain ploughing the red mould," too, is beautifully fancied. "Benlomond's lofty, pathless top," is a good expression; and the surrounding view from it is truly great: the silver mist,

Beneath the beaming sun,

is well described; and here he has contrived to enliven his poem with a little of that passion which bids fair, I think, to usurp the modern muses altogether. I know not how far this episode is a beauty on the whole, but the swain's wish to carry "some faint idea of the vision bright," to entertain her "partial listening ear," is a pretty thought. But, in my opinion, the most beautiful passages in the whole poem are the fowls crowding, in wintry frosts, to Lochlomond's "hospitable flood;" their wheeling round; their lighting, mixing, diving, etc.; and the glorious description of the sportsman. This last is equal to anything in the "Seasons." The idea of "the floating tribes distant seen, far glistering to the moon," provoking his eye as he is obliged to leave them, is a noble ray of poetic genius.

 The "howling winds," the "hideous roar" of "the white cascades," are all in the same style.

 I forget that while I am thus holding forth, with the heedless warmth of an enthusiast, I am perhaps tiring you with nonsense. I must, however, mention that the last verse of the sixteenth page is one of the most elegant compliments I have ever seen. I must likewise notice that beautiful paragraph beginning "The gleaming lake," etc. I dare not go into the particular beauties of the last two paragraphs, but they are admirably fine, and truly Ossianic. I must beg your pardon for this lengthened scrawl. I had no idea of it when I began—I should like to know who the author is; but, whoever he be, please present him with my grateful thanks for the entertainment he has afforded me.[90]

92

A friend of mine desired me to commission for him two books, *Letters on the Religion essential to Man*, a book you sent me before; and *The World Unmasked, or the Philosopher the greatest Cheat*. Send me them by the first opportunity. The Bible you sent me is truly elegant; I only wish it had been in two volumes. R. B.

[90] The poem, entitled "An Address to Lochlomond," is said to have been written by one of the masters of the High School of Edinburgh.

CVIIL—To THE EDITOR OF THE "STAR".
November 8th, 1788.

Sir,—Notwithstanding the opprobrious epithets with which some of our philosophers and gloomy sectarians have branded our nature—the principle of universal selfishness, the proneness to all evil, they have given us—still, the detestation in which inhumanity to the distressed, or insolence to the fallen, are held by all mankind, shows that they are not natives of the human heart. Even the unhappy partner of our kind who is undone, the bitter consequence of his follies or his crimes—who but sympathises with the miseries of this ruined profligate brother? We forget the injuries, and feel for the man.

I went, last Wednesday, to my parish church, most cordially to join in grateful acknowledgment to the AUTHOR OF ALL GOOD for the consequent blessings of the glorious Revolution. To that auspicious event we owe no less than our liberties, civil and religious; to it we are likewise indebted for the present Royal Family, the ruling features of whose administration have ever been mildness to the subject, and tenderness of his rights.

Bred and educated in revolution principles, the principles of reason and common sense, it could not be any silly political prejudice which made my heart revolt at the harsh, abusive manner in which the reverend gentleman mentioned the House of Stuart, and which, I am afraid, was too much the language of the day. We may rejoice sufficiently in our deliverance from past evils, without cruelly raking up the ashes of those whose misfortune it was, perhaps as much as their crime, to be the authors of those evils; and we may bless GOD for all His goodness to us as a nation, without, at the same time, cursing a few ruined, powerless exiles, who only harboured ideas, and made attempts, that most of us would have done, had we been in their situation.

"The bloody and tyrannical House of Stuart" may be said with propriety and justice, when compared with the present Royal Family, and the sentiments of our days; but is there no allowance to be made for the manners of the times? Were the royal contemporaries of the Stuarts more attentive to their subjects' rights? Might not the epithets of "bloody and tyrannical" be, with at least equal justice, applied to the House of Tudor, of York, or any other of their predecessors?

The simple state of the case, Sir, seems to be this:—At that period, the science of government, the knowledge of the true relation between king and subject, was, like other sciences and other knowledge, just in its infancy, emerging from dark ages of ignorance and barbarity.

The Stuarts only contended for prerogatives which they knew their predecessors enjoyed, and which they saw their contemporaries enjoying; but these prerogatives were inimical to the happiness of a nation and the rights of subjects.

In this contest between prince and people, the consequence of that light of science which had lately dawned over Europe, the monarch of France, for example, was victorious over the struggling liberties of his people: with us, luckily, the monarch failed, and his unwarrantable pretensions fell a sacrifice to our rights and happiness. Whether it was owing to the wisdom of leading individuals, or to the justling of parties, I cannot pretend to determine; but, likewise, happily for us, the kingly power was shifted into another branch of the family, who, as they owed the throne solely to the call of a free people, could claim nothing inconsistent with the covenanted terms which placed them there.

The Stuarts have been condemned and laughed at, for the folly and impracticability of their attempts in 1715, and 1745. That they failed, I bless GOD; but cannot join in the ridicule against them. Who does not know that the abilities or defects of leaders and commanders are often hidden, until put to the touchstone of exigency; and that there is a caprice of fortune, an omnipotence in particular accidents and conjunctures of circumstances, which exalt us as heroes, or brand us as madmen, just as they are for or against us?

Man, Mr. Publisher, is a strange, weak, inconsistent being: who would believe, Sir, that in this our Augustan age of liberality and refinement, while we seem so justly sensible and jealous of our rights and liberties, and animated with such indignation against the very memory of those who would have subverted them—that a certain people under our national protection should complain, not against our monarch and a few favourite advisers, but against our WHOLE LEGISLATIVE BODY, for similar oppression, and almost in the very same terms, as our forefathers did of the House of Stuart! I will not, I cannot, enter into the merits of the cause; but I dare say the American Congress, in 1776, will be allowed to be as able and enlightened as the English Convention was in 1688; and that their posterity will celebrate the centenary of their deliverance from us, as duly and sincerely, as we do ours from the oppressive measures of the wrong-headed House of Stuart.

To conclude, Sir; let every man who has a tear for the many miseries incident to humanity, feel for a family illustrious as any in Europe, and unfortunate beyond historic precedent; and let every Briton (and particularly every Scotsman) who ever looked with reverential pity on the dotage of a parent, cast a veil over the fatal mistake of the Kings of his forefathers.

R. B.

CIX.—TO MRS. DUNLOP, AT MOREHAM MAINS.
MAUCHLINE, 13*th November* 1788.

Madam,—I had the very great pleasure of dining at Dunlop yesterday. Men are said to flatter women because they are weak, if it is so, poets must be weaker still; for Misses R. and K. and Miss G. M'K., with their flattering attentions, and artful compliments, absolutely turned my head. I own they did not lard me over as many a poet does his patron, but they so intoxicated me with their sly insinuations and delicate innuendos of compliment, that if it had not been for a lucky recollection, how much additional weight and lustre your good opinion and friendship must give me in that circle, I had certainly looked upon myself as a person of no small consequence. I dare not say one word how much I was charmed with the Major's friendly welcome, elegant manner, and acute remark, lest I should be thought to balance my orientalisms of applause over-against the finest heifer in Ayrshire, which he made me a present of to help and adorn my farm-stock. As it was on hallow-day, I am determined annually as that day returns, to decorate her horns with an ode of gratitude to the family of Dunlop.

So soon as I know of your arrival at Dunlop, I will take the first conveniency to dedicate a day, or perhaps two, to you and friendship, under the guarantee of the Major's hospitality. There will soon be three score and ten miles of permanent distance between us; and now that your friendship and friendly correspondence is entwisted with the heart-strings of my enjoyment of life, I must indulge myself in a happy day of "the feast of reason and the flow of soul."

R. B.

CX.—TO DR. BLACKLOCK.
MAUCHLINE, *November* 15*th*, 1788.

Reverend and dear Sir,—As I hear nothing of your motions, but that you are, or were, out of town, I do not know where this may find you, or whether it will find you at all. I wrote you a long letter, dated from the land of matrimony, in June; but either it had not found you, or, what I dread more, it found you or Mrs. Blacklock in too precarious a state of health and spirits to take notice of an idle packet.

I have done many little things for Johnson since I had the pleasure of seeing you; and I have finished one piece, in the way of Pope's "Moral Epistles;" but, from your silence, I have everything to fear, so I have only sent you two melancholy things, which I tremble to fear may too well suit the tone of your present feelings.

94

In a fortnight I move, bag and baggage, to Nithsdale; till then, my direction is at this place; after that period, it will be at Ellisland, near Dumfries. It would extremely oblige me, were it but half a line, to let me know how you are, and where you are. Can I be indifferent to the fate of a man to whom I owe so much—a man whom I not only esteem, but venerate?

My warmest good wishes and most respectful compliments to Mrs. Blacklock, and Miss Johnson, if she is with you.

I cannot conclude without telling you that I am more and more pleased with the step I took respecting "my Jean." Two things, from my happy experience, I set down as apophthegms in life,—a wife's head is immaterial, compared with her heart; and "Virtue's (for wisdom, what poet pretends to it?) ways are ways of pleasantness, and all her paths are peace." Adieu!

R. B.[91]

[91] Here follow "The mother's lament for the loss of her son," and the song beginning "The lazy mist hangs from the brow of the hill."

CXI.—TO MRS. DUNLOP.

ELLISLAND, 17*th December* 1788.

My dear honoured friend,—Yours, dated Edinburgh, which I have just read, makes me very unhappy. "Almost blind and wholly deaf" are melancholy news of human nature; but when told of a much-loved and honoured friend, they carry misery in the sound. Goodness on your part, and gratitude on mine, began a tie which has gradually entwisted itself among the dearest chords of my bosom, and I tremble at the omens of your late and present ailing habit and shattered health. You miscalculate matters widely, when you forbid my waiting on you, lest it should hurt my worldly concerns. My small scale of farming is exceedingly more simple and easy than what you have lately seen at Moreham Mains. But, be that as it may, the heart of the man and the fancy of the poet are the two grand considerations for which I live: if miry ridges and dirty dunghills are to engross the best part of the functions of my soul immortal, I had better been a rook or a magpie at once, and then I should not have been plagued with any ideas superior to breaking of clods and picking up grubs; not to mention barn-door cocks of mallards, creatures with which I could almost exchange lives at any time. If you continue so deaf, I am afraid a visit will be no great pleasure to either of us; but if I hear you are got so well again as to be able to relish conversation, look you to it, Madam, for I will make my threatenings good. I am to be at the New-year-day fair of Ayr, and, by all that is sacred in the world, friend, I will come and see you.

Your meeting, which you so well describe, with your old schoolfellow and friend, was truly interesting. Out upon the ways of the world! They spoil these "social offsprings of the heart." Two veterans of the "men of the world" would have met with little more heart-workings than two old hacks worn out on the road. Apropos, is not the Scotch phrase, "Auld lang syne," exceedingly expressive? There is an old song and tune which has often thrilled through my soul. You know I am an enthusiast in old Scotch song. I shall give you the verses on the other sheet, as I suppose Mr. Kerr[92] will save you the postage.

Should auld acquaintance be forgot?

Light be the turf on the breast of the Heaven-inspired poet who composed this glorious fragment! There is more of the fire of native genius in it than in half a dozen of modern English Bacchanalians! Now I am on my hobbyhorse, I cannot help inserting two other old stanzas, which please me mightily:—

Go fetch to me a pint o' wine, etc.

R. B.

[92] Postmaster in Edinburgh.

CXII.—TO MR. JOHN TENNANT.

December 22*nd*, 1788.

95

I yesterday tried my cask of whisky for the first time, and I assure you it does you great credit. It will bear five waters, strong: or six ordinary toddy. The whisky of this country is a most rascally liquor; and, by consequence, only drunk by the most rascally part of the inhabitants. I am persuaded, if you once get a footing here, you might do a great deal of business, in the way of consumpt; and should you commence distiller again, this is the native barley country. I am ignorant if, in your present way of dealing, you would think it worth your while to extend your business so far as this country-side. I write you this on the account of an accident, which I must take the merit of having partly designed too. A neighbour of mine, a John Currie, miller, in Carse Mill—a man who is, in a word, a very good man, even for a £500 bargain—he and his wife were in my house the time I broke open the cask. They keep a country public-house and sell a great deal of foreign spirits, but all along thought that whisky would have degraded their house. They were perfectly astonished at my whisky, both for its taste and strength; and, by their desire, I write you to know if you could supply them with liquor of an equal quality, and what price. Please write me by first post, and direct to me at Ellisland, near Dumfries. If you could take a jaunt this way yourself, I have a spare spoon, knife, and fork, very much at your service. My compliments to Mrs. Tennant, and all the good folks in Glenconnel and Barguharrie.

R. B.

CXIII.—TO MRS. DUNLOP.

ELLISLAND, *New-year-day Morning*, 1789.

This, dear Madam, is a morning of wishes, and would to God that I came under the Apostle James's description!—*the prayer of a righteous man availeth much.* In that case, Madam, you should welcome in a year full of blessings: everything that obstructs or disturbs tranquillity and self-enjoyment should be removed, and every pleasure that frail humanity can taste, should be yours. I own myself so little a Presbyterian, that I approve of set times and seasons of more than ordinary acts of devotion, for breaking in on that habituated routine of life and thought, which is so apt to reduce our existence to a kind of instinct, or even sometimes, and with some minds, to a state very little superior to mere machinery.

This day; the first Sunday of May; a breezy blue-skyed noon some time about the beginning, and a hoary morning and calm sunny day about the end of autumn; these, time out of mind, have been with me a kind of holiday.

I believe I owe this to that glorious paper in the *Spectator* "The Vision of Mirza," a piece that struck my young fancy before I was capable of fixing an idea to a word of three syllables: "On the fifth day of the moon, which, according to the custom of my forefathers, I always *keep holy*, after having washed myself, and offered up my morning devotions, I ascended the high hill of Bagdat, in order to pass the rest of the day in meditation and prayer."

We know nothing, or next to nothing, of the substance or structure of our souls, so cannot account for those seeming caprices in them, that one should be particularly pleased with this thing, or struck with that, which, on minds of a different cast, makes no extraordinary impression. I have some favourite flowers in spring, among which are the mountain-daisy, the hare-bell, the fox-glove, the wild brier-rose, the budding birch, and the hoary hawthorn, that I view and hang over with particular delight. I never hear the loud, solitary whistle of the curlew in a summer noon, or the wild mixing cadence of a troop of grey plovers, in an autumnal morning, without feeling an elevation of soul like the enthusiasm of devotion or poetry. Tell me, my dear friend, to what can this be owing? Are we a piece of machinery, which, like the Æolian harp, passive, takes the impression of the passing accident? Or do these workings argue something within us above the trodden clod? I own myself partial to such proofs of those awful and important realities—a God that made all things—man's immaterial and immortal nature—and a world of weal or woe beyond death and the grave.

R. B.

CXIV.-TO DR. MOORE, LONDON.

ELLISLAND, *4th Jan.* 1789.

Sir,—As often as I think of writing to you, which has been three or four times every week these six months, it gives me something so like the idea of an ordinary-sized statue offering at a conversation with the Rhodian Colossus, that my mind misgives me, and the affair always miscarries somewhere between purpose and resolve. I have at last got some business with you, and business letters are written by the style-book. I say my business is with you, Sir, for you never had any with me, except the business that benevolence has in the mansion of poverty.

The character and employment of a poet were formerly my pleasure, but are now my pride. I know that a very great deal of my late éclat was owing to the singularity of my situation, and the honest prejudice of Scotsmen; but still, as I said in the preface to my first edition, I do look upon myself as having some pretensions from nature to the poetic character. I have not a doubt but the knack, the aptitude, to learn the Muses' trade, is a gift bestowed by Him "who forms the secret bias of the soul;" but I as firmly believe that *excellence* in the profession is the fruit of industry, labour, attention, and pains. At least I am resolved to try my doctrine by the test of experience. Another appearance from the press I put off to a very distant day, a day that may never arrive—but poesy I am determined to prosecute with all my vigour. Nature has given very few, if any, of the profession, the talents of shining in every species of composition. I shall try (for until trial it is impossible to know) whether she has qualified me to shine in any one. The worst of it is, by the time one has finished a piece, it has been so often viewed and reviewed before the mental eye, that one loses in a good measure the powers of critical discrimination. Here the best criterion I know is a friend—not only of abilities to judge, but with good-nature enough, like a prudent teacher with a young learner, to praise perhaps a little more than is exactly just, lest the thin-skinned animal fall into that most deplorable of all poetic diseases—heart-breaking despondency of himself. Dare I, Sir, already immensely indebted to your goodness, ask the additional obligation of your being that friend to me? I inclose you an essay of mine in a walk of poesy to me entirely new; I mean the epistle addressed to R. G., Esq., or Robert Graham, of Fintry, Esq., a gentleman of uncommon worth, to whom I lie under very great obligations. The story of the poem, like most of my poems, is connected with my own story, and to give you the one, I must give you something of the other. I cannot boast of Mr. Creech's ingenuous fair dealing to me. He kept me hanging about Edinburgh from the 7th August 1787 until the 13th April 1788 before he would condescend to give a statement of affairs; nor had I got it even then, but for an angry letter I wrote him, which irritated his pride. "I could" not a "tale," but a detail "unfold"; but what am I that should speak against the Lord's anointed Bailie of Edinburgh?[23]

I believe I shall, in whole, £100 copyright included, clear about £400, some little odds; and even part of this depends upon what the gentleman has yet to settle with me. I give you this information, because you did me the honour to interest yourself much in my welfare. I give you this information, but I give it to yourself only, for I am still much in the gentleman's mercy. Perhaps I injure the man in the idea I am sometimes tempted to have of him—God forbid I should. A little time will try, for in a month I shall go to town to wind up the business, if possible.

To give the rest of my story in brief, I have married "my Jean," and taken a farm; with the first step I have every day more and more reason to be satisfied; with the last, it is rather the reverse. I have a younger brother, who supports my aged mother, another still younger brother, and three sisters, in a farm. On my last return from Edinburgh it cost me about £180 to save them from ruin.

Not that I have lost so much—I only interposed between my brother and his impending fate by the loan of so much. I give myself no airs on this, for it was mere selfishness on my part; I was conscious that the wrong scale of the balance was pretty heavily charged, and I thought that throwing a little filial piety and fraternal affection into the scale in my favour, might help to smooth matters at the *grand reckoning*. There is still one thing would make my circumstances quite easy—I have an excise officer's commission, and I live in the midst of a country division. My request to Mr. Graham, who is one of the commissioners of excise, was, if in his power, to procure me that division. If I were very sanguine, I might hope that some of my great patrons might procure me a treasury warrant for supervisor, surveyor-general, etc.

Thus, secure of a livelihood, "to thee, sweet poetry, delightful maid,"[94] I would consecrate my future days.

R. B.

[93] Creech; remarkable for his reluctance to settle accounts.

[94] Goldsmith's "Deserted Village."

CXV.—TO MR. ROBERT AINSLIE.

ELLISLAND, *January 6th*, 1789.

Many happy returns of the season to you, my dear Sir! May you be comparatively happy, up to your comparative worth among the sons of men; which wish would, I am sure, make you one of the most blessed of the human race.

I do not know if passing a "Writer to the Signet" be a trial of scientific merit, or a mere business of friends and interest. However it be, let me quote you my two favourite passages, which, though I have repeated them ten thousand times, still they rouse my manhood and steel my resolution like inspiration.

On Reason build resolve.

That column of true majesty in man.

YOUNG.

Hear, Alfred, hero of the slate,
Thy genius heaven's high will declare;
The triumph of the truly great,
Is never, never to despair!
Is never to despair!

MASQUE OF ALFRED.

I grant you enter the lists of life, to struggle for bread, business, notice, and distinction, in common with hundreds. But who are they? Men like yourself, and of that aggregate body your compeers, seven-tenths of them come short of your advantages, natural and accidental; while two of those that remain, either neglect their parts, as flowers blooming in a desert, or misspend their strength like a bull goring a bramble bush.

But to change the theme: I am still catering for Johnson's publication; and among others, I have brushed up the following old favourite song a little, with a view to your worship. I have only altered a word here and there; but if you like the humour of it, we shall think of a stanza or two to add to it. R. B.

CXVI.—TO PROFESSOR DUGALD STEWART.

ELLISLAND, *20th Jan*. 1789.

Sir,—The inclosed sealed packet I sent to Edinburgh, a few days after I had the happiness of meeting you in Ayrshire, but you were gone for the Continent. I have now added a few more of my productions, those for which I am indebted to the Nithsdale Muses. The piece inscribed to R. G., Esq., is a copy of verses I sent Mr. Graham, of Fintry, accompanying a request for his assistance in a matter to me of very great moment. To that gentleman I am already doubly indebted; for deeds of kindness of serious import to my dearest interests, done in a manner grateful to the delicate feelings of sensibility. This poem is a species of composition new to me, but I do not intend it shall be my last essay of the kind, as you will see by the "Poet's Progress." These fragments, if my design succeed, are but a small part of the intended whole. I propose it shall be the work of my utmost exertions, ripened by years; of course I do not wish it much known. The fragment beginning "A little upright, pert, tart," etc., I have not shown to man living, till I now send it you. It forms the postulata, the axioms, the definition of a character, which, if it appear at all, shall be placed in a variety of lights. This particular part I send you merely as a sample of my hand at portrait-sketching; but, lest idle conjecture should pretend to point out the original, please to let it be for your single, sole inspection.

Need I make any apology for this trouble, to a gentleman who has treated me with such marked benevolence and peculiar kindness; who has entered into my interests with so much zeal, and on whose critical decisions I can so fully depend? A poet as I am by trade, these decisions are to me of the last consequence. My late transient acquaintance among some of the mere rank and file of greatness, I resign with ease; but to the distinguished champions of genius and learning, I shall be ever ambitious of being known. The native genius and accurate discernment in Mr. Stewart's critical strictures; the justness (iron justice, for he has no bowels of compassion for a poor poetic sinner) of Dr. Gregory's remarks, and the delicacy of Professor Dalzel's taste, I shall ever revere.

I shall be in Edinburgh some time next month.—I have the honour to be, Sir, your highly obliged, and very humble servant, R. B.

CXVII.—TO MR. ROBERT CLEGHORN, SAUGHTON MILLS.
ELLISLAND, *23rd Jan.* 1789.

I must take shame and confusion of face to myself, my dear friend and brother Farmer, that I have not written you much sooner. The truth is I have been so tossed about between Ayrshire and Nithsdale that, till now I have got my family here, I have had time to think of nothing except now and then a stanza or so as I rode along. Were it not for our gracious monarch's cursed tax of postage I had sent you one or two pieces of some length that I have lately done. I have no idea of the *Press*. I am more able to support myself and family, though in a humble, yet an independent way; and I mean, just at my leisure, to pay court to the tuneful sisters in the hope that they may one day enable me to carry on a work of some importance. The following are a few verses which I wrote in a neighbouring gentleman's *hermitage* to which he is so good as let me have a key.

CXVIII.—To BISHOP GEDDES, EDINBURGH.
ELLISLAND, *3rd Feb.* 1789.

VENERABLE FATHER,—As I am conscious that wherever I am, you do me the honour to interest yourself in my welfare, it gives me pleasure to inform you, that I am here at last, stationary in the serious business of life, and have now not only the retired leisure, but the hearty inclination, to attend to those great and important questions,—what I am? where I am? and for what I am destined.

In that first concern, the conduct of the man, there was ever but one side on which I was habitually blameable, and there I have secured myself in the way pointed out by nature and nature's God. I was sensible that, to so helpless a creature as a poor poet, a wife and family were incumbrances, which a species of prudence would bid him shun; but when the alternative was, being at eternal warfare with myself, on account of habitual follies, to give them no worse name, which no general example, no licentious wit, no sophistical infidelity, would, to me, ever justify, I must have been a fool to have hesitated, and a madman to have made another choice. Besides, I had in "my Jean" a long and much-loved fellow-creature's happiness or misery among my hands, and who could trifle with such a deposit?

In the affair of a livelihood, I think myself tolerably secure: I have good hopes of my farm, but should they fail, I have an excise commission, which, on my simple petition, will, at any time, procure me bread. There is a certain stigma affixed to the character of an excise officer, but I do not pretend to borrow honour from my profession; and though the salary be comparatively small, it is luxury to anything that the first twenty-five years of my life taught me to expect.

Thus, with a rational aim and method in life, you may easily guess, my reverend and much-honoured friend, that my characteristical trade is not forgotten. I am, if possible, more than ever an enthusiast to the Muses. I am determined to study man and nature, and in that view incessantly; and to try if the ripening and corrections of years can enable me to produce something worth preserving.

You will see in your book, which I beg your pardon for detaining so long, that I have been tuning my lyre on the banks of Nith. Some large poetic plans that are floating in my imagination, or partly put in execution, I shall impart to you when I have the pleasure of meeting with you; which, if you are then in Edinburgh, I shall have about the beginning of March.

That acquaintance, worthy Sir, with which you were pleased to honour me, you must still allow me to challenge; for, with whatever unconcern I give up my transient connection with the merely great, I cannot lose the patronising notice of the learned and good without the bitterest regret.

R. B.

CXIX.—TO MR. JAMES BURNESS.

ELLISLAND, *9th Feb.* 1789.

MY DEAR SIR,—Why I did not write to you long ago is what, even on the rack, I could not answer. If you can in your mind form an idea of indolence, dissipation, hurry, cares, change of country, entering on untried scenes of life, all combined, you will save me the trouble of a blushing apology. It could not be want of regard for a man for whom I had a high esteem before I knew him—an esteem which has much increased since I did know him; and this caveat entered, I shall plead guilty to any other indictment with which you shall please to charge me.

After I parted from you, for many months my life was one continued scene of dissipation. Here at last I am become stationary, and have taken a farm and—a wife.

The farm is beautifully situated on the Nith, a large river that runs by Dumfries, and falls into the Solway frith. I have gotten a lease of my farm as long as I please; but how it may turn out is just a guess, and it is yet to improve and inclose, etc.; however, I have good hopes of my bargain on the whole.

My wife is my Jean, with whose story you are partly acquainted. I found I had a much-loved fellow-creature's happiness or misery among my hands, and I durst not trifle with so sacred a deposit. Indeed, I have not any reason to repent the step I have taken, as I have attached myself to a very good wife, and have shaken myself loose of every bad failing.

I have found my book a very profitable business, and with the profits of it I have begun life pretty decently. Should fortune not favour me in farming, as I have no great faith in her fickle ladyship, I have provided myself in another resource, which, however some folks may affect to despise it, is still a comfortable shift in the day of misfortune. In the hey-day of my fame, a gentleman, whose name at least I daresay you know, as his estate lies somewhere near Dundee, Mr. Graham, of Fintry, one of the commissioners of Excise, offered me the commission of an excise officer. I thought it prudent to accept the offer; and, accordingly, I took my instructions, and have my commission by me. Whether I may ever do duty, or be a penny the better for it, is what I do not know; but I have the comfortable assurance that, come whatever ill fate will, I can, on my simple petition to the Excise Board, get into employ.

We have lost poor uncle Robert this winter. He has long been very weak, and with very little alteration on him; he expired 3rd January.

His son William has been with me this winter, and goes in May to be an apprentice to a mason. His other son, the eldest, John, comes to me I expect in summer. They are both remarkably stout young fellows, and promise to do well. His only daughter, Fanny, has been with me ever since her father's death, and I purpose keeping her in my family till she is woman grown, and fit for better service. She is one of the cleverest girls, and has one of the most amiable dispositions I have ever seen.

All friends in this country and Ayrshire are well. Remember me to all friends in the north. My wife joins me in compliments to Mrs. B. and family.—I am ever, my dear cousin, yours sincerely,

R. B.[95]

[95] "Fanny Burns, the Poet's relation, merited all the commendations he has here bestowed.

I remember her while she lived at Ellisland, and better still as the wife of Adam Armour, the brother of bonnie Jean."—CUNNINGHAM.

CXX.-To MRS. DUNLOP.
ELLISLAND, 4*th March* 1789.

Here am I, my honoured friend, returned safe from the capital. To a man who has a home, however humble or remote—if that home is like mine, the scene of domestic comfort—the bustle of Edinburgh will soon be a business of sickening disgust.

Vain pomp and glory of this world, I hate you!

When I must skulk into a corner, lest the rattling equipage of some gaping blockhead should mangle me in the mire, I am tempted to exclaim—"What merits has he had, or what demerit have I had, in some state of pre-existence, that he is ushered into this state of being with the sceptre of rule, and the key of riches in his puny fist, and I am kicked into the world, the sport of folly, or the victim of pride?" I have read somewhere of a monarch (in Spain I think it was) who was so out of humour with the Ptolemean system of astronomy, that he said, had he been of the Creator's council, he could have saved him a great deal of labour and absurdity. I will not defend this blasphemous speech; but often, as I have glided with humble stealth through the pomp of Princes Street, it has suggested itself to me, as an improvement on the present human figure, that a man, in proportion to his own conceit of his consequence in the world, could have pushed out the longitude of his common size, as a snail pushes out his horns, or as we draw out a perspective. This trifling alteration, not to mention the prodigious saving it would be in the tear and wear of the neck and limb-sinews of many of his majesty's liege-subjects, in the way of tossing the head and tip-toe strutting, would evidently turn out a vast advantage, in enabling us at once to adjust the ceremonials in making a bow, or making way to a great man, and that too within a second of the precise spherical angle of reverence, or an inch of the particular point of respectful distance, which the important creature itself requires, as a measuring-glance at its towering altitude would determine the affair like instinct.

You are right, Madam, in your idea of poor Mylne's poem, which he has addressed to me. The piece has a good deal of merit, but it has one great fault—it is, by far, too long. Besides, my success has encouraged such a shoal of ill-spawned monsters to crawl into public notice, under the title of Scottish Poets, that the very term Scottish Poetry borders on the burlesque. When I write to Mr. Carfrae, I shall advise him rather to try one of his deceased friend's English pieces. I am prodigiously hurried with my own matters, else I would have requested a perusal of all Mylne's poetic performances, and would have offered his friends my assistance in either selecting or correcting what would be proper for the press. What it is that occupies me so much, and perhaps a little oppresses my present spirits, shall fill up a paragraph in some future letter. In the meantime, allow me to close this epistle with a few lines done by a friend of mine.... I give you them, that, as you have seen the original, you may guess whether one or two alterations I have ventured to make in them, be any real improvement.

Like the fair plant that from our touch withdraws,
Shrink, mildly fearful, even from applause,
Be all a mother's fondest hope can dream,
And all you are, my charming Rachel, seem.
Straight as the fox-glove, ere her bells disclose,
Mild as the maiden-blushing hawthorn blows,
Fair as the fairest of each lovely kind,
Your form shall be the image of your mind;
Your manners shall so true your soul express,
That all shall long to know the worth they guess;

Congenial hearts shall greet with kindred love,
And even sick'ning envy must approve.[96]

R. B.

[96] These lines are Mrs. Dunlop's own, addressed to her daughter.

CXXI.—TO MRS. M'LEHOSE (FORMERLY CLARINDA).

ELLISLAND, *Mar. 9th,* 1789.

Madam,—The letter you wrote me to Heron's carried its own answer. You forbade me to write you unless I was willing to plead guilty to a certain indictment you were pleased to bring against me. As I am convinced of my own innocence, and, though conscious of high imprudence and egregious folly, can lay my hand on my breast and attest the rectitude of my heart, you will pardon me, Madam, if I do not carry my complaisance so far as humbly to acquiesce in the name of "Villain" merely out of compliment to your opinion, much as I esteem your judgment and warmly as I regard your worth.

I have already told you, and I again aver it, that, at the time alluded to, I was not under the smallest moral tie to Mrs. Burns; nor did I, nor could I, then know all the powerful circumstances that omnipotent necessity was busy laying in wait for me. When you call over the scenes that have passed between us, you will survey the conduct of an honest man struggling successfully with temptations the most powerful that ever beset humanity, and preserving untainted honour in situations where the austerest virtue would have forgiven a fall; situations that, I will dare to say not a single individual of all his kind, even with half his sensibility and passion, could have encountered without ruin; and I leave you, Madam, to guess how such a man is likely to digest an accusation of "perfidious treachery."

When I shall have regained your good opinion, perhaps I may venture to solicit your friendship; but, be that as it may, the first of her sex I ever knew shall always be the object of my warmest good wishes.

ROBT. BURNS.

CXXII—TO DR. MOORE.

ELLISLAND, *23rd March* 1789.

Sir,—The gentleman who will deliver you this is a Mr. Nielson, a worthy clergyman in my neighbourhood, and a very particular acquaintance of mine. As I have troubled him with this packet, I must turn him over to your goodness, to recompense him for it in a way in which he much needs your assistance, and where you can effectually serve him. Mr. Nielson is on his way for France, to wait on his Grace of Queensberry, on some little business of a good deal of importance to him, and he wishes for your instructions respecting the most eligible mode of travelling, etc., for him, when he has crossed the channel. I should not have dared to take this liberty with you, but that I am told, by those who have the honour of your personal acquaintance, that to be a poor honest Scotsman is a letter of recommendation to you, and that to have it in your power to serve such a character, gives you much pleasure.

The inclosed ode is a compliment to the memory of the late Mrs. Oswald of Auchencruive. You probably knew her personally, an honour of which I cannot boast; but I spent my early years in the neighbourhood, and among her servants and tenants. I know that she was detested with the most heartfelt cordiality. However, in the particular part of her conduct which roused my poetic wrath, she was much less blameable. In January last, on my road to Ayrshire, I had put up at Bailie Whigham's, in Sanquhar, the only tolerable inn in the place. The frost was keen, and the grim evening and howling wind were ushering in a night of snow and drift. My horse and I were both much fatigued with the labours of the day, and just as my friend the Bailie and I were bidding defiance to the storm, over a smoking bowl, in wheels the funeral pageantry of the late great Mrs. Oswald, and poor I am forced to brave all the horrors of the tempestuous night, and jade my horse, my young favourite horse, whom I had just christened Pegasus, twelve miles farther on, through the wildest moors and hills of Ayrshire, to New Cumnock, the next inn. The powers of poesy and prose sink under me, when I would describe what I felt. Suffice it to say, that when a good fire at New Cumnock had so far recovered my frozen sinews, I sat down and wrote the inclosed ode.

I was at Edinburgh lately, and settled finally with Mr. Creech; and I must own, that at last, he has been amicable and fair with me.

R. B.

CXXIII.—To HIS BROTHER, MR. WILLIAM BURNS.

ISLE, March 25th 1789.

I have stolen from my corn-sowing this minute to write a line to accompany your shirt and hat, for I can no more. Your sister Nannie arrived yesternight, and begs to be remembered to you. Write me every opportunity—never mind postage. My head, too, is as addle as an egg this morning, with dining abroad yesterday. I received yours by the mason. Forgive me this foolish looking scrawl of an epistle.—I am ever, my dear William, yours,

R. B.

P.S.—If you are not then gone from Longtown, I'll write you a long letter by this day se'ennight. If you should not succeed in your tramps, don't be dejected, or take any rash step—return to us in that case, and we will court Fortune's better humour. Remember this, I charge you.

R. B.

CXXIV.—To MR. HILL, BOOKSELLER, EDINBURGH.

ELLISLAND, *2nd April* 1789.

I will make no excuse, my dear Bibliopolus (God forgive me for murdering language!) that I have sat down to write you on this vile paper.

It is economy, Sir; it is that cardinal virtue, prudence; so I beg you will sit down, and either compose or borrow a panegyric. If you are going to borrow, apply to[97] ... to compose, or rather to compound, something very clever on my remarkable frugality; that I write to one of my most esteemed friends on this wretched paper, which was originally intended for the venal fist of some drunken exciseman, to take dirty notes in a miserable vault of an ale-cellar.

O Frugality! thou mother of ten thousand blessings—thou cook of fat beef and dainty greens!—thou manufacturer of warm Shetland hose, and comfortable surtouts!—thou old housewife, darning thy decayed stockings with thy ancient spectacles on thy aged nose!—lead me, hand me in thy clutching palsied fist, up those heights, and through those thickets, hitherto inaccessible, and impervious to my anxious, weary feet:—not those Parnassian crags, bleak and barren, where the hungry worshippers of fame are, breathless, clambering, hanging between heaven and hell; but those glittering cliffs of Potosi, where the all-sufficient, all-powerful deity, wealth, holds his immediate court of joy and pleasures; where the sunny exposure of plenty, and the hot walls of profusion, produce those blissful fruits of luxury, exotics in this world, and natives of paradise!—Thou withered sibyl, my sage conductress, usher me into thy refulgent, adored presence!—The power, splendid and potent as he now is, was once the puling nursling of thy faithful care and tender arms! Call me thy son, thy cousin, thy kinsman, or favourite, and adjure the god by the scenes of his infant years, no longer to repulse me as a stranger, or an alien, but to favour me with his peculiar countenance and protection! He daily bestows his great kindness on the undeserving and the worthless—assure him that I bring ample documents of meritorious demerits! Pledge yourself for me, that, for the glorious cause of lucre, I will do anything, be anything; but the horse-leech of private oppression, or the vulture of public robbery!

But to descend from heroics.

I want a Shakespeare; I want likewise an English dictionary,—Johnson's, I suppose, is best. In these and all my prose commissions, the cheapest is always the best for me. There is a small debt of honour that I owe Mr. Robert Cleghorn, in Saughton Mills, my worthy friend, and your well-wisher. Please give him, and urge him to take it, the first time you see him, ten shillings worth of anything you have to sell, and place it to my account.

The library scheme that I mentioned to you is already begun under the direction of Captain Riddel. There is another in emulation of it going on at Closeburn, under the auspices of Mr. Monteith of Closeburn, which will be on a greater scale than ours. Captain Riddel gave his infant society a great many of his old books, else I had written you on that subject; but, one of these days, I shall trouble you with a commission for "The Monkland Friendly Society," a copy of *The Spectator, Mirror*, and *Lounger, Man of Feeling,Man of the World, Guthrie's Geographical Grammar*, with some religious pieces, will likely be our first order.

When I grow richer, I will write to you on gilt-post, to make amends for this sheet. At present every guinea has a five guinea errand with, my dear Sir, your faithful, poor, but honest friend,

R. B.

[97] Creech? or Ramsay of *The Courant?*

CXXV.—TO MRS. M'MURDO, DRUMLANRIG.

ELLISLAND, *2nd May* 1789.

Madam,—I have finished the piece which had the happy fortune to be honoured with your approbation; and never did little Miss, with more sparkling pleasure, show her applauded sampler to partial Mamma, than I now send my poem to you and Mr. M'Murdo,[98] if he is returned to Drumlanrig. You cannot easily imagine what thin-skinned animals—what sensitive plants poor poets are. How do we shrink into the imbittered corner of self-abasement, when neglected or condemned by those to whom we look up! and how do we, in erect importance, add another cubit to our stature on being noticed and applauded by those whom we honour and respect! My late visit to Drumlanrig has, I can tell you, Madam, given me a balloon waft up Parnassus, where, on my fancied elevation, I regard my poetic self with no small degree of complacency. Surely with all their sins, the rhyming tribe are not ungrateful creatures—I recollect your goodness to your humble guest—I see Mr. M'Murdo adding to the politeness of the gentleman, the kindness of a friend, and my heart swells as it would burst, with warm emotions and ardent wishes! It may be it is not gratitude—it may be a mixed sensation. That strange, shifting, doubling animal, MAN, is so generally, at best, but a negative, often a worthless creature, that we cannot see real goodness and native worth, without feeling the bosom glow with sympathetic approbation. With every sentiment of grateful respect, I have the honour to be, Madam, your obliged and grateful humble servant,

R. B.

[98] The piece beginning—There was a lass and she was fair.

CXXVI.—TO MR. CUNNINGHAM.

ELL ISLAND, *4th May* 1789.

My dear Sir,—Your *duty-free* favour of the 25th April I received two days ago; I will not say I perused it with pleasure; that is the cold compliment of ceremony; I perused it, Sir, with delicious satisfaction;—in short, it is such a letter, that not you, nor your friend, but the legislature, by express proviso in their postage laws, should frank. A letter informed with the soul of friendship is such an honour to human nature, that they should order it free ingress and egress to and from their bags and mails, as an encouragement and mark of distinction to supereminent virtue.

I have just put the last hand to a little poem, which I think will be something to your taste.[99] One morning lately, as I was out pretty early in the fields, sowing some grass seeds, I heard the burst of a shot from a neighbouring plantation, and presently a poor little wounded hare came crippling by me. You will guess my indignation at the inhuman fellow who could shoot a hare at this season, when all of them have young ones. Indeed there is something in that business of destroying, for our sport, individuals in the animal creation that do not injure us materially, which I could never reconcile to my ideas of virtue.

Let me know how you like my poem. I am doubtful whether it would not be an improvement to keep out the last stanza but one altogether.

Cruikshank is a glorious production of the author of man. You, he, and the noble Colonel[100] of the Crochallan Fencibles are to me

Dear as the ruddy drops which warm my heart.

I have got a good mind to make verses on you all, to the tune of "*Three guid fellows ayont the glen*"

R. B.

[99] See the poem on the "Wounded Hare."

[100] That is, William Dunbar, W.S.

CXXVIL—TO MR. RICHARD BROWN.
MAUCHLINE, *21st May* 1789.

My Dear Friend,—I was in the country by accident, and hearing of your safe arrival, I could not resist the temptation of wishing you joy on your return—wishing you would write to me before you sail again—wishing that you would always set me down as your bosom friend—wishing you long life and prosperity, and that every good thing may attend you— wishing Mrs. Brown and your little ones as free of the evils of this world as is consistent with humanity—wishing you and she were to make two at the ensuing lying-in, with which Mrs. B. threatens very soon to favour me—wishing I had longer time to write to you at present; and, finally, wishing that if there is to be another state of existence, Mrs. Brown, Mrs. Burns, our little ones of both families, and you and I, in some snug retreat, may make a jovial party to all eternity!

My direction is at Ellisland, near Dumfries.—Yours,

R. B.

CXXVIIL—To MR. ROBERT AINSLIE.
ELLISLAND, *8th June* 1789.

MY DEAR FRIEND,—I am perfectly ashamed of myself when I look at the date of your last. It is not that I forget the friend of my heart and the companion of my peregrinations; but I have been condemned to drudgery beyond sufferance, though not, thank God, beyond redemption. I have had a collection of poems by a lady put into my hands to prepare them for the press; which horrid task, with sowing corn with my own hand, a parcel of masons, wrights, plasterers, etc., to attend to, roaming on business through Ayrshire—all this was against me, and the very first dreadful article was of itself too much for me.

13th. I have not had a moment to spare from incessant toil since the 8th. Life, my dear Sir, is a serious matter. You know by experience that a man's individual self is a good deal, but believe me, a wife and family of children, whenever you have the honour to be a husband and a father, will show you that your present and most anxious hours of solitude are spent on trifles. The welfare of those who are very dear to us, whose only support, hope, and stay we are—this, to a generous mind, is another sort of more important object of care than any concerns whatever which centre merely in the individual. On the other hand, let no young, rakehelly dog among you, make a song of his pretended liberty and freedom from care. If the relations we stand in to king, country, kindred, and friends, be anything but the visionary fancies of dreaming metaphysicians; if religion, virtue, magnanimity, generosity, humanity and justice, be ought but empty sounds; then the man who may be said to live only for others, for the beloved, honourable female, whose tender faithful embrace endears life, and for the helpless little innocents who are to be the men and women, the worshippers of his God, the subjects of his king, and the support, nay the very vital existence of his COUNTRY, in the ensuing age;—compare such a man with any fellow whatever, who, whether he bustle and push in business among labourers, clerks, statesmen; or whether he roar and rant, and drink and sing in taverns—a fellow over whose grave no one will breathe a single heigh-ho, except from the cobweb-tie of what is called good fellowship—who has no view nor aim but what terminates in himself—if there be any grovelling earth-born wretch of our species, a renegade to common sense, who would fain believe that the noble creature, man, is no better than a sort of fungus, generated out of nothing, nobody knows how, and soon dissipating in nothing, nobody knows where; such a stupid beast, such a crawling reptile, might balance the foregoing unexaggerated comparison, but no one else would have the patience.

Forgive me, my dear Sir, for this long silence. *To make you amends*, I shall send you soon, and more encouraging still, without any postage, one or two rhymes of my later manufacture.

R. B.

CXXIX.—TO MRS. DUNLOP.

ELLISLAND, 21*st June* 1789.

Dear Madam,—Will you take the effusions, the miserable effusions of low spirits, just as they flow from their bitter spring? I know not of any particular cause for this worst of all my foes besetting me; but for some time my soul has been beclouded with a thickening atmosphere of evil imaginations and gloomy presages.

Monday Evening.

I have just heard Mr. Kilpatrick preach a sermon. He is a man famous for his benevolence, and I revere him; but from such ideas of my Creator, good Lord, deliver me! Religion, my honoured friend, is surely a simple business, as it equally concerns the ignorant and the learned, the poor and the rich. That there is an incomprehensible Great Being, to whom I owe my existence, and that He must be intimately acquainted with the operations and progress of the internal machinery, and consequent outward deportment of this creature which He has made; these are, I think, self-evident propositions. That there is a real and eternal distinction between virtue and vice, and consequently, that I am an accountable creature; that from the seeming nature of the human mind, as well as from the evident imperfection, nay, positive injustice, in the administration of affairs, both in the natural and moral worlds, there must be a retributive scene of existence beyond the grave; must, I think, be allowed by every one who will give himself a moment's reflection. I will go farther, and affirm, that from the sublimity, excellence, and purity of his doctrine and precepts, unparalleled by all the aggregated wisdom and learning of many preceding ages, though, to *appearance* he, himself, was the obscurest and most illiterate of our species; therefore Jesus Christ was from God.

Whatever mitigates the woes, or increases the happiness of others, this is my criterion of goodness; and whatever injures society at large, or any individual in it, this is my measure of iniquity.

What think you, Madam, of my creed? I trust that I have said nothing that will lessen me in the eye of one, whose good opinion I value almost next to the approbation of my own mind.

R. B.

CXXX.—TO MISS HELEN MARIA WILLIAMS.

ELLISLAND, 1789.

Madam,—Of the many problems in the nature of that wonderful creature, man, this is one of the most extraordinary—that he shall go on from day to day, from week to week, from month to month, or perhaps from year to year, suffering a hundred times more in an hour from the impotent consciousness of neglecting what he ought to do, than the very doing of it would cost him. I am deeply indebted to you, first, for a most elegant poetic compliment; then for a polite, obliging letter; and, lastly, for your excellent poem on the Slave Trade; and yet, wretch that I am! though the debts were debts of honour, and the creditor a lady, I have put off and put off even the very acknowledgment of the obligation, until you must indeed be the very angel I take you for, if you can forgive me.

Your poem I have read with the highest pleasure. I have a way whenever I read a book—I mean a book in our own trade, Madam, a poetic one, and when it is my own property—that I take a pencil and mark at the ends of verses, or note on margins and odd paper, little criticisms of approbation or disapprobation as I peruse along. I will make no apology for presenting you with a few unconnected thoughts that occurred to me in my repeated perusals of your poem. I want to show you that I have honesty enough to tell you what I take to be truths, even when they are not quite on the side of approbation; and I do it in the firm faith that you have equal greatness of mind to hear them with pleasure. [Here follows a list of strictures.]

I had lately the honour of a letter from Dr. Moore, where he tells me that he has sent me some books; they are not yet come to hand, but I hear they are on the way.

Wishing you all success in your progress in the path of fame, and that you may equally escape the danger of stumbling through incautious speed, or losing ground through loitering neglect, I am, etc.

R. B.

CXXXI.—To MR. ROBERT GRAHAM, OF FINTRY.

ELLISLAND, 31st *july* 1789.

Sir,—The language of gratitude has been so prostituted by servile adulation and designing flattery that I know not how to express myself when I would acknowledge receipt of your last letter. I beg and hope, ever-honoured "Friend of my life and patron of my rhymes," that you will always give me credit for the sincerest, chastest gratitude. I dare call the Searcher of hearts and Author of all Goodness to witness how truly grateful I am.

Mr. Mitchell[101] did not wait my calling on him, but sent me a kind letter, giving me a hint of the business; and yesterday he entered with the most friendly ardour into my views and interests. He seems to think, and from my private knowledge I am certain he is right, that removing the officer who now does, and for these many years has done, duty in the Division in the middle of which I live, will be productive of at least no disadvantage to the revenue, and may likewise be done without any detriment to him. Should the Honourable Board [of Excise] think so, and should they deem it eligible to appoint me to officiate in his present place, I am then at the top of my wishes. The emoluments in my office will enable me to carry on, and enjoy those improvements on my farm, which but for this additional assistance, I might in a year or two have abandoned. Should it be judged improper to place me in this Division, I am deliberating whether I had not better give up my farming altogether, and go into the Excise whenever I can find employment. Now that the salary is £50 per annum, the Excise is surely a much superior object to a farm, which, without some foreign assistance, must for half a lease be a losing bargain. The worst of it is—I know there are some respectable characters who do me the honour to interest themselves in my welfare and behaviour, and, as leaving the farm so soon may have an unsteady, giddy-headed appearance, I had better perhaps lose a little money than hazard their esteem.

You see, Sir, with what freedom I lay before you all my little matters—little indeed to the world, but of the most important magnitude to me.... Were it not for a very few of our kind, the very existence of magnanimity, generosity, and all their kindred virtues, would be as much a question with metaphysicians as the existence of witchcraft. Perhaps the nature of man is not so much to blame for this, as the situation in which by some miscarriage or other he is placed in this world. The poor, naked, helpless wretch, with such voracious appetites and such a famine of provision for them, is under a cursed necessity of turning selfish in his own defence. Except a few instances of original scoundrelism, thorough-paced selfishness is always the work of time. Indeed, in a little time, we generally grow so attentive to ourselves and so regardless of others that I have often in poetic frenzy looked on this world as one vast ocean, occupied and commoved by innumerable vortices, each whirling round its centre. These vortices are the children of men. The great design and, if I may say so, merit of each particular vortex consists in how widely it can extend the influence of its circle, and how much floating trash it can suck in and absorb.

I know not why I have got into this preaching vein, except it be to show you that it is not my ignorance but my knowledge of mankind which makes me so much admire your goodness to me.

I shall return your books very soon. I only wish to give Dr. Adam Smith one other perusal, which I will do in one or two days.

R. B.

[101] A collector in the Excise.

CXXXIL—TO DAVID SILLAR, MERCHANT, IRVINE.[102]

ELLISLAND, 5 *Aug.* 1789.

My Dear Sir,—I was half in thoughts not to have written to you at all, by way of revenge for the two damn'd business letters you sent me. I wanted to know all about your publications—your news, your hopes, fears, etc., in commencing poet in print. In short, I wanted you to write to Robin like his old acquaintance Davie, and not in the style of Mr. Tare to Mr. Tret, as thus:—

"Mr. Tret.—Sir,—This comes to advise you that fifteen barrels of herrings were, by the blessing of God, shipped safe on board the *Lovely Janet*, Q.D.C., Duncan Mac-Leerie, master, etc."

I hear you have commenced married man—so much the better. I know not whether the nine gipsies are jealous of my lucky, but they are a good deal shyer since I could boast the important relation of husband.

I have got about eleven subscribers for your book.... My best compliments to Mrs. Sillar, and believe me to be, dear Davie, ever yours,

ROBT. BURNS.

[102] This letter was first published in 1879. The original is probably lost, but a copy is to be found in the minute-book of the Irvine Burns Club. Sillar was "Davie, a brother poet."

CXXXIII.—TO MR. JOHN LOGAN, OF KNOCK SHINNOCK.

ELLISLAND, NEAR DUMFRIES, 7*th Aug.* 1789.

Dear Sir,—I intended to have written you long ere now, and, as I told you, I had gotten three stanzas on my way in a poetic epistle to you; but that old enemy of all *good works*, the Devil, threw me into a prosaic mire, and for the soul of me I cannot get out of it. I dare not write you a long letter, as I am going to intrude on your time with a long ballad. I have, as you will shortly see, finished "The Kirk's Alarm;" but now that it is done, and that I have laughed once or twice at the conceits in some of the stanzas, I am determined not to let it get into the public; so I send you this copy, the first that I have sent to Ayrshire, except some few of the stanzas, which I wrote off in embryo for Gavin Hamilton, under the express provision and request that you will only read it to a few of us, and do not on any account give, or permit to be taken, any copy of the ballad. If I could be of any service to Dr. M'Gill, I would do it, though it should be at a much greater expense than irritating a few bigoted priests, but I am afraid serving him in his present *embarras* is a task too hard for me. I have enemies enow, God knows, though I do not wantonly add to the number. Still, as I think there is some merit in two or three of the thoughts, I send it to you as a small, but sincere testimony how much, and with what respectful esteem, I am, dear Sir, your obliged humble servant

R. B.

CXXXIV.—TO MR. PETER STUART, EDITOR, LONDON.

End of Aug. 1789.

My dear Sir,—The hurry of a farmer in this particular season, and the indolence of a poet at all seasons, will, I hope, plead my excuse for neglecting so long to answer your obliging letter of the 5th August.

... When I received your letter I was transcribing for *The Star* my letter to the magistrates of the Canongate of Edinburgh, begging their permission to place a tombstone over poor Fergusson. [124]. Poor Fergusson! if there be a life beyond the grave, which I trust there is; and if there be a good God presiding over all nature, which I am sure there is, thou art now enjoying existence in a glorious world where worth of heart alone is distinction in the man; where riches, deprived of their pleasure-purchasing powers, return to their native sordid matter; where titles and honours are the disregarded reveries of an idle dream; and where that heavy virtue, which is the negative consequence of steady dulness, and those thoughtless though often destructive follies, which are the unavoidable aberrations of frail human nature, will be thrown into equal oblivion as if they had never been!

R. B.

[112a]: A young Scottish poet of undoubted ability who perished miserably in Edinburgh at the age of twenty-four. He was the senior of Burns, who greatly admired and mourned him, by about eight year

CXXXV.—To HIS BROTHER, WILLIAM BURNS, SADDLER, NEWCASTLE-ON-TYNE.

ELLISLAND, 14*th Aug.* 1789.

My Dear William,—I received your letter, and am very happy to hear that you have got settled for the winter. I enclose you the two guinea-notes of the Bank of Scotland, which I hope will serve your need. It is, indeed, not quite so convenient for me to spare money as it once was, but I know your situation, and, I will say it, in some respects your worth. I have no time to write at present, but I beg you will endeavour to pluck up a *little* more of the Man than you used to have. Remember my favourite quotations:

On reason build resolve,
That pillar of true majesty in man.[103]

and

What proves the hero truly great,
Is never, never to despair![103a]

Your mother and sisters desire their compliments. A Dieu je vous commende,

ROBT. BURNS.

[103] From Young.

[103a] From Thomson.

CXXXVL—TO MRS. DUNLOP.

ELLISLAND, *6th Sept.* 1789.

Dear Madam,—I have mentioned, in my last, my appointment to the Excise, and the birth of little Frank; who, by the bye, I trust will be no discredit to the honourable name of Wallace, as he has a fine manly countenance, and a figure that might do credit to a litlle fellow two months older; and likewise an excellent good temper, though when he pleases he has a pipe, only not quite so loud as the horn that his immortal namesake blew as a signal to take out the pin of Stirling bridge.

I had some time ago an epistle, part poetic, and part prosaic, from your poetess Miss. J. Little,[104] a very ingenious, but modest composition. I should have written her as she requested, but for the hurry of this new business. I have heard of her and her compositions in this country; and I am happy to add, always to the honour of her character. The fact is, I knew not well how to write to her: I should sit down to a sheet of paper that I knew not how to stain. I am no dab at fine-drawn letter-writing; and, except when prompted by friendship or gratitude, or, which happens extremely rarely, inspired by the Muse (I know not her name) that presides over epistolary writing, I sit down, when necessitated to write, as I would sit down to beat hemp.

Some parts of your letter of the 2oth August struck me with the most melancholy concern for the state of your mind at present.

Would I could write you a letter of comfort, I would sit down to it with as much pleasure as I would to write an epic poem of my own composition that should equal the *Iliad!* Religion, my dear friend, is the true comfort. A strong persuasion in a future state of existence; a proposition so obviously probable, that, setting revelation aside, every nation and people, so far as investigation has reached, for at least near four thousand years, have, in some mode or other, firmly believed it. In vain would we reason and pretend to doubt. I have myself done so to a very daring pitch; but, when I reflected that I was opposing the most ardent wishes and the most darling hopes of good men, and flying in the face of all human belief, in all ages, I was shocked at my own conduct.

I know not whether I have ever sent you the following lines; or if you have ever seen them; but it is one of my favourite quotations, which I keep constantly by me in my progress through life, in the language of the book of Job,

Against the day of battle and of war—
spoken of religion:
'Tis *this*, my friend, that streaks our morning bright,
'Tis *this* that gilds the horror of our night,
When wealth forsakes us, and when friends are few;
When friends are faithless, or when foes pursue;
'Tis this that wards the blow, or stills the smart,
Disarms affliction, or repels his dart;
Within the breast bids purest raptures rise,
Bids smiling conscience spread her cloudless skies.

I have been busy with *Zeluco*. The Doctor is so obliging as to request my opinion of it; and I have been revolving in my mind some kind of criticisms on novel-writing, but it is a depth beyond my research. I shall, however, digest my thoughts on the subject as well as I can. *Zeluco* is a most sterling performance.

Farewell! *A Dieu, le bon Dieu, je vous commende!*

[104] A maid servant at Loudon house.

CXXXVIL—To CAPTAIN RIDDEL, FRIARS CARSE.

ELLISLAND, *16th October* 1789.

Sir,—Big with the idea of this important day at Friars Carse, I have watched the elements and skies, in the full persuasion that they would announce it to the astonished world by some phenomena of terrific portent. Yesternight until a very late hour, did I wait with anxious horror for the appearance of some comet firing half the sky, or aerial armies of sanguinary Scandinavians, darting athwart the startled heavens, rapid as the ragged lightning, and horrid as those convulsions of nature that bury nations.

The elements, however, seem to take the matter very quietly; they did not even usher in this morning with triple suns and a shower of blood, symbolical of the three potent heroes[105] and the mighty claret-shed of the day. For me—as Thomson in his Winter says of the storm—I shall "hear astonished, and astonished sing"

The WHISTLE and the man I sing,
The man that won the whistle, etc.

To leave the heights of Parnassus and come to the humble vale of prose. I have some misgivings that I take too much upon me, when I request you to get your guest, Sir Robert Lawrie, to frank the two inclosed covers for me, the one of them to Sir William Cunningham, of Robertland, Bart., at Kilmarnock,—the other, to Mr. Allan Masterton, Writing-Master, Edinburgh. The first has a kindred claim on Sir Robert, as being a brother Baronet, and likewise a keen Foxite; the other is one of the worthiest men in the world, and a man of real genius; so, allow me to say, he has a fraternal claim on you. I want them franked for to-morrow, as I cannot get them to the post to-night. I shall send a servant again for them in the evening. Wishing that your head may be crowned with laurels to-night, and free from aches to-morrow, I have the honour to be, Sir, your deeply indebted humble Servant,

R. B.

[105] Sir Robert Lawrie of Maxwellton, the holder of the Whistle, Alexander Fergusson of Craigdarroch, and Captain Riddel. *See* the Poem. Burns was apparently absent.

CXXXVIII—To MR. ROBERT AINSLIE, W.S.

ELLISLAND, *1st Nov.* 1789.

My Dear Friend,—I had written you ere now, could I have guessed where to find you, for I am sure you have more good sense than to waste the precious days of vacation time in the dirt of business and Edinburgh. Wherever you are, God bless you, and lead you not into temptation, but deliver you from evil!

I do not know if I have informed you that I am now appointed to an Excise division, in the middle of which my house and farm lie. In this I was extremely lucky. Without ever having been an expectant, as they call their journeymen excisemen, I was directly planted down to all intents and purposes an officer of Excise; there to flourish and bring forth fruits—worthy of repentance.

You need not doubt that I find several very unpleasant and disagreeable circumstances in my business; but I am tired with and disgusted at the language of complaint against the evils of life. Human existence in the most favourable situations does not abound with pleasures, and has its inconveniences and ills: capricious foolish man mistakes these inconveniences and ills as if they were the peculiar property of his particular situation; and hence that eternal fickleness, that love of change, which has ruined, and daily does ruin many a fine fellow, as well as many a blockhead, and is almost, without exception, a constant source of disappointment and misery.

I long to hear from you how you go on-not so much in business as in life. Are you pretty well satisfied with your own exertions, and tolerably at ease in your internal reflections? 'Tis much to be a great character as a lawyer, but beyond comparison more to be a great character as a man. That you may be both the one and the other is the earnest wish, and that you *will* be both is the firm persuasion of, my dear Sir, etc.

R. B.

CXXXIX.—To MR. RICHARD BROWN, PORT-GLASGOW.

ELLISLAND, *4th November* 1789.

I have been so hurried, my ever dear friend, that though I got both your letters, I have not been able to command an hour to answer them as I wished; and even now, you are to look on this as merely confessing debt, and craving days. Few things could have given me so much pleasure as the news that you were once more safe and sound on terra firma, and happy in that place where happiness is alone to be found, in the fireside circle. May the benevolent Director of all things peculiarly bless you in all those endearing connections consequent on the tender and venerable names of husband and father! I have indeed been extremely lucky in getting an additional income of £50 a-year, while, at the same time, the appointment will not cost me above £10 or £12 per annum of expenses more than I must have inevitably incurred. The worst circumstance is, that the Excise division which I have got is so extensive, no less than ten parishes to ride over; and it abounds besides with so much business, that I can scarcely steal a spare moment. However, labour endears rest, and both together are absolutely necessary for the proper enjoyment of human existence. I cannot meet you anywhere.

No less than an order from the Board of Excise, at Edinburgh, is necessary before I can have so much time as to meet you in Ayrshire. But do you come, and see me. We must have a social day, and perhaps lengthen it out with half the night, before you go again to sea. You are the earliest friend I now have on earth, my brothers excepted; and is not that an endearing circumstance? When you and I first met, we were at the green period of human life. The twig would easily take a bent, but would as easily return to its former state. You and I not only took a mutual bent, but, by the melancholy, though strong influence of being both of the family of the unfortunate, we were entwined with one another in our growth towards advanced age; and blasted be the sacrilegious hand that shall attempt to undo the union! You and I must have one bumper to my favourite toast, "May the companions of our youth be the friends of our old age!" Come and see me one year; I shall see you at Port-Glasgow the next, and if we can contrive to have a gossiping between our two bed-fellows, it will be so much additional pleasure. Mrs. Burns joins me in kind compliments to you and Mrs. Brown. Adieu!—I am ever, my dear Sir, yours,

R. B.

CXL.—To MR. R. GRAHAM, OF FINTRY.

9th December 1789.

Sir,—I have a good while had a wish to trouble you with a letter, and had certainly done it long ere now, but for a humiliating something that throws cold water on the resolution, as if one should say, "You have found Mr. Graham a very powerful and kind friend indeed, and that interest he is so kindly taking in your concerns, you ought by everything in your power to keep alive and cherish." Now, though since God has thought proper to make one powerful and another helpless, the connection of obliger and obliged is all fair; and though my being under your patronage is to me highly honourable, yet, Sir, allow me to flatter myself that,—as a poet and an honest man you first interested yourself in my welfare, and principally as such still, you permit me to approach you.

I have found the Excise business go on a great deal smoother with me than I expected; owing a good deal to the generous friendship of Mr. Mitchell, my collector, and the kind assistance of Mr. Findlater, my supervisor. I dare to be honest, and I fear no labour. Nor do I find my hurried life greatly inimical to my correspondence with the Muses. Their visits to me, indeed, and I believe to most of their acquaintance, like the visits of good angels, are short and far between; but I meet them now and then as I jog through the hills of Nithsdale, just as I used to do on the banks of Ayr. I take the liberty to inclose you a few bagatelles, all of them the productions of my leisure thoughts in my excise rides.

If you know or have ever seen Captain Grose, the antiquarian, you will enter into any humour that is in the verses on him. Perhaps you have seen them before, as I sent them to a London newspaper. Though, I dare say, you have none of the solemn-league-and-covenant fire, which shone so conspicuous in Lord George Gordon, and the Kilmarnock weavers, yet I think you must have heard of Dr. M'Gill, one of the clergymen of Ayr, and his heretical book. God help him, poor man! Though he is one of the worthiest, as well as one of the ablest of the whole priesthood of the Kirk of Scotland, in every sense of that ambiguous term, yet the poor Doctor and his numerous family are in imminent danger of being thrown out to the mercy of the winter-winds. The inclosed ballad on that business is, I confess, too local, but I laughed myself at some conceits in it, though I am convinced in my conscience that there are a good many heavy stanzas in it too.[106]

The election ballad,[107] as you will see, alludes to the present canvass in our string of boroughs. I do not believe there will be such a hard run match in the whole general election.

I am too little a man to have any political attachments; I am deeply indebted to, and have the warmest veneration for, individuals of both parties; but a man[108] who has it in his power to be the father of a country, and who is only known to that country by the mischiefs he does in it, is a character that one cannot speak of with patience.

Sir J. J. does "what man can do," but yet I doubt his fate.

R. B.

[106] The Kirk's Alarm.

   [107] *The Five Carlines.*

   [108] Duke of Queensbury.

CXLL—To MRS. DUNLOP.

ELLISLAND, *13th December* 1789.

Many thanks, dear Madam, for your sheetful of rhymes. Though at present I am below the veriest prose, yet from you everything pleases. I am groaning under the miseries of a diseased nervous system; a system, the state of which is most conducive to our happiness—or the most productive of our misery. For now near three weeks I have been so ill with a nervous headache, that I have been obliged for a time to give up my excise-books, being scare able to lift my head, much less to ride once a week over ten muir parishes. What is man? To-day, in the luxuriance of health, exulting in the enjoyment of existence; in a few days, perhaps in a few hours, loaded with conscious painful being, counting the tardy pace of the lingering moments by the repercussions of anguish, and refusing or denied a comforter. Day follows night, and night comes after day, only to curse him with life which gives him no pleasure; and yet the awful, dark termination of that life, is something at which he recoils.

Tell us, ye dead; will none of you in pity
Disclose the secret
What'tis you are, and we must shortly be?
'Tis no matter:
A little time will make us learn'd as you are.

Can it be possible, that when I resign this frail, feverish being, I shall still find myself in conscious existence? When the last gasp of agony has announced that I am no more to those that knew me, and the few who loved me; when the cold, stiffened, unconscious, ghastly corse is resigned into the earth, to be the prey of unsightly reptiles, and to become in time a trodden clod, shall I be yet warm in life, seeing and seen, enjoying and enjoyed? Ye venerable sages, and holy flamens, is there probability in your conjectures, truth in your stories, of another world beyond death; or are they all alike, baseless visions, and fabricated fables? If there is another life, it must be only for the just, the benevolent, the amiable, and the humane; what a flattering idea, then, is a world to come! Would to God I as firmly believed it, as I ardently wish it! There I should meet an aged parent, now at rest from the many buffetings of an evil world, against which he so long and so bravely struggled. There should I meet the friend, the disinterested friend of my early life; the man who rejoiced to see me, because he loved me and could serve me. Muir, thy weaknesses were the aberrations of human nature, but thy heart glowed with everything generous, manly, and noble; and if ever emanation from the All-good Being animated a human form, it was thine! There should I, with speechless agony of rapture, again recognise my lost, my ever dear Mary! whose bosom was fraught with truth, honour, constancy, and love.

My Mary, dear departed shade!
Where is thy place of heavenly rest?
Seest thou thy lover lowly laid?
Hear'st thou the groans that rend his breast?

Jesus Christ, thou amiablest of characters! I trust thou art no impostor, and that thy revelation of blissful scenes of existence beyond death and the grave, is not one of the many impositions which time after time have been palmed on credulous mankind. I trust that in thee "shall all the families of the earth be blessed," by being yet connected together in a better world, where every tie that bound heart to heart, in this state of existence, shall be, far beyond our present conceptions, more endearing.

I am a good deal inclined to think with those who maintain, that what are called nervous affections are in fact diseases of the mind. I cannot reason, I cannot think; and but to you I would not venture to write anything above an order to a cobbler. You have felt too much of the ills of life not to sympathise with a diseased wretch, who has impaired more than half of any faculties he possessed. Your goodness will excuse this distracted scrawl, which the writer dare scarcely read, and which he would throw into the fire, were he able to write anything better, or indeed anything at all.

Rumour told me something of a son of yours, who was returned from the East or West Indies. If you have gotten news from James or Anthony, it was cruel in you not to let me know; as I promise you, on the sincerity of a man, who is weary of one world, and anxious about another, that scarce anything could give me so much pleasure as to hear of any good thing befalling my honoured friend.

If you have a minute's leisure, take up your pen in pity to LE PAUVRE MISERABLE.
R. B.

CXLII.—To LADY WINIFRED M. CONSTABLE.
ELLISLAND, 16th DECEMBER 1789.

My Lady,—In vain have I from day to day expected to hear from Mis. Young, as she promised me at Dalswinton that she would do me the honour to introduce me at Tinwald;

and it was impossible, not from your Ladyship's accessibility, but from my own feelings, that I could go alone. Lately, indeed, Mr. Maxwell, of Currachan, in his usual goodness, offered to accompany me, when an unlucky indisposition on my part hindered my embracing the opportunity. To court the notice or the tables of the great, except where I sometimes have had a little matter to ask of them, or more often the pleasanter task of witnessing my gratitude to them, is what I never have done, and I trust never shall do. But with your Ladyship I have the honour to be connected by one of the strongest and most endearing ties in the whole moral world. Common sufferings, in a cause where even to be unfortunate is glorious—the cause of heroic loyalty! Though my fathers had not illustrious honours and vast properties to hazard in the contest, though they left their humble cottages only to add so many units more to the unnoted crowd that followed their leaders, yet what they could they did, and what they had they lost; with unshaken firmness and unconcealed political attachments, they shook hands with Ruin for what they esteemed the cause of their king and their country. This language and the inclosed verses are for your Ladyship's eye alone. Poets are not very famous for their prudence; but as I can do nothing for a cause which is now nearly no more, I do not wish to hurt myself.—I have the honour to be, my lady, your Ladyship's obliged and obedient humble servant.

R. B.

CXLIII.—To MR. CHARLES K. SHARPE, OF HODDAM.

Under a fictitious Signature, inclosing a Ballad, 1790 or 1791.[109]

It is true, Sir, you are a gentleman of rank and fortune, and I am a poor devil; you are a feather in the cap of society, and I am a very hobnail in his shoes; yet I have the honour to belong to the same family with you, and on that score I now address you. You will perhaps suspect that I am going to claim affinity with the ancient and honourable house of Kirkpatrick. No, no, Sir. I cannot indeed be properly said to belong to any house, or even any province or kingdom; as my mother, who for many years was spouse to a marching regiment, gave me into this bad world, aboard the packet-boat, somewhere between Donaghadee and Portpatrick. By our common family, I mean, Sir, the family of the Muses. I am a fiddler and a poet; and you, I am told, play an exquisite violin, and have a standard taste in the belles lettres. The other day, a brother catgut gave me a charming Scots air of your composition. If I was pleased with the tune, I was in raptures with the title you have given it, and, taking up the idea, I have spun it into the three stanzas inclosed. Will you allow me, Sir, to present you them, as the dearest offering that a misbegotten son of poverty and rhyme has to give? I have a longing to take you by the hand and unburden my heart by saying, "Sir, I honour you as a man who supports the dignity of human nature, amid an age when frivolity and avarice have, between them, debased us below the brutes that perish!" But, alas, Sir! to me you are unapproachable. It is true, the Muses baptised me in Castalian streams; but the thoughtless gipsies forgot to give me a name. As the sex have served many a good fellow, the Nine have given me a great deal of pleasure; but, bewitching jades! they have beggared me. Would they but spare me a little of their cast-linen! Were it only to put it in my power to say, that I have a shirt on my back! But the idle wenches, like Solomon's lilies, "they toil not, neither do they spin;" so I must e'en continue to tie my remnant of a cravat, like the hangman's rope, round my naked throat, and coax my galligaskins to keep together their many-coloured fragments. As to the affair of shoes, I have given that up. My pilgrimages in my ballad-trade, from town to town, and on your stony-hearted turnpikes too, are not what even the hide of Job's behemoth could bear. The coat on my back is no more: I shall not speak evil of the dead. It would be equally unhandsome and ungrateful to find fault with my old surtout, which so kindly supplies and conceals the want of that coat. My hat, indeed, is a great favourite; and though I got it literally for an old song, I would not exchange it for the best beaver in Britain. I was, during several years, a kind of fac-totum servant to a country clergyman, where I picked up a good many scraps of learning, particularly—in some branches of the mathematics. Whenever I feel inclined to rest myself on my way, I take my seat under a hedge, laying my poetic wallet on the one side, and my fiddle-case on the other, and placing my hat between my legs, I can by means of its brim, or rather brims, go through the whole doctrine of the Conic Sections. However, Sir, don't let me mislead you, as if I would interest your pity. Fortune has so much forsaken me, that she has taught me to live without her; and, amid all my rags and poverty, I am as independent, and much more happy than a monarch of the world. According to the hackneyed metaphor, I value the several actors in the great drama of life, simply as they act their parts. I can look on a worthless fellow of a duke with unqualified contempt, and can regard an honest scavenger with sincere respect. As you, Sir, go through your role with such distinguished merit, permit me to make one in the chorus of universal applause, and assure you that with the highest respect, I have the honour to be, etc.

[109] "Here Burns plays high Jacobite to that singular old curmudgeon, Lady Constable. I imagine his Jacobitism, like my own, belonged to the fancy rather than the reason."—Scott.

CXLIV.—To HIS BROTHER, GILBERT BURNS, MOSSGIEL.

ELLISLAND, *11th January 1790.*

Dear Brother,—I mean to take advantage of the frank, though I have not in my present frame of mind much appetite for exertion in writing. My nerves are in a cursed state. I feel that horrid hypochondria pervading every atom of both body and soul. This farm has undone my enjoyment of myself. It is a ruinous affair on all hands. But let it go to hell! I'll fight it out and be off with it.

We have gotten a set of very decent players here just now. I have seen them an evening or two. David Campbell, in Ayr, wrote to me by the manager of the company, a Mr. Sutherland, who is a man of apparent worth. On New-year-day evening I gave him the following prologue, which he spouted to his audience with applause:—

No song nor dance I bring from yon great city, etc.

I can no more. If once I was clear of this curst farm, I should respire more at ease.

CXLV.—To MR. WILLIAM DUNBAR, W.S.

ELLISLAND, 14th Jan. 1790.

Since we are here creatures of a day, since "a few summer days, a few winter nights, and the life of man is at an end," why, my dear much esteemed Sir, should you and I let negligent indolence, for I know it is nothing worse, step in between us and bar the enjoyment of a mutual correspondence? We are not shapen out of the common, heavy, methodical clod, the elemental stuff of the plodding selfish race, the sons of Arithmetic and Prudence; our feelings and hearts are not benumbed and poisoned by the cursed influence of riches, which, whatever blessing they may be in other respects, are no friends to the nobler qualities of the heart; in the name of random sensibility, then, let never the moon change on our silence any more. I have had a tract of bad health the most part of this winter, else you had heard from me long ere now. Thank heaven, I am now got so much better as to be able to partake a little in the enjoyments of life.

Our friend, Cunningham, will perhaps have told you of my going into the Excise. The truth is, I found it a very convenient business to have £50 per annum, nor have I yet felt any of these mortifying circumstances in it that I was led to fear.

Feb. 2nd.—I have not for sheer hurry of business been able to spare five minutes to finish my letter. Besides my farm business, I ride on my Excise matters at least two hundred miles every week. I have not by any means given up the Muses. You will see in the third volume of Johnson's Scots songs that I have contributed my mite there.

But, my dear Sir, little ones that look up to you for paternal protection are an important charge. I have already two fine healthy stout little fellows, and I wish to throw some light upon them. I have a thousand reveries and schemes about them, and their future destiny. Not that I am an Utopian projector in these things. I am resolved never to breed up a son of mine to any of the learned professions. I know the value of independence; and since I cannot give my sons an independent fortune, I shall give them an independent line of life. What a chaos of hurry, chance, and changes is this world, when one sits soberly down to reflect on it! To a father, who himself knows the world, the thought that he shall have sons to usher into it, must fill him with dread; but if he have daughters, the prospect in a thoughtful moment is apt to shock him.

I hope Mrs. Fordyce and the two young ladies are well. Do let me forget that they are nieces of yours, and let me say that I never saw a more interesting, sweeter pair of sisters in my life. I am the fool of my feelings and attachments. I often take up a volume of my Spenser to realise you to my imagination, [109a]. and think over the social scenes we have had together. God grant that there may be another world more congenial for honest fellows beyond this; a world where these rubs and plagues of absence, distance, misfortunes, ill-health, etc., shall no more damp hilarity and divide friendship. This I know is your throng season, but half a page will much oblige, my dear Sir, yours sincerely,
R. B.

[109a] Mr. Dunbar had made him a present of a Spenser's Poems

CXLVL.—To MRS. DUNLOP.

ELLISLAND, *25th January 1790.*

It has been owing to unremitting hurry of business that I have not written to you, Madam, long ere now. My health is greatly better, and I now begin once more to share in satisfaction and enjoyment with the rest of my fellow-creatures.

Many thanks, my much esteemed friend, for your kind letters; but why will you make me run the risk of being contemptible and mercenary in my own eyes? When I pique myself on my independent spirit, I hope it is neither poetic licence, nor poetic rant; and I am so flattered with the honour you have done me in making me your compeer in friendship and friendly correspondence, that I cannot without pain, and a degree of mortification, be reminded of the real inequality between our situations.

Most sincerely do I rejoice with you, dear Madam, in the good news of Anthony. Not only your anxiety about his fate, but my own esteem for such a noble, warm-hearted, manly young fellow, in the little I had of his acquaintance, has interested me deeply in his fortunes.

Falconer, the unfortunate author of the "Shipwreck," which you so much admire, is no more. After witnessing the dreadful catastrophe he so feelingly describes in his poem, and after weathering many hard gales of fortune, he went to the bottom with the *Aurora* frigate!

I forget what part of Scotland had the honour of giving him birth; but he was the son of obscurity and mis'ortune.[110] He was one of those daring, adventurous spirits, which Scotland, beyond any other country, is remarkable for producing. Little does the fond mother think, as she hangs delighted over the sweet little leech at her bosom, where the poor fellow may hereafter wander, or what may be his fate. I remember a stanza in an old Scottish ballad, which, notwithstanding its rude simplicity, speaks feelingly to the heart:—
Little did my mother think,

That day she cradled me,

What land I was to travel in,

Or what death I should dee!

Old Scottish songs are, you know, a favourite study and pursuit of mine, and now I am on that subject, allow me to give you two stanzas of another old simple ballad, which I am sure will please you. The catastrophe of the piece is a poor ruined female, lamenting her fate, She concludes with this pathetic wish:—
O that my father had ne'er on me smil'd;

O that my mother had ne'er to me sung!

O that my cradle had never been rock'd;

But that I had died when I was young!

O that the grave it were my bed;

My blankets were my winding sheet;

The clocks and the worms my bedfellows a';

And O sad sound as I should sleep!

I do not remember in all my reading to have met with anything more truly the language of misery than the exclamation in the last line. Misery is like love; to speak its language truly, the author must have felt it.

I am every day expecting the doctor to give your little godson the small-pox. They are *rife* in the country, and I tremble for his fate. By the way, I cannot help congratulating you on his looks and spirit. Every person who sees him, acknowledges him to be the finest, handsomest child he has ever seen. I am myself delighted with the manly swell of his little chest, and a certain miniature dignity in the carriage of his head, and the glance of his fine black eye, which promise the undaunted gallantry of an independent mind.

I thought to have sent you some rhymes, but time forbids. I promise you poetry until you are tired of it, next time I have the honour of assuring you how truly I am, etc.

R. B.

[110] He was of poor parentage, and a native of Edinburgh.

CXLVII.—To MR. PETER HILL, BOOKSELLER, EDINBURGH.

ELLISLAND, *2nd Feb. 1790.*

No! I will not say one word about apologies or excuses for not writing—I am a poor, rascally gauger, condemned to gallop at least 200 miles every week to inspect dirty ponds and yeasty barrels, and where can I find time to write to, or importance to interest anybody? The upbraidings of my conscience, nay, the upbraidings of my wife, have persecuted me on your account these two or three months past. I wish to God I was a great man, that my correspondence might throw light upon you, to let the world see what you really are: and then I would make your fortune, without putting my hand in my pocket for you, which, like all other great men, I suppose I would avoid as much as possible. What are you doing, and how are you doing? Have you lately seen any of my few friends? What has become of the borough reform, or how is the fate of my poor namesake Mademoiselle Burns decided? O man! but for thee and thy selfish appetites, and dishonest artifices, that beauteous form, and that once innocent and still ingenuous mind, might have shone conspicuous and lovely in the faithful wife, and the affectionate mother; and shall the unfortunate sacrifice to thy pleasures have no claim on thy humanity!

I saw lately, in a review, some extracts from a new poem, called the "Village Curate;" send it me. I want likewise a cheap copy of *The World*. Mr. Armstrong, the young poet, who does me the honour to mention me so kindly in his works, please give him my best thanks for the copy of his book.[111]—I shall write him, my first leisure hour. I like his poetry much, but I think his style in prose quite astonishing.

Your book came safe, and I am going to trouble you with farther commissions. I call it troubling you, because I want only books; the cheapest way, the best; so you may have to hunt for them in the evening auctions. I want Smollett's Works, for the sake of his incomparable humour. I have already *Roderick Random* and *Humphrey Clinker;—Peregrine Pickle, Launcelot Greaves,* and *Ferdinand, Count Fathom,* I still want; but, as I said, the veriest ordinary copies will serve me. I am nice only in the appearance of my poets. I forget the price of Cowper's *Poems,* but, I believe, I must have them. I saw the other day, proposals for a publication, entitled *Banks's New and Complete Christian Family Bible,* printed for C. Cooke, Paternoster Row, London. He promises at least to give in the work, I think it is three hundred and odd engravings, to which he has put the names of the first artists in London. You will know the character of the performance, as some numbers of it are published, and if it is really what it pretends to be, set me down as a subscriber, and send me the published numbers.

Let me hear from you, your first leisure minute, and trust me, you shall in future have no reason to complain of my silence. The dazzling perplexity of novelty will dissipate, and leave me to pursue my course in the quiet path of methodical routine.

R. B.

[111] John Armstrong, student in the University of Edinburgh, who had recently published a volume of Juvenile Poems.

CXLVIII.—To MR. W. NICOL.

ELLISLAND, *Feb. 9th, 1790.*

My Dear Sir,—That damn'd mare of yours is dead. I would freely have given her price to have saved her; she has vexed me beyond description. Indebted as I was to your goodness beyond what I can ever repay, I eagerly grasped at your offer to have the mare with me. That I might at least show my readiness in wishing to be grateful, I took every care of her in my power. She was never crossed for riding above half a score of times by me or in my keeping. I drew her in the plough, one of three, for one poor week. I refused fifty-five shillings for her, which was the highest bode I could squeeze for her. I fed her up and had her in fine order for Dumfries fair, when, four or five days before the fair, she was seized with an unaccountable disorder in the sinews, or somewhere in the bones of the neck—with a weakness or total want of power in her fillets; and, in short, the whole vertebrae of her spine seemed to be diseased and unhinged, and in eight and forty hours, in spite of the two best farriers in the country, she died and be damn'd to her! The farriers said that she had been quite strained in the fillets beyond cure before you had bought her; and that the poor devil, though she might keep a little flesh, had been jaded and quite worn out with fatigue and oppression. While she was with me she was under my own eye, and I assure you, my much valued friend, everything was done for her that could be done; and the accident has vexed me to the heart. In fact, I could not pluck up spirits to write to you, on account of the unfortunate business.

There is little new in this country. Our theatrical company, of which you must have heard, leave us this week. Their merit and character are indeed very great, both on the stage and in private life; not a worthless creature among them; and their encouragement has been accordingly. Their usual run is from eighteen to twenty-five pounds a night; seldom less than the one, and the house will hold no more than the other. There have been repeated instances of sending away six, and eight, and ten pounds a night for want of room. A new theatre is to be built by subscription; the first stone is to be laid on Friday first to come. Three hundred guineas have been raised by thirty subscribers, and thirty more might have been got if wanted. The manager, Mr. Sutherland, was introduced to me by a friend from Ayr; and a worthier or cleverer fellow I have rarely met with. Some of our clergy have slipt in by stealth now and then; but they have got up a farce of their own. You must have heard how the Rev. Mr. Lawson of Kirkmahoe, seconded by the Rev. Mr. Kirkpatrick of Dunscore, and the rest of that faction, have accused, in formal process, the unfortunate and Rev. Mr. Heron of Kirkgunzeon, that in ordaining Mr. Nielson to the cure of souls in Kirkbean, he, the said Heron, feloniously and treasonably bound the said Nielson to the confession of faith, *so far as it was agreeable to reason and the word of God!*

Mrs. B. begs to be remembered most gratefully to you. Little Bobby and Frank are charmingly well and healthy. I am jaded to death with fatigue. For these two or three months, on an average, I have not ridden less than two hundred miles per week. I have done little in the poetic way. I have given Mr. Sutherland two Prologues, one of which was delivered last week. I have likewise strung four or five barbarous stanzas, to the tune of Chevy Chase, by way of Elegy on your poor unfortunate mare, beginning (the name she got here was Peg Nicholson),—

Peg Nicholson was a good bay mare,
As ever trod on airn;
But now she's floating down the Nith,
And past the mouth o' Cairn.

My best compliments to Mrs. Nicol, and little Neddy, and all the family; I hope Ned is a good scholar, and will come out to gather nuts and apples with me next harvest.

R. B.

CXLIX.—To MR. CUNNINGHAM, WRITER, EDINBURGH.

ELLISLAND, *13th February 1790*.

I beg your pardon, my dear and much valued friend, for writing to you on this very unfashionable, unsightly sheet—

My poverty but not my will consents.

But to make amends, since of modish post I have none, except one poor widowed half-sheet of gilt, which lies in my drawer, among my plebeian foolscap pages, like the widow of a man of fashion, whom that unpolite scoundrel, Necessity, has driven from Burgundy and Pineapple to a dish of Bohea, with the scandal-bearing help-mate of a village-priest; or a glass of whisky-toddy with a ruby-nosed yokefellow of a foot-padding exciseman—I make a vow to inclose this sheet-full of epistolary fragments in that my only scrap of gilt paper.

I am, indeed, your unworthy debtor for three friendly letters. I ought to have written to you long ere now, but it is a literal fact, I have scarcely a spare moment. It is not that I *will not* write to you: Miss Burnet is not more dear to her guardian angel, nor his grace the Duke of Queensberry to the powers of darkness, than my friend Cunningham to me. It is not that I cannot write to you; should you doubt it, take the following fragment, which was intended for you some time ago, and be convinced that I can antithesize sentiment, and circumvolute periods, as well as any coiner of phrase in the regions of philology.

December 1789.

My Dear Cunningham,—Where are you? And what are you doing? Can you be that son of levity, who takes up a friendship as he takes up a fashion; or are you, like some other of the worthiest fellows in the world, the victim of indolence, laden with fetters of ever-increasing weight?

What strange beings we are! Since we have a portion of conscious existence, equally capable of enjoying pleasure, happiness, and rapture, or of suffering pain, wretchedness, and misery, it is surely worthy of an inquiry, whether there be not such a thing as a science of life; whether method, economy, and fertility of expedients, be not applicable to enjoyment; and whether there be not a want of dexterity in pleasure, which renders our little scantling of happiness still less; and a profuseness, an intoxication in bliss, which leads to satiety, disgust, and self-abhorrence. There is not a doubt but that health, talents, character, decent competency, respectable friends, are real substantial blessings; and yet do we not daily see those who enjoy many or all of these good things, contrive, notwithstanding, to be as unhappy as others to whose lot few of them have fallen? I believe one great source of this mistake or misconduct is owing to a certain stimulus, with us called ambition, which goads us up the hill of life, not as we ascend other eminences; for the laudable curiosity of viewing an extended landscape, but rather for the dishonest pride of looking down on others of our fellow-creatures, seemingly diminutive in humbler stations, etc., etc.

Sunday, 14th February 1790.

God help me! I am now obliged to join

Night to day, and Sunday to the week.

If there be any truth in the orthodox faith of these churches, I am damn'd past redemption, and what is worse, damn'd to all eternity. I am deeply read in Boston's *Four-fold State*, Marshal *On Sanctification*, Guthrie's *Trial of a Saving Interest*, etc., but "there is no balm in Gilead, there is no physician there," for me; so I shall e'en turn Arminian, and trust to "Sincere though imperfect obedience."

Tuesday, 16th.

Luckily for me, I was prevented from the discussion of the knotty point at which I had just made a full stop. All my fears and cares are of this world; if there is another, an honest man has nothing to fear from it. I hate a man that wishes to be a deist; but I fear, every fair, unprejudiced inquirer must in some degree be a sceptic. It is not that there are any very staggering arguments against the immortality of man; but, like electricity, phlogiston, etc., the subject is so involved in darkness, that we want data to go upon. One thing frightens me much: that we are to live for ever seems *too good news to be true*. That we are to enter into a new scene of existence, where, exempt from want and pain, we shall enjoy ourselves and our friends without satiety or separation—how much should I be indebted to any one who could fully assure me that this was certain!

My time is once more expired. I will write to Mr. Cleghorn soon. God bless him and all his concerns! And may all the powers that preside over conviviality and friendship, be present with all their kindest influence, when the bearer of this, Mr. Syme, and you meet! I wish I could also make one.

Finally, brethren, farewell! Whatsoever things are lovely, whatsoever things are gentle, whatsoever things are charitable, whatsoever things are kind, think on these things, and think on

R. B.

CL.—To MR. HILL, BOOKSELLER, EDINBURGH.
ELLISLAND, *2nd March 1790.*

At a late meeting of the Monkland Friendly Society, it was resolved to augment their library by the following books, which you are to send us as soon as possible:—*The Mirror, The Lounger, Man of Feeling, Man of the World,* (these, for my own sake, I wish to have by the first carrier), Knox's *History of the Reformation,* Rae's *History of the Rebellion in 1715,* any good History of the Rebellion in 1745, *A Display of the Secession Act and Testimony,* by Mr. Gib, Hervey's *Meditations,* Beveridge's *Thoughts,* and another copy of Watson's *Body of Divinity.*

I wrote to Mr. A. Masterton three or four months ago, to pay some money he owed me into your hands, and lately I wrote to you to the same purpose, but I have heard from neither one nor other of you.

In addition to the books I commissioned in my last, I want very much, an Index to the Excise Laws, or an Abridgment of all the statutes now in force, relative to the Excise, by Jellinger Symons; I want three copies of this book: if it is now to be had, cheap or dear, get it for me. An honest country neighbour of mine wants too a Family Bible, the larger the better, but second-handed, for he does not choose to give above ten shillings for the book. I want likewise for myself, as you can pick them up, second-handed or cheap, copies of Otway's Dramatic Works, Ben Jonson's, Dryden's, Congreve's, Wycherley's, Vanbrugh's, Gibber's, or any Dramatic Works of the more modern Macklin, Garrick, Foote, Colman, or Sheridan. A good copy too of Moliere, in French, I much want. Any other good dramatic authors in that language I want also; but comic authors chiefly, though I should wish to have Racine, Corneille, and Voltaire too. I am in no hurry for all, or any of these, but if you accidentally meet with them very-cheap, get them for me.

And now, to quit the dry walk of business, how do you do, my dear friend? and how is Mrs. Hill? I trust, if now and then not so *elegantly* handsome, at least as amiable, and sings as divinely as ever. My good wife too has a charming "wood-note wild;" now could we four get together, etc.

I am out of all patience with this vile world, for one thing. Mankind are by nature benevolent creatures, except in a few scoundrelly instances. I do not think that avarice of the good things we chance to have, is born with us; but we are placed here amid so much nakedness, and hunger, and poverty, and want, that we are under a cursed necessity of studying selfishness, in order that we may exist! Still there are, in every age, a few souls that all the wants and woes of life cannot debase to selfishness, or even to the necessary alloy of caution and prudence. If ever I am in danger of vanity, it is when I contemplate myself on this side of my disposition and character. God knows I am no saint; I have a whole host of follies and sins to answer for; but if I could—and I believe I do it as far as I can—I would wipe away all tears from all eyes. Adieu!

R. B.

CLI.—To MRS. DUNLOP.
ELLISLAND, *10th April 1790.*

I have just now, my ever honoured friend, enjoyed a very high luxury, in reading a paper of the *Lounger.* You know my national prejudices. I had often read and admired the *Spectator, Adventurer, Rambler,* and *World,* but still with a certain regret, that they were so

thoroughly and entirely English. Alas! have I often said to myself, what are all the boasted advantages which my country reaps from the Union, that can counterbalance the annihilation of her independence, and even her very name? I often repeat that couplet of my favourite poet, Goldsmith—
States of native liberty possest,
Tho' very poor, may yet be very blest.

Nothing can reconcile me to the common terms, "English ambassador," "English court," etc., and I am out of all patience to see that equivocal character, Hastings, impeached by "the Commons of England." Tell me, my friend, is this weak prejudice? I believe in my conscience such ideas as "my country; her independence; her honour; the illustrious names that mark the history of my native land," etc.—I believe these, among your *men of the world*, men who, in fact, guide for the most part and govern our world, are looked on as so many modifications of wrong-headedness. They know the use of bawling out such terms, to rouse or lead THE RABBLE; but for their own private use, with almost all the *able statesmen* that ever existed, or now exist, when they talk of right and wrong they only mean proper and improper; and their measure of conduct is, not what they ought, but what they dare. For the truth of this I shall not ransack the history of nations, but appeal to one of the ablest judges of men that ever lived—the celebrated Earl of Chesterfield. In fact, a man who could thoroughly control his vices whenever they interfered with his interests, and who could completely put on the appearance of every virtue as often as it suited his purposes, is, on the Stanhopian plan, the *perfect man*; a man to lead nations. But are great abilities, complete without a flaw, and polished without a blemish, the standard of human excellence? This is certainly the staunch opinion of *men of the world*; but I call on honour, virtue, and worth, to give the Stygian doctrine a loud negative! However, this must be allowed, that, if you abstract from man the idea of an existence beyond the grave, *then*, the true measure of human conduct is, *proper* and *improper*: virtue and vice, as dispositions of the heart, are, in that case, of scarcely the same import and value to the world at large, as harmony and discord in the modifications of sound; and a delicate sense of honour, like a nice ear for music, though it may sometimes give the possessor an ecstacy unknown to the coarser organs of the herd, yet, considering the harsh gratings, and inharmonic jars, in this ill-tuned state of being, it is odds but the individual would be as happy, and certainly would be as much respected by the true judges of society as it would then stand, without either a good ear or a good heart.

You must know I have just met with the *Mirror* and *Lounger* for the first time, and I am quite in raptures with them; I should be glad to have your opinion of some of the papers. The one I have just read, *Lounger*, No. 61, has cost me more honest tears than anything I have read for a long time. Mackenzie has been called the Addison of the Scots, and in my opinion, Addison would not be hurt at the comparison. If he has not Addison's exquisite humour, he as certainly outdoes him in the tender and the pathetic. His *Man of Feeling* (but I am not counsel learned in the laws of criticism) I estimate as the first performance in its kind I ever saw. From what book, moral or even pious, will the susceptible young mind receive impressions more congenial to humanity and kindness, generosity and benevolence; in short, more of all that ennobles the soul to herself, or endears her to others—than from the simple affecting tale of poor Harley?

Still, with all my admiration of Mackenzie's writings, I do not know if they are the fittest reading for a young man who is about to set out, as the phrase is, to make his way into life. Do you not think, Madam, that among the few favoured of Heaven in the structure of their minds (for such there certainly are) there may be a purity, a tenderness, a dignity, an elegance of soul, which are of no use, nay, in some degree, absolutely disqualifying for the truly important business of making a man's way into life? If I am not much mistaken, my gallant young friend, Antony, is very much under these disqualifications; and for the young females of a family I could mention, well may they excite parental solicitude; for I, a common acquaintance, or as my vanity will have it, an humble friend, have often trembled for a turn of mind which may render them eminently happy—or peculiarly miserable!

I have been manufacturing some verses lately; but as I have got the most hurried season of Excise business over, I hope to have more leisure to transcribe any thing that may show how much I have the honour to be, Madam, yours, etc.

R. B.

CLII.—To DR. JOHN MOORE, LONDON.

DUMFRIES, *Excise-Office, 14th July 1790.*

Sir,—Coming into town this morning to attend my duty in this office, it being collection-day, I met with a gentleman who tells me he is on his way to London; so I take the opportunity of writing to you, as franking is at present under a temporary death. I shall have some snatches of leisure through the day, amid our horrid business and bustle, and I shall improve them as well as I can; but let my letter be as stupid as..., as miscellaneous as a newspaper, as short as a hungry grace-before-meat, or as long as a law-paper in the Douglas cause; as ill spelt as country John's billet-doux, or as unsightly a scrawl as Betty Byre-Mucker's answer to it; I hope, considering circumstances, you will forgive it; and as it will put you to no expense of postage, I shall have the less reflection about it.

I am sadly ungrateful in not returning you my thanks for your most valuable present, *Zeluco.* In fact, you are in some degree blameable for my neglect. You were pleased to express a wish for my opinion of the work, which so flattered me, that nothing less would serve my over-weening fancy, than a formal criticism on the book. In fact, I have gravely planned a comparative view of you, Fielding, Richardson, and Smollett, in your different qualities and merits as novel-writers. This, I own, betrays my ridiculous vanity, and I may probably never bring the business to bear; but I am fond of the spirit young Elihu shows in the book of Job—"And I said, I will also declare my opinion." I have quite disfigured my copy of the book with my annotations. I never take it up without at the same time taking my pencil, and marking with asterisms, parentheses, etc., wherever I meet with an original thought, a nervous remark on life and manners, a remarkably well-turned period, or a character sketched with uncommon precision.

Though I should hardly think of fairly writing out my "Comparative View," I shall certainly trouble you with my remarks, such as they are.

I have just received from my gentleman that horrid summons in the Book of Revelation—"that time shall be no more."

The little collection of sonnets have some charming poetry in them. If *indeed* I am indebted to the fair author for the book, and not, as I rather suspect, to a celebrated author of the other sex, I should certainly have written to the lady, with my grateful acknowledgments, and my own idea of the comparative excellence of her pieces.[112] I would do this last, not from any vanity of thinking that my remarks could be of much consequence to Mrs. Smith, but merely from my own feelings as an author, doing as I would be done by.
R. B.

[112] Sonnets of Charlotte Smith.

CLIII.—To MR. MURDOCH,[113] TEACHER OF FRENCH, LONDON.

ELLISLAND, *July 16th,* 1790.

My Dear Sir,—I received a letter from you a long time ago, but unfortunately, as it was in the time of my peregrinations and journeyings through Scotland, I mislaid or lost it, and by consequence your direction along with it. Luckily my good star brought me acquainted with Mr. Kennedy, who, I understand, is an acquaintance of yours: and by his means and mediation I hope to replace that link, which my unfortunate negligence had so unluckily broke, in the chain of our correspondence. I was the more vexed at the vile accident, as my brother William, a journeyman saddler, has been for some time in London; and wished above all things for your direction, that he might have paid his respects to his father's friend.

His last address he sent me was, "Wm. Burns, at Mr. Barber's, saddler, No. 181 Strand." I writ him by Mr. Kennedy, but neglected to ask him for your address; so, if you find a spare half minute, please let my brother know by a card where and when he will find you, and the poor fellow will joyfully wait on you, as one of the few surviving friends of the man whose name, and Christian name too, he has the honour to bear.

The next letter I write you shall be a long one. I have much to tell you of "hair-breadth 'scapes in th' imminent deadly breach," with all the eventful history of a life, the early years of which owed so much to your kind tutorage; but this at an hour of leisure. My kindest compliments to Mrs. Murdoch and family.—I am ever, my dear Sir, your obliged friend,

R. B.

|113| He had been Burns's schoolmaster at Mount Oliphant.

CLIV.—To MR. CUNNINGHAM.

ELLISLAND, *8th August 1790.*

Forgive me, my once dear, and ever dear friend, my seeming negligence. You cannot sit down and fancy the busy life I lead.

I laid down my goose feather to beat my brains for an apt simile, and had some thoughts of a country grannum at a family christening; a bride on the market-day before her marriage; or a tavern-keeper at an election dinner; but the resemblance that hits my fancy best is, that blackguard miscreant, Satan, who roams about like a roaring lion, seeking, searching, whom he may devour. However, tossed about as I am, if I choose (and who would not choose) to bind down with the crampets of attention the brazen foundation of integrity, I may rear up the superstructure of Independence, and from its daring turrets bid defiance to the storms of fate. And is not this a "consummation devoutly to be wished?"

Thy spirit, Independence, let me share;
Lord of the lion-heart, and eagle-eye!
Thy steps I follow with my bosom bare,
Nor heed the storm that howls along the sky!

Are not these noble verses? They are the introduction of Smollett's Ode to Independence: if you have not seen the poem, I will send it to you. How wretched is the man that hangs on by the favours of the great! To shrink from every dignity of man, at the approach of a lordly piece of self-consequence, who, amid all his tinsel glitter, and stately hauteur, is but a creature formed as thou art—and perhaps not so well formed as thou art—came into the world a puling infant as thou didst, and must go out of it as all men must, a naked corse...

R. B.

CLV.—To MR. CRAUFORD TAIT,|114| W.S., EDINBURGH.

ELLISLAND, 15th *October* 1790.

Dear Sir,—Allow me to introduce to your acquaintance the bearer, Mr. Wm. Duncan, a friend of mine, whom I have long known and long loved. His father, whose only son he is, has a decent little property in Ayrshire, and has bred the young man to the law, in which department he comes up an adventurer to your good town. I shall give you my friend's character in two words: as to his head, he has talents enough, and more than enough for common life; as to his heart, when nature had kneaded the kindly clay that composes it, she said, "I can no more."

You, my good Sir, were born under kinder stars; but your fraternal sympathy, I well know, can enter into the feelings of the young man who goes into life with the laudable ambition to do something, and to be something among his fellow-creatures; but whom the consciousness of friendless obscurity presses to the earth and wounds to the soul!

Even the fairest of his virtues are against him. That independent spirit, and that ingenuous modesty, qualities inseparable from a noble mind, are, with the million, circumstances not a little disqualifying. What pleasure is in the power of the fortunate and the happy, by their notice and patronage, to brighten the countenance and glad the heart of such depressed youth! I am not so angry with mankind for their deaf economy of the purse—the goods of this world cannot be divided without being lessened—but why be a niggard of that which bestows bliss on a fellow-creature, yet takes nothing from our own means of enjoyment? We wrap ourselves up in the cloak of our own better fortune, and turn

123

away our eyes, lest the wants and woes of our brother-mortals should disturb the selfish apathy of our souls!

I am the worst hand in the world at asking a favour. That indirect address, that insinuating implication, which, without any positive request, plainly expresses your wish, is a talent not to be acquired at a plough-tail. Tell me, then, for you can, in what periphrasis of language, in what circumvolution of phrase, I shall envelope, yet not conceal, the plain story. "My dear Mr, Tait, my friend, Mr. Duncan, whom I have the pleasure of introducing to you, is a young lad of your own profession, and a gentleman of much modesty and great worth. Perhaps it may be in your power to assist him in the, to him, important consideration of getting a place; but, at all events, your notice and acquaintance will be a very great acquisition to him; and I dare pledge myself that he will never disgrace your favour."

You may possibly be surprised, Sir, at such a letter from me; 'tis, I own, in the usual way of calculating these matters, more than our acquaintance entitles me to; but my answer is short: Of all the men at your time of life whom I knew in Edinburgh, you are the most accessible on the side on which I have assailed you. You are very much altered indeed from what you were when I knew you, if generosity point the path you will not tread, or humanity call to you in vain.

As to myself, a being to whose interest I believe you are still a well-wisher; I am here, breathing at all times, thinking sometimes, and rhyming now and then. Every situation has its share of the cares and pains of life, and my situation I am persuaded has a full ordinary allowance of its pleasures and enjoyments.

My best compliments to your father and Miss Tait. If you have an opportunity, please remember me in the solemn league and covenant of friendship to Mrs. Lewis Hay.[115] I am a wretch for not writing her; but I am so hackneyed with self-accusation in that way, that my conscience lies in my bosom with scarce the sensibility of an oyster in its shell. Where is Lady M'Kenzie? wherever she is, God bless her! I likewise beg leave to trouble you with compliments to Mr. Wm. Hamilton; Mrs. Hamilton and family; and Mrs. Chalmers, when you are in that country. Should you meet with Miss Nimmo, please remember me kindly to her.

R. B.

[114] Son of Mr. Tait of Harviestoun, where Burns was a happy guest in the Autumn of 1787. He was also father of the late Archbishop Tait.

[115] Miss Peggy Chalmers.

CLVL.—To MRS. DUNLOP.

ELLISLAND, *November* 1790.

"As cold waters to a thirsty soul, so is good news from a far country."

Fate has long owed me a letter of good news from you, in return for the many tidings of sorrow which I have received. In this instance I most cordially obey the apostle—"Rejoice with them that do rejoice;" for me, to sing for joy, is no new thing; but to preach for joy, as I have done in the commencement of this epistle, is a pitch of extravagant rapture to which I never rose before.

I read your letter—I literally jumped for joy. How could such a mercurial creature as a poet lumpishly keep his seat on the receipt of the best news from his best friend. I seized my gilt-headed Wangee rod, an instrument indispensably necessary in the moment of inspiration and rapture; and stride, stride-quick and quicker-out skipt I among the broomy banks of Nith to muse over my joy by retail. To keep within the bounds of prose was impossible. Mrs. Little's is a more elegant, but not a more sincere compliment to the sweet little fellow, than I, extempore almost, poured out to him in the following verses:—

Sweet flow'ret, pledge o' meikle love, etc.[116]

I am much flattered by your approbation of my "Tam o' Shanter," which you express in your former letter; though, by-the-bye, you load me in that said letter with accusations heavy and many; to all which I plead, *not guilty!* Your book is, I hear, on the road to reach me. As to printing of poetry, when you prepare it for the press, you have only to spell it right, and place the capital letters properly: as to the punctuation, the printers do that themselves.

I have a copy of "Tam o' Shanter" ready to send you by the first opportunity: it is too heavy to send by post.

I heard of Mr. Corbet lately. [116a] He, in consequence of your recommendation, is most zealous to serve me. Please favour me soon with an account of your good folks; if Mrs. H. is recovering, and the young gentleman doing well.

R. B.

[116] See Poems.

[116a] A Supervisor of Excise.

CLVIL.—To MR. WILLIAM DUNBAR, W.S.

ELLISLAND, 17*th January* 1791.

I am not gone to Elysium, most noble Colonel,[117] but am still here in this sublunary world, serving my God by propagating His image, and honouring my king by begetting him loyal subjects.

Many happy returns of the season await my friend. May the thorns of care never beset his path! May peace be an inmate of his bosom, and rapture a frequent visitor of his soul! May the blood-hounds of misfortune never track his steps, nor the screech-owl of sorrow alarm his dwelling! May enjoyment tell thy hours, and pleasure number thy days, thou friend of the Bard! "Blessed be he that blesseth thee, and cursed be he that curseth thee!!!"

As a farther proof that I am still in the land of existence, I send you a poem, the latest I have composed. I have a particular reason for wishing you only to show it to select friends, should you think it worthy a friend's perusal: but if at your first leisure hour you will favour me with your opinion of, and strictures on the performance, it will be an additional obligation on, dear Sir, your deeply indebted humble servant,

R. B.

[117] Colonel of Volunteers.

CLVIIL.—To MR. PETER HILL.

ELLISLAND, 17*th January* 1791.

Take these two guineas, and place them over against that damn'd account of yours which has gagged my mouth these five or six months. I can as little write good things as apologies to the man I owe money to. O the supreme misery of making three guineas do the business of five! Not all the labours of Hercules not all the Hebrews' three centuries of Egyptian bondage, were such an insuperable business, such an infernal task! Poverty, thou half-sister of death, thou cousin-german of hell! where shall I find force or execration equal to the amplitude of thy demerits? Oppressed by thee, the venerable ancient, grown hoary in the practice of every virtue, laden with years and wretchedness, implores a little, little aid to support his existence, from a stony-hearted son of Mammon, whose sun of prosperity never knew a cloud; and is by him denied and insulted. Oppressed by thee, the man of sentiment, whose heart glows with independence, and melts with sensibility, inly pines under the neglect, or writhes in bitterness of soul under the contamely of arrogant unfeeling wealth. Oppressed by thee, the son of genius, whose ill-starred ambition plants him at the tables of the fashionable and polite, must see in suffering silence his remark neglected and his person despised, while shallow greatness, in his idiot attempts at wit, shall meet with countenance and applause. Nor is it only the family of worth that have reason to complain of thee; the children of folly and vice, though in common with thee the offspring of evil, smart equally under thy rod. Owing to thee, the man of unfortunate disposition and neglected education, is condemned as a fool for his dissipation, despised and shunned as a needy wretch, when his follies as usual bring him to want; and when his unprincipled necessities drive him to dishonest practices, he is abhorred as a miscreant, and perishes by the justice of his country. But far otherwise is the lot of the man of family and fortune. *His* early follies and extravagance are spirit and fire; *his* consequent wants are the embarrassments of an honest fellow; and when, to remedy the matter, he has gained a legal commission to plunder distant provinces, or massacre peaceful nations, he returns, perhaps, laden with the spoils of rapine and murder; lives wicked and respected; and dies a scoundrel and a lord. Nay, worst of all, alas for helpless woman!...

Well! divines may say of it what they please; but execration is to the mind, what phlebotomy is to the body; the overloaded sluices of both are wonderfully relieved by their respective evacuations.
R. B.

CLIX.—To DR. MOORE.
ELLISLAND, 28*th January* 1791.

I do not know, Sir, whether you are a subscriber to Grose's *Antiquities of Scotland*. If you are, the inclosed poem will not be altogether new to you. Captain Grose did me the favour to send me a dozen copies of the proof sheet, of which this is one. Should you have read the piece before, still this will answer the principal end I have in view: it will give me another opportunity of thanking you for all your goodness to the rustic bard; and also of showing you, that the abilities you have been pleased to commend and patronise, are still employed in the way you wish.

The *Elegy on Captain Henderson* is a tribute to the memory of the man I loved much. Poets have in this the same advantage as Roman Catholics; they can be of service to their friends after they have passed that bourne where all other kindness ceases to be of avail. Whether, after all, either the one or the other be of any real service to the dead, is, I fear, very problematical; but I am sure they are highly gratifying to the living: and as a very orthodox text, I forget where in Scripture, says, "whatsoever is not of faith is sin;" so say I, whatsoever is not detrimental to society, and is of positive enjoyment, is of God, the giver of all good things, and ought to be received and enjoyed by His creatures with thankful delight. As almost all my religious tenets originate from my heart, I am wonderfully pleased with the idea, that I can still keep up a tender intercourse with the dearly beloved friend, or still more dearly beloved mistress, who is gone to the world of spirits.

The ballad on Queen Mary was begun while I was busy with *Percy's Reliques of English Poetry*. By the way, how much is every honest heart, which has a tincture of Caledonian prejudice, obliged to you for your glorious story of Buchanan and Targe! 'Twas an unequivocal proof of your loyal gallantry of soul giving Targe the victory. I should have been mortified to the ground if you had not.

I have just read over, once more of many times, your *Zeluco*. I marked with my pencil as I went along, every passage that pleased me above the rest; and one or two, which, with humble deference, I am disposed to think unequal to the merits of the book. I have sometimes thought to transcribe these marked passages, or at least so much of them as to point where they are, and send them to you. Original strokes that strongly depict the human heart, is your and Fielding's province, beyond any other novelist I have ever perused. Richardson, indeed, might, perhaps, be excepted; but unhappily, his *dramatis personæ* are beings of another world; and however they may captivate the unexperienced romantic fancy of a boy or a girl, they will ever, in proportion as we have made human nature our study, dissatisfy our riper years.

As to my private concerns, I am going on, a mighty tax-gatherer before the Lord, and have lately had the interest to get myself ranked on the list of excise as a supervisor. T am not yet employed as such, but in a few years I shall fall into the file of supervisorship by seniority. I have had an immense loss in the death of the Earl of Glencairn—the patron from whom all my fame and fortune took its rise. Independent of my grateful attachment to him, which was indeed so strong that it pervaded my very soul, and was entwined with the thread of my existence; so soon as the prince's friends had got in, (and every dog, you know, has his day) my getting forward in the excise would have been an easier business than otherwise it will be. Though this was a consummation devoutly to be wished, yet, thank Heaven, I can live and rhyme as I am; and as to my boys, poor little fellows! if I cannot place them on as high an elevation in life as I could wish, I shall, if I am favoured so much of the Disposer of events as to see that period, fix them on as broad and independent a basis as possible. Among the many wise adages which have been treasured up by our Scottish ancestors, this is one of the best—*Better be the head o' the commonalty than the tail o' the gentry*.

But I am got on a subject which, however interesting to me, is of no manner of consequence to you; so I shall give you a short poem on the other page, and close this with assuring you how sincerely I have the honour to be, yours, etc.,

R. B.

Written on the blank leaf of a book which I presented to a very young lady, whom I had formerly characterised under the denomination of *The Rose Bud*.[118]

[118] See Poems—-"Lines to Miss Cruikshank."

CLX.—To MRS. DUNLOP.

ELLISLAND, *7th Feb. 1791.*

When I tell you, Madam, that by a fall, not from my horse, but with my horse, I have been a cripple some time, and that this is the first day my arm and hand have been able to serve me in writing,—you will allow that it is too good an apology for my seemingly ungrateful silence. I am now getting better, and am able to rhyme a little, which implies some tolerable ease; as I cannot think that the most poetic genius is able to compose on the rack.

I do not remember if ever I mentioned to you my having an idea of composing an elegy on the late Miss Burnet, of Monboddo. I had the honour of being pretty well acquainted with her, and have seldom felt so much at the loss of an acquaintance, as when I heard that so amiable and accomplished a piece of God's work was no more. I have, as yet, gone no farther than the following fragment, of which please let me have your opinion. You know that elegy is a subject so much exhausted, that any new idea on the business is not to be expected: 'tis well if we can place an old idea in a new light. How far I have succeeded as to this last, you will judge from what follows. I have proceeded no further.

Your kind letter, with your kind *remembrance* of your godson, came safe. This last, Madam, is scarcely what my pride can bear. As to the little fellow,[118a] he is, partiality apart, the finest boy I have of a long time seen. He is now seventeen months old, has the small-pox and measles over, has cut several teeth, and never had a grain of doctor's drugs in his bowels.

I am truly happy to hear that the "little floweret" is blooming so fresh and fair, and that the "mother plant" is rather recovering her drooping head. Soon and well may her "cruel wounds" be healed! I have written thus far with a good deal of difficulty. When I get a little abler you shall hear farther from, Madam, yours,

R. B.

[118a] The infant was Francis Wallace, the Poet's second son.

CLXI.—To THE REV. ARCH. ALISON.

ELLISLAND, *near Dumfries 14th Feb. 1791.*

Sir,—You must by this time have set me down as one of the most ungrateful of men. You did me the honour to present me with a book, which does honour to science and the intellectual powers of man, and I have not even so much as acknowledged the receipt of it. The fact is, you yourself are to blame for it. Flattered as I was by your telling me that you wished to have my opinion of the work, the old spiritual enemy of mankind, who knows well that vanity is one of the sins that most easily beset me, put it into my head to ponder over the performance with the look-out of a critic, and to draw up forsooth a deep learned digest of strictures on a composition, of which, in fact, until I read the book, I did not even know the first principles. I own, Sir, that at first glance, several of your propositions startled me as paradoxical. That the martial clangour of a trumpet had something in it vastly more grand, heroic, and sublime, than the twingle twangle of a Jews-harp; that the delicate flexure of a rose-twig, when the half-blown flower is heavy with the tears of the dawn, was infinitely more beautiful and elegant than the upright stub of a burdock; and that from something innate and independent of all associations of ideas;-these I had set down as irrefragable, orthodox truths, until perusing your book shook my faith. In short, Sir, except Euclid's Elements of Geometry, which I made a shift to unravel by my father's fire-side, in the winter evening of the first season I held the plough, I never read a book which gave me such a quantum of information, and added so much to my stock of ideas, as your *Essays on the Principles of Taste*. One thing, Sir, you must forgive my mentioning as an uncommon merit in the work, I mean the language. To clothe abstract philosophy in elegance of style, sounds something like a contradiction in terms; but you have convinced me that they are quite compatible.

I inclose you some poetic bagatelles of my late composition. The one in print is my first essay in the way of telling a tale.—I am, Sir, etc.

R. B.

CLXII.—TO THE REV. G. BAIRD.

ELLISLAND, 1791.

Reverend Sir,—Why did you, my dear Sir, write to me in such a hesitating style on the business of poor Bruce?[119] Don't I know, and have I not felt, the many ills, the peculiar ills, that poetic flesh is heir to? You shall have your choice of all the unpublished poems[120] I have; and had your letter had my direction so as to have reached me sooner (it only came to my hand this moment) I should have directly put you out of suspense on the subject. I only ask, that some prefatory advertisement in the book, as well as the subscription bills, may bear, that the publication is solely for the benefit of Bruce's mother. I would not put it in the power of ignorance to surmise, or malice to insinuate, that I clubbed a share in the work from mercenary motives. Nor need you give me credit for any remarkable generosity in my part of the business. I have such a host of peccadilloes, failings, follies, and backslidings (anybody but myself might perhaps give some of them a worse appellation), that by way of some balance, however trifling, in the account, I am fain to do any good that occurs in my very limited power to a fellow-creature, just for the selfish purpose of clearing a little the vista of retrospection.

R. B.

[119] Michael Bruce, a young poet of Kinross-Shire.
[120] *Tam o' Shanter* included! It was refused!!

CLXIII.—TO MR. CUNNINGHAM, WRITER, EDINBURGH.

ELLISLAND, 2*th March* 1791.

If the foregoing piece be worth your strictures, let me have them. For my own part, a thing I have just composed always appears through a double portion of that partial medium in which an author will ever view his own works. I believe, in general, novelty has something in it that inebriates the fancy, and not unfrequently dissipates and fumes away like other intoxication, and leaves the poor patient, as usual, with an aching heart. A striking instance of this might be adduced, in the revolution of many a hymeneal honeymoon. But lest I sink into stupid prose, and so sacrilegiously intrude on the office of my parish priest, I shall fill up the page in my own way, and give you another song of my late composition, which will appear perhaps in Johnson's work, as well as the former.

You must know a beautiful Jacobite air, *There'll never be peace till Jamie comes hame*. When political combustion ceases to be the object of princes and patriots, it then, you know, becomes the lawful prey of historians and poets.

By yon castle wa' at the close of the day,
I heard a man sing, tho' his head it was grey;
And as he was singing, the tears fast down came—
There'll never be peace till Jamie comes hame.

If you like the air, and if the stanzas hit your fancy, you cannot imagine, my dear friend, how much you would oblige me, if, by the charms of your delightful voice, you would give my honest effusion, to "the memory of joys that are past," to the few friends whom you indulge in that pleasure. But I have scribbled on till I hear the clock has intimated the near approach of

That hour, o' night's black arch the key-stane.

So good night to you! Sound be your sleep, and delectable your dreams! Apropos, how do you like this thought in a ballad I have just now on the tapis?—

I look to the west when I gae to my rest,
That happy my dreams and my slumbers may be;
Far, far in the west is he I lo'e best,
The lad that is dear to my babie and me!

Good night once more, and God bless you!
    R. B.

CLXIV.—TO MRS. DUNLOP.
ELLISLAND, 11*th April* 1791.

I am once more able, my honoured friend, to return you, with my own hand, thanks for the many instances of your friendship, and particularly for your kind anxiety in this last disaster that my evil genius had in store for me. However, life is chequered—joy and sorrow—for on Saturday morning last, Mrs. Burns made me a present of a fine boy; rather stouter, but not so handsome as your godson was at his time of life. Indeed, I look on your little namesake to be my *chef d'oeuvre* in that species of manufacture, as I look on "Tam o' Shanter" to be my standard performance in the poetical line. 'Tis true, both the one and the other discover a spice of roguish waggery, that might perhaps be as well spared; but then they also show, in my opinion, a force of genius, and a finishing polish, that I despair of ever excelling. Mrs. Burns is getting stout again, and laid as lustily about her to-day at breakfast, as a reaper from the corn-ridge. That is the peculiar privilege and blessing of our hale sprightly damsels, that are bred among the *hay* and *heather*. We cannot hope for that highly polished mind, that charming delicacy of soul, which is found among the female world in the more elevated stations of life, and which is certainly by far the most bewitching charm in the famous cestus of Venus, It is indeed such an inestimable treasure, that where it can be had in its native heavenly purity, unstained by some one or other of the many shades of affectation, and unalloyed by some one or other of the many species of caprice, I declare to Heaven I should think it cheaply purchased at the expense of every other earthly good! But as this angelic creature is, I am afraid, extremely rare in any station and rank of life, and totally denied to such an humble one as mine, we meaner mortals must put up with the next rank of female excellence. As fine a figure and face we can produce as any rank of life whatever; rustic, native grace; unaffected modesty and unsullied purity; nature's mother-wit and the rudiments of taste, a simplicity of soul, unsuspicious of, because unacquainted with, the crooked ways of a selfish, interested, disingenuous world; and the dearest charm of all the rest, a yielding sweetness of disposition, and a generous warmth of heart, grateful for love on our part, and ardently glowing with a more than equal return; these, with a healthy frame, a sound, vigorous constitution, which your higher ranks can scarcely ever hope to enjoy, are the charms of lovely woman in my humble walk of life.

This is the greatest effort my broken arm has yet made. Do let me hear, by first post, how *cher petit Monsieur* comes on with his small-pox. May Almighty goodness preserve and restore him!
    R. B.

CLXV.—TO MR. CUNNINGHAM.
11*th June* 1791.

Let me interest you, my dear Cunningham, in behalf of the gentleman who waits on you with this. He is a Mr. Clarke, of Moffat, principal schoolmaster there, and is at present suffering severely under the persecution of one or two powerful individuals of his employers. He is accused of harshness to boys that were placed under his care. God help the teacher, if a man of sensibility and genius, and such is my friend Clarke, when a booby father presents him with his booby son, and insists on lighting up the rays of science in a fellow's head whose skull is impervious and inaccessible by any other way than a positive fracture with a cudgel: a fellow whom in fact it savours of impiety to attempt making a scholar of, as he has been marked a blockhead in the book of fate, at the almighty fiat of his Creator.

The patrons of Moffat school are the ministers, magistrates, and town council of Edinburgh; and as the business comes now before them, let me beg my dearest friend to do every thing in his power to serve the interests of a man of genius and worth, and a man whom I particularly respect and esteem. You know some good fellows among the magistracy and council, but particularly you have much to say with a reverend gentleman to whom you have the honour of being very nearly related, and whom this country and age have had the honour to produce. I need not name the historian of Charles V.[121] I tell him through the medium of his nephew's influence, that Mr. Clarke is a gentleman who will not disgrace even his patronage. I know the merits of the cause thoroughly, and say it, that my friend is falling a sacrifice to prejudiced ignorance.

God help the children of dependence! Hated and persecuted by their enemies, and too often, alas! almost unexceptionally always, received by their friends with disrespect and reproach, under the thin disguise of cold civility and humiliating advice. O! to be a sturdy savage, stalking in the pride of his independence, amid the solitary wilds of his deserts, rather than in civilised life, helplessly to tremble for a subsistence precarious as the caprice of a fellow-creature! Every man has his virtues, and no man is without his failings; and plague on that privileged plain-dealing of friendship, which, in the hour of my calamity, cannot reach forth the helping hand without at the same time pointing out those failings, and apportioning them their share in procuring my present distress. My friends, for such the world calls ye, and such ye think yourselves to be, pass by my virtues if you please, but do, also, spare my follies; the first will witness in my breast for themselves, and the last will give pain enough to the ingenuous mind without you. And since deviating more or less from the paths of propriety and rectitude must be incident to human nature, do thou, Fortune, put it in my power, always from myself, and of myself, to bear the consequence of those errors! I do not want to be independent that I may sin, but I want to be independent in my sinning.

To return in this rambling letter to the subject I set out with, let me recommend my friend, Mr. Clarice, to your acquaintance and good offices; his worth entitles him to the one, and his gratitude will merit the other. I long much to hear from you. Adieu!

R. B.

[121] Dr. Robertson, uncle to Mr. Alexander Cunningham.

CLXVL—To MR. THOMAS SLOAN
[122]

ELLISLAND, *Sept. 1st*, 1791.

My Dear Sloan,—Suspense is worse than disappointment; for that reason I hurry to tell you that I just now learn that Mr. Ballantine does not choose to interfere more in the business. I am truly sorry for it, but cannot help it.

You blame me for not writing you sooner, but you will please to recollect that you omitted one little necessary piece of information;—your address.

However, you know equally well my hurried life, indolent temper, and strength of attachment. It must be a longer period than the longest life "in the world's hale and undegenerate days," that will make me forget so dear a friend as Mr. Sloan. I am prodigal enough at times, but I will not part with such a treasure as that.

I can easily enter into the *embarras* of your present situation. You know my favourite quotation from Young—

On Reason build RESOLVE!

That column of true majesty in man,—

and that other favourite one from Thomson's "Alfred"—

What proves the hero truly GREAT,

Is, never, never to despair.

Or, shall I quote you an author of your acquaintance?—

  Whether DOING, SUFFERING, or FORBEARING,
You may do miracles by—PERSEVERING.

I have nothing new to tell you. The few friends we have are going on in the old way. I sold my crop on this day se'ennight, and sold it very well. A guinea an acre, on an average, above value. But such a scene of drunkenness was hardly ever seen in this country. After the roup was over, about thirty people engaged in a battle, every man for his own hand, and fought it out for three hours. Nor was the scene much better in the house. No fighting, indeed, but folks lying drunk on the floor, and decanting, until both my dogs got so drunk by attending them, that they could not stand. You will easily guess how I enjoyed the scene, as I was no farther over than you used to see me.

  Mrs. B. and family have been in Ayrshire these many weeks.

  Farewell! and God bless you, my dear Friend! R.B.

[122] Of Wanlockhead. Burns got to know him during his frequent journeys between Ellisland and Mauchline in 1788-9.

CLXVII—TO MR. AINSLIE.
ELLISLAND, 1791.

  My Dear Ainslie,—Can you minister to a mind diseased? can you, amid the horrors of penitence, regret, remorse, head-ache, nausea, and all the rest of the damn'd hounds of hell that beset a poor wretch who has been guilty of the sin of drunkenness—can you speak peace to a troubled soul?

  Miserable perdu that I am, I have tried every thing that used to amuse me, but in vain; here must I sit, a monument of the vengeance laid up in store for the wicked, slowly counting every click of the clock as it slowly, slowly numbers over these lazy scoundrels of hours, who, damn them, are ranked up before me, every one at his neighbour's backside, and every one with a burthen of anguish on his back, to pour on my devoted head—and there is none to pity me. My wife scolds me, my business torments me, and my sins come staring me in the face, every one telling a more bitter tale than his fellow.—When I tell you even ———— has lost its power to please, you will guess something of my hell within, and all around me.—I began *Elibanks and Elibraes*, but the stanzas fell unenjoyed and unfinished from my listless tongue: at last I luckily thought of reading over an old letter of yours, that lay by me in my bookcase, and I felt something for the first time since I opened my eyes, of pleasurable existence.——Well—I begin to breathe a little, since I began to write to you. How are you, and what are you doing? How goes Law? Apropos, for correction's sake do not address to me supervisor, for that is an honour I cannot pretend to—I am on the list, as we call it, for a supervisor, and will be called out by-and-by to act as one; but at present I am a simple gauger, tho' t'other day I got an appointment to an excise division of £25 *per annum* better than the rest. My present income, down money, is £70 *per annum*.

  I have one or two good fellows here whom you would be glad to know.

  R. B.

CLXVIII.—TO MISS DAVIES.

  It is impossible, Madam, that the generous warmth and angelic purity of your youthful mind can have any idea of that moral disease under which I unhappily must rank as the chief of sinners; I mean a torpitude of the moral powers that may be called a lethargy of conscience. In vain Remorse rears her horrent crest, and rouses all her snakes: beneath the deadly-fixed eye and leaden hand of Indolence their wildest ire is charmed into the torpor of the bat, slumbering out the rigours of winter in the chink of a ruined wall. Nothing less, Madam, could have made me so long neglect your obliging commands. Indeed, I had one apology—the bagatelle was not worth presenting. Besides, so strongly am I interested in Miss Davies's fate and welfare in the serious business of life, amid its chances and changes, that to make her the subject of a silly ballad is downright mockery of these ardent feelings; 'tis like an impertinent jest to a dying friend.

Gracious Heaven! why this disparity between our wishes and our powers? Why is the most generous wish to make others blest impotent and ineffectual as the idle breeze that crosses the pathless desert? In my walks of life I have met with a few people to whom how gladly would I have said—"Go, be happy! I know that your hearts have been wounded by the scorn of the proud, whom accident has placed above you; or worse still, in whose hands are, perhaps, placed many of the comforts of your life. But there! ascend that rock, Independence, and look justly down on their littleness of soul. Make the worthless tremble under your indignation, and the foolish sink before your contempt; and largely impart that happiness to others which, I am certain, will give yourselves so much pleasure to bestow."

Why, dear Madam, must I wake from this delightful reverie, and find it all a dream? Why, amid my generous enthusiasm, must I find myself poor and powerless, incapable of wiping one tear from the eye of pity, or of adding one comfort to the friend I love? Out upon the world! say I, that its affairs are administered so ill! They talk of reform;—good Heaven! what a reform would I make among the sons, and even the daughters of men! Down, immediately, should go fools from the high places where misbegotten chance has perked them up, and through life should they skulk, ever haunted by their native insignificance, as the body marches accompanied by its shadow. As for a much more formidable class, the knaves, I am at a loss what to do with them: had I a world, there should not be a knave in it.

But the hand that could give, I would liberally fill: and I would pour delight on the heart that could kindly forgive, and generously love.

Still the inequalities of life are, among men, comparatively tolerable; but there is a delicacy, a tenderness, accompanying every view in which we can place lovely Woman, that are grated and shocked at the rude, capricious distinctions of Fortune. Woman is the blood-royal of life: let there be slight degrees of precedency among them—but let them be ALL sacred. Whether this last sentiment be right or wrong, I am not accountable; it is an original component feature of my mind.

R. B.

CLXIX.—To MRS. DUNLOP.
5th January 1792.

You see my hurried life, Madam: I can only command starts of time; however, I am glad of one thing; since I finished the other sheet, the political blast that threatened my welfare is overblown. I have corresponded with Commissioner Graham, for the Board had made me the subject of their animadversions; and now I have the pleasure of informing you that all is set to rights in that quarter. Now as to these informers, may the devil be let loose to—but, hold! I was praying most fervently in my last sheet, and I must not so soon fall a swearing in this.

Alas! how little do the wantonly or idly officious think what mischief they do by their malicious insinuations, indirect impertinence, or thoughtless babblings. What a difference there is in intrinsic worth, candour, benevolence, generosity, kindness,—in all the charities and all the virtues—between one class of human beings and another!

For instance, the amiable circle I so lately mixed with in the hospitable hall of Dunlop, their generous hearts—their uncontaminated dignified minds—their informed and polished understandings—what a contrast, when compared—if such comparing were not downright sacrilege—with the soul of the miscreant who can deliberately plot the destruction of an honest man that never offended him, and with a grin of satisfaction see the unfortunate being, his faithful wife, and prattling innocents, turned over to beggary and ruin!

Your cup, my dear Madam, arrived safe. I had two worthy fellows dining with me the other day, when I, with great formality, produced my whigmeleerie cup, and told them that it had been a family-piece among the descendants of William Wallace, This roused such an enthusiasm, that they insisted on bumpering the punch round in it; and by-and-by, never did your great ancestor lay a *Southron* more completely to rest than for a time did your cup my two friends. Apropos, this is the season of wishing. May God bless you, my dear friend, and bless me, the humblest and sincerest of your friends, by granting you yet many returns of the season! May all good things attend you and yours wherever they are scattered over the earth!

R.B.

CLXX.—TO MR. WILLIAM SMELLIE, PRINTER.

DUMFRIES, *22nd January* 1792.

I sit down, my dear Sir, to introduce a young lady[123] to you, and a lady in the first ranks of fashion, too. What a task! to you—who care no more for the herd of animals called young ladies than you do for the herd of animals called young gentlemen; to you—who despise and detest the groupings and combinations of fashion, as an idiot painter that seems industrious to place staring fools and unprincipled knaves in the foreground of his picture, while men of sense and honesty are too often thrown in the dimmest shades. Mrs. Riddell, who will take this letter to town with her, and send it to you, is a character that, even in your own way as a naturalist and a philosopher, would be an acquisition to your acquaintance. The lady, too, is a votary of the muses; and as I think myself somewhat of a judge in my own trade, I assure you that her verses, always correct, and often elegant, are much beyond the common run of the *lady poetesses* of the day. She is a great admirer of your book; and, hearing me say that I was acquainted with you, she begged to be known to you, as she is just going to pay her first visit to our Caledonian capital. I told her that her best way was to desire her near relation, and your intimate friend, Craigdarroch, to have you at his house while she was there; and lest you might think of a lively West Indian girl of eighteen, as girls of eighteen too often deserve to be thought of, I should take care to remove that prejudice. To be impartial, however, in appreciating the lady's merits, she has one unlucky failing—a failing which you will easily discover, as she seems rather pleased with indulging in it; and a failing that you will easily pardon, as it is a sin which very much besets yourself;—where she dislikes, or despises, she is apt to make no more a secret of it, than where she esteems and respects.

I will not present you with the unmeaning *compliments of the season*, but I will send you my warmest wishes and most ardent prayers, that Fortune may never throw your subsistence to the mercy of a knave, or set your character on the judgment of a fool; but that, upright and erect, you may walk to an honest grave, where men of letters shall say, here lies a man who did honour to science, and men of worth shall say, here lies a man who did honour to human nature.

R. B.

[123] Maria Riddell, a gay, clever, young Creole, wife of Walter, brother of Captain Riddell.

CLXXL—TO MR. WILLIAM NICOL.

20*th February* 1792.

O thou wisest among the wise, meridian blaze of prudence, full moon of discretion, and chief of many counsellors! How infinitely is thy puddle-headed, rattleheaded, wrong-headed, round-headed slave indebted to thy super-eminent goodness, that from the luminous path of thy own right-lined rectitude, thou lookest benignly down on an erring wretch, of whom the zig-zag wanderings defy all the powers of calculation, from the simple copulation of units, up to the hidden mysteries of fluxions! May one feeble ray of that light of wisdom which darts from thy sensorium, straight as the arrow of heaven, and bright as the meteor of inspiration, may it be my portion, so that I may be less unworthy of the face and favour of that father of proverbs and master of maxims, that antipode of folly, and magnet among the sages, the wise and witty Willie Nicol! Amen! Amen! Yea, so be it!

For me! I am a beast, a reptile, and know nothing! From the cave of my ignorance, amid the fogs of my dulness, and pestilential fumes of my political heresies, I look up to thee, as doth a toad through the iron-barred lucarne of a pestiferous dungeon, to the cloudless glory of a summer sun! Sorely sighing in bitterness of soul, I say, When shall my name be the quotation of the wise, and my countenance be the delight of the godly, like the illustrious lord of Laggan's many hills?[124] As for him, his works are perfect: never did the pen of calumny blur the fair page of his reputation, nor the bolt of hatred fly at his dwelling.

Thou mirror of purity, when shall the elfin lamp of my glimmerous understanding, purged from sensual appetites and gross desires, shine like the constellation of thy intellectual powers. As for thee, thy thoughts are pure and thy lips are holy. Never did the unhallowed breath of the powers of darkness, and the pleasures of darkness, pollute the sacred flame of thy sky-descended and heaven-bound desires: never did the vapours of impurity stain the unclouded serene of thy cerulean imagination. O that like thine were the tenor of my life, like thine the tenor of my conversation! then should no friend fear for my strength, no enemy rejoice in my weakness! Then should I lie down and rise up, and none to make me afraid. May thy pity and thy prayer be exercised for, O thou lamp of wisdom and mirror of morality! thy devoted slave,

R. B.

[124] Mr. Nicol had purchased a small piece of ground called Laggan, on the Nith. There took place the Bacchanalian scene which called forth "Willie brew'd a peck o' Maat."

CLXXII.—TO MR. FRANCIS GROSE, F.S A.
DUMFRIES, 1792.

Among the many witch stories I have heard, relating to Alloway Kirk, I distinctly remember only two or three.

Upon a stormy night, amid whistling squalls of wind, and bitter blasts of hail; in short, on such a night as the devil would choose to take the air in; a farmer or farmer's servant was plodding and plashing homeward with his plough-irons on his shoulder, having been getting some repairs on them at a neighbouring smithy. His way lay by the kirk of Alloway, and being rather on the anxious look out in approaching a place so well known to be a favourite haunt of the devil and the devil's friends and emissaries, he was struck aghast by discovering through the horrors of the storm and stormy night, a light, which on his nearer approach plainly showed itself to proceed from the haunted edifice. Whether he had been fortified from above on his devout supplication, as is customary with people when they suspect the immediate presence of Satan; or whether, according to another custom, he got courageously drunk at the smithy, I will not pretend to determine; but so it was that he ventured to go up to, nay, into the very kirk. As luck would have it his temerity came off unpunished.

The members of the infernal junto were all out on some midnight business or other, and he saw nothing but a kind of kettle or caldron, depending from the roof, over the fire, simmering some heads of unchristened children, limbs of executed malefactors, etc., for the business of the night. It was in for a penny, in for a pound, with the honest ploughman: so without ceremony he unhooked the caldron from off the fire, and, pouring out the damn'd ingredients, inverted it on his head, and carried it fairly home, where it remained long in the family, a living evidence of the truth of the story.

Another story, which I can prove to be equally authentic, is as follows:

On a market day in the town of Ayr a farmer from Carrick, and consequently whose way lay by the very gate of Alloway kirk-yard, in order to cross the river Doon at the old Bridge, which is about two or three hundred yards farther on than the said gate, had been detained by his business, till by the time he reached Alloway it was the wizard hour, between night and morning.

Though he was terrified with a blaze streaming from the kirk, yet as it is a well-known fact that to turn back on these occasions is running by far the greatest risk of mischief, he prudently advanced on his road. When he had reached the gate of the kirk-yard, he was surprised and entertained, through the ribs and arches of an old gothic window, which still faces the highway, to see a dance of witches merrily footing it round their old sooty blackguard master, who was keeping them all alive with the power of his bagpipe. The farmer stopping his horse to observe them a little, could plainly descry the faces of many old women of his acquaintance and neighbourhood. How the gentleman was dressed tradition does not say; but that the ladies were all in their smocks: and one of them happening unluckily to have a smock which was considerably too short to answer all the purpose of that piece of dress, our farmer was so tickled that he involuntarily burst out with a loud laugh, "Weel luppen, Maggy wi' the short sark!" and recollecting himself, instantly spurred his horse to the top of his speed. I need not mention the universally known fact, that no diabolical power can pursue you beyond the middle of a running stream. Lucky it was for the poor farmer that the river Doon was so near, for, notwithstanding the speed of his horse, which was a good one, against he reached the middle of the arch of the bridge, and consequently the middle of the stream, the pursuing, vengeful hags were so close at his heels, that one of them actually sprung to seize him; but it was too late; nothing was on her side of the stream but the horse's tail, which immediately gave way at her infernal grip, as if blasted by a stroke of lightning; but the farmer was beyond her reach. However, the unsightly, tailless condition of the vigorous steed was to the last hour of the noble creature's life, an awful warning to the Carrick farmers, not to stay too late in Ayr markets.

The last relation I shall give, though equally true, is not so well identified as the two former, with regard to the scene; but as the best authorities give it for Alloway, I shall relate it.

On a summer's evening, about the time nature puts on her sables to mourn the expiry of the cheerful day, a shepherd boy, belonging to a farmer in the immediate neighbourhood of Alloway kirk, had just folded his charge, and was returning home. As he passed the kirk, in the adjoining field he fell in with a crew of men and women, who were busy pulling stems of the plant ragwort. He observed that as each person pulled a ragwort, he or she got astride of it, and called out, "Up, horsie!" on which the ragwort flew off, like Pegasus, through the air with its rider. The foolish boy likewise pulled his ragwort, and cried with the rest, "Up, horsie!" and, strange to tell, away he flew with the company. The first stage at which the cavalcade stopt was a merchant's wine-cellar in Bourdeaux, where, without saying "By your leave," they quaffed away at the best the cellar could afford, until the morning, foe to the imps and works of darkness, threatened to throw light on the matter, and frightened them from their carousals.

The poor shepherd lad, being equally a stranger to the scene and the liquor, heedlessly got himself drunk; and when the rest took horse, he fell asleep, and was found so next day by some of the people belonging to the merchant. Somebody that understood Scotch, asking him what he was, he said such a-one's herd in Alloway, and by some means or other getting home again, he lived long to tell the world the wondrous tale.[125]

R. B.

[125] Cp.Hogg's *Witch of Fife.*

CLXXIIL.—TO MRS. DUNLOP.

ANNAN WATER FOOT, 22nd *August* 1792.

Do not blame me for it, Madam—my own conscience, hackneyed and weather-beaten as it is, in watching and reproving my vagaries, follies, indolence, etc., has continued to punish me sufficiently.

Do you think it possible, my dear and honoured friend, that I could be so lost to gratitude for many favours; to esteem for much worth; and to the honest, kind, pleasurable tie of, now old acquaintance, and I hope and am sure of progressive, increasing friendship—as, for a single day, not to think of you nor to ask the Fates what they are doing and about to do with my much loved friend and her wide scattered connections, and to beg of them to be as kind to you and yours as they possibly can?

Apropos! (though how it is apropos I have not leisure to explain) do you know that I am almost in love with an acquaintance of yours?—Almost! said I—I *am* in love, souse! over head and ears, deep as the most unfathomable abyss of the boundless ocean; but the word Love, owing to the *intermingledoms* of the good and the bad, the pure and the impure, in this world, being rather an equivocal term for expressing one's sentiments and sensations, I must do justice to the sacred purity of my attachment. Know, then, that the heart-struck awe the distant humble approach; the delight we should have in gazing upon and listening to a Messenger of Heaven, appearing in all the unspotted purity of his celestial home, among the coarse, polluted, far inferior sons of men, to deliver to them tidings that make their hearts swim in joy, and their imaginations soar in transport—such, so delighting and so pure, were the emotions of my soul on meeting the other day with Miss Lesley Baillie, your neighbour at Mayfield. Mr. B., with his two daughters, accompanied by Mr. H. of G., passing through Dumfries a few days ago, on their way to England, did me the honour of calling on me; on which I took my horse (though God knows I could ill spare the time), and accompanied them fourteen or fifteen miles, and dined and spent the day with them. Twas about nine, I think, when I left them, and, riding home, I composed the following ballad, of which you will probably think you have a dear bargain, as it will cost you another groat of postage. You must know that there is an old ballad beginning with—

My bonnie Lizzie Bailie,
I'll lowe thee in my plaidie, (etc,)

So I parodied it as follows, which is literally the first copy, "unanointed, unanneal'd," as Hamlet says,—

O saw ye bonny Lesley
As she gaed o'er the border?
She's gane, like Alexander,
To spread her conquests farther, (etc.)

So much for ballads. I regret that you are gone to the east country, as I am to be in Ayrshire in about a fortnight. This world of ours, notwithstanding it has many good things in it, yet it has ever had this curse, that two or three people, who would be the happier the oftener they met together, are, almost without exception, always so placed as never to meet but once or twice a-year, which, considering the few years of a man's life, is a very great "evil under the sun," which I do not recollect that Solomon has mentioned in his catalogue of the miseries of man. I hope and believe that there is a state of existence beyond the grave, where the worthy of this life will renew their former intimacies, with this endearing addition, that "we meet to part no more"

Tell us, ye dead,
Will none of you in pity disclose the secret
What 'tis you are, and we must shortly be!

A thousand times have I made this apostrophe to the departed sons of men, but not one of them has ever thought fit to answer the question. "O that some courteous ghost would blab it out!" but it cannot be; you and I, my friend, must make the experiment by ourselves, and for ourselves. However, I am so convinced that an unshaken faith in the doctrines of religion is not only necessary, by making us better men, but also by making us happier men, that I shall take every care that your little godson, and every little creature that shall call me father, shall be taught them. So ends this heterogeneous letter, written at this wild place of the world, in the intervals of my labour of discharging a vessel of rum from Antigua.
R. B.

CLXXIV.—TO MR. CUNNINGHAM.
DUMFRIES, 10th September 1792.

No! I will not attempt an apology. Amid all my hurry of business, grinding the faces of the publican and the sinner on the merciless wheels of the Excise; making ballads, and then drinking, and singing them; and, over and above all, the correcting the press-work of two different publications; still, still I might have stolen five minutes to dedicate to one of the first of my friends and fellow-creatures. I might have done, as I do at present-snatched an hour near "witching time of night," and scrawled a page or two; I might have congratulated my friend on his marriage; or I might have thanked the Caledonian archers for the honour they have done me (though, to do myself justice, I intended to have done both in rhyme, else I had done both long ere now). Well, then, here is to your good health! for you must know, I have set a nipperkin of toddy by me, just by way of spell, to keep away the meikle horned deil, or any of his subaltern imps who may be on their nightly rounds.

But what shall I write to you?—"The voice said, cry," and I said, "What shall I cry?"—O, thou spirit! whatever thou art, or wherever thou makest thyself visible! be thou a bogle by the eerie side of an auld thorn, in the dreary glen through which the herd-callan maun bicker in his gloamin route frae the fauld!—Be thou a brownie, set, at dead of night, to thy task by the blazing ingle, or in the solitary barn, where the repercussions of thy iron flail half affright thyself, as thou performest the work of twenty of the sons of men, ere the cock-crowing summon thee to thy ample cog of substantial brose. Be thou a kelpie, haunting the ford or ferry, in the starless night, mixing thy laughing yell with the howling of the storm and the roaring of the flood, as thou viewest the perils and miseries of man on the foundering horse, or in the tumbling boat!—Or, lastly, be thou a ghost, paying thy nocturnal visits to the hoary ruins of decayed grandeur; or performing thy mystic rites in the shadow of the time-worn church, while the moon looks, without a cloud, on the silent, ghastly dwellings of the dead around thee; or taking thy stand by the bedside of the villain, or the murderer, portraying on his dreaming fancy, pictures, dreadful as the horrors of unveiled hell, and terrible as the wrath of incensed Deity!—Come, thou spirit, but not in these horrid forms; come with the milder, gentle, easy inspirations, which thou breathest round the wig of a prating advocate, or the tête of a tea-sipping gossip, while their tongues run at the light-horse gallop of clish-maclaver for ever and ever—come and assist a poor devil who is quite jaded in the attempt to share half an idea among half a hundred words; to fill up four quarto pages, while he has not got one single sentence of recollection, information, or remark worth putting pen to paper for.

I feel, I feel the presence of supernatural assistance! Circled in the embrace of my elbow-chair, my breast labours, liked the bloated Sibyl on her three-footed stool, and like her too, labours with Nonsense. Nonsense, auspicious name! Tutor, friend, and finger-post in the mystic mazes of law; the cadaverous paths of physic: and particularly in the sightless soarings of SCHOOL DIVINITY, who, leaving Common Sense confounded at the strength of his pinion; Reason delirious with eyeing his giddy flight; and Truth creeping back into the bottom of her well, cursing the hour that ever she offered her scorned alliance to the wizard power of Theologic Vision-raves abroad on all the winds:— "On earth discord! a gloomy Heaven above, opening her jealous gates to the nineteen-thousandth part of the tithe of mankind! and below, an inescapable and inexorable hell, expanding its leviathan jaws for the vast residue of mortals!!! "—O doctrine! comfortable and healing to the weary wounded soul of man! Ye sons and daughters of affliction, ye *pauvres miserables,* to whom day brings no pleasure, and night yields no rest, be comforted! 'Tis but *one* to nineteen hundred thousand that your situation will mend in this world; so, alas, the experience of the poor and needy too often affirms; and 'tis nineteen hundred thousand to *one,* by the dogmas of Theology, that you will be condemned eternally in the world to come!

But of all Nonsense, Religious Nonsense is the most nonsensical; so enough, and more than enough, of it. Only, by-the-bye, will you, or can you tell me, my dear Cunningham, why a sectarian turn of mind has always a tendency to narrow and illiberalise the heart? They are orderly; they may be just; nay, I have known them merciful: but still your children of sanctity move among their fellow-creatures with a nostril snuffing putrescence, and a foot spurning filth—in short, with a conceited dignity that your titled Douglases, or any other of your Scottish lordlings of seven centuries standing, display when they accidentally mix among the many-aproned sons of mechanical life. I remember, in my plough-boy days, I could not conceive it possible that a noble lord could be a fool, or a godly man could be a knave. How ignorant are plough-boys!—Nay, I have since discovered that a *godly woman* may be a—!—But hold—here's t'ye again—this rum is generous Antigua, so a very unfit menstruum for scandal.

Apropos, how do you like, I mean *really* like, the married life? Ah, my friend! matrimony is quite a different thing from what your love-sick youths and sighing girls take it to be! But marriage, we are told, is appointed by God, and I shall never quarrel with any of His institutions. I am a husband of older standing than you, and shall give you my ideas of the conjugal state, (*en passant*—you know I am no Latinist-is not *conjugal* derived from *jugum,* a yoke?) Well, then, the scale of good wifeship I divide into ten parts. Good-nature, four; Good Sense, two; Wit, one; Personal Charms, viz., a sweet face, eloquent eyes, fine limbs, graceful carriage (I would add a fine waist too, but that is so soon spoilt, you know), all these, one; as for the other qualities belonging to, or attending on, a wife, such as Fortune, Connections, Education (I mean education extraordinary), Family blood, etc., divide the two remaining degrees among them as you please; only, remember that all these minor properties must be expressed by *fractions*, for there is not any one of them, in the aforesaid scale, entitled to the dignity of an *integer*.

As for the rest of my fancies and reveries—how I lately met with Miss Lesley Baillie, the most beautiful, elegant woman in the world—how I accompanied her and her father's family fifteen miles on their journey, out of pure devotion, to admire the loveliness of the works of God, in such an unequalled display of them—how, in galloping home at night, I made a ballad on her, of which these two stanzas make a part—

Thou, bonnie Lesley, art a queen,
Thy subjects we before thee;
Thou, bonnie Lesley, art divine,
The hearts o' men adore thee.
The very deil he could na scathe
Whatever wad belang thee!
He'd look into thy bonnie face
And say, "I canna wrang thee"—

behold all these things are written in the chronicles of my imagination, and shall be read by thee, my dear friend, and by thy beloved spouse, my other dear friend, at a more convenient season.

Now to thee and thy wife [*etc.*—a mock benediction.]
R.B.

CLXXV.—To MRS. DUNLOP.
DUMFRIES, *24th September 1792.*

I have this moment, my dear Madam, yours of the twenty-third. All your other kind reproaches, your news, etc., are out of my head when I read and think of Mrs. Henri's[126] situation. Good God! a heart-wounded helpless young woman—in a strange, foreign land, and that land convulsed with every horror that can harrow the human feelings—sick-looking, longing for a comforter, but finding none—a mother's feelings, too:—but it is too much: He who wounded (He only can) may He heal!

I wish the farmer great joy of his new acquisition to his family.... I cannot say that I give Him joy of his life as a farmer. 'Tis, as a farmer paying a dear, unconscionable rent, a *cursed life!* As to a laird farming his own property; sowing his own corn in hope; and reaping it, in spite of brittle weather, in gladness; knowing that none can say unto him, "What dost thou?"—fattening his herds; shearing his flocks; rejoicing at Christmas; and begetting sons and daughters, until he be the venerated, grey-haired leader of a little tribe—'tis a heavenly life! but devil take the life of reaping the fruits that another must eat!

Well, your kind wishes will be gratified, as to seeing me when I make my Ayrshire visit. I cannot leave Mrs. Burns until her nine months' race is run, which may perhaps be in three or four weeks. She, too, seems determined to make me the patriarchal leader of a band. However, if Heaven will be so obliging as to let me have them in the proportion of three boys to one girl, I shall be so much the more pleased. I hope, if I am spared with them, to show a set of boys that will do honour to my cares and name; but I am not equal to the task of rearing girls. Besides, I am too poor; a girl should always have a fortune. Apropos, your little godson is thriving charmingly, but is a very deil. He, though two years younger, has completely mastered his brother. Robert is indeed the mildest, gentlest creature I ever saw. He has a most surprising memory, and is quite the pride of his schoolmaster.

138

You know how readily we get into prattle upon a subject dear to our heart: you can excuse it. God bless you and yours!

[126] Her daughter, ill in France.

CLXXVI.—To MRS. DUNLOP.

Supposed to have been written on the Death of Mrs. Henri, her daughter, at Muges.

I had been from home, and did not receive your letter until my return the other day. What shall I say to comfort you, my much-valued, much-afflicted friend! I can but grieve with you; consolation I have none to offer, except that which religion holds out to the children of affliction—*children of affliction!*—how just the expression! and like every other family, they have matters among them which they hear, see, and feel in a serious, all-important manner, of which the world has not, nor cares to have, any idea. The world looks indifferently on, makes the passing remark, and proceeds to the next novel occurrence.

Alas, Madam! who would wish for many years? What is it but to drag existence until our joys gradually expire, and leave us in a night of misery: like the gloom which blots out the stars, one by one, from the face of night, and leaves us, without a ray of comfort, in the howling waste!

I am interrupted, and must leave off. You shall soon hear from me again.

R. B.

CLXXVII.—To MRS. DUNLOP.

DUMFRIES, *6th December 1792.*

I shall be in Ayrshire, I think, next week; and, if at all possible, I shall certainly, my much esteemed friend, have the pleasure of visiting at Dunlop House.

Alas, Madam! how seldom do we meet in this world, that we have reason to congratulate ourselves on accessions of happiness! I have not passed half the ordinary term of an old man's life, and yet I scarcely look over the obituary of a newspaper that I do not see some names that I have known, and which I and other acquaintances little thought to meet with there so soon. Every other instance of the mortality of our kind makes us cast an anxious look into the dreadful abyss of uncertainty, and shudder with apprehension for our own fate. But of how different an importance are the lives of different individuals! Nay, of what importance is one period of the same life more than another? A few years ago I could have lain down in the dust, "careless of the voice of the morning;" and now not a few, and these most helpless individuals, would, on losing me and my exertions, lose both "staff and shield." By the way, these helpless ones have lately got an addition—Mrs. B. having given me a fine girl since I wrote you. There is a charming passage in Thomson's" Edward and Eleanora:"

The valiant, *in himself* what can he suffer?
Or what need he regard his *single* woes? (etc.)

I do not remember to have heard you mention Thomson's dramas. I pick up favourite quotations, and store them in my mind as ready armour, offensive or defensive, amid the struggle of this turbulent existence. Of these is one, a very favourite one, from his "Alfred:"

Attach thee firmly to the virtuous deeds
And offices of life; to life itself,
With all its vain and transient joys, sit loose.

Probably I have quoted these to you formerly, as indeed, when I write from the heart, I am apt to be guilty of repetitions. The compass of the heart, in the musical style of expression, is much more bounded than that of the imagination; so the notes of the former are extremely apt to run into one another; but in return for the paucity of its compass, its few notes are much more sweet....

I see you are in for double postage, so I shall e'en scribble out t'other sheet. We in this country here have many alarms of the reforming, or rather the republican spirit, of your part of the kingdom. Indeed, we are a good deal in commotion ourselves. For me, I am a placeman, you know; a very humble one indeed, Heaven knows, but still so much as to gag me. What my private sentiments are, you will find out without an interpreter.

I have taken up the subject, and the other day, for a pretty actress's benefit night, I wrote an address, which I will give on the other page, called "The Rights of Woman." I shall have the honour of receiving your criticisms in person at Dunlop.

R. B.

CLXXVIII.—To MR. R. GRAHAM, FINTRY.

December 1792.

Sir,—I have been surprised, confounded, and distracted, by Mr. Mitchel, the collector, telling me that he has received an order from your Board to inquire into my political conduct, and blaming me as a person disaffected to government.

Sir, you are a husband—and a father. You know what you would feel, to see the much-loved wife of your bosom, and your helpless, prattling little ones, turned adrift into the world, degraded and disgraced from a situation in which they had been respectable and respected, and left almost without the necessary support of a miserable existence. Alas, Sir! must I think that such, soon, will be my lot! and from the damn'd, dark insinuations of hellish, groundless envy too! I believe, Sir, I may aver it, and in the sight of Omniscience, that I would not tell a deliberate falsehood, no, not though even worse horrors, if worse can be, than those I have mentioned, hung over my head; and I say, that the allegation, whatever villain has made it, is a lie! To the British Constitution, on revolution principles, next after my God, I am most devoutly attached. You, Sir, have been much and generously my friend: Heaven knows how warmly I have felt the obligation, and how gratefully I have thanked you. Fortune, Sir, has made you powerful, and me impotent; has given you patronage, and me dependence. I would not for my single self call on your humanity; were such my insular, unconnected situation, I would despise the tear that now swells in my eye—I could brave misfortune, I could face ruin; for at the worst, "Death's thousand doors stand open;" but, good God! the tender concerns that I have mentioned, the claims and ties that I see at this moment, and feel around me, how they unnerve Courage, and wither Resolution! To your patronage, as a man of some genius, you have allowed me a claim; and your esteem, as an honest man, I know is my due: to these, Sir, permit me to appeal; by these may I adjure you to save me from that misery which threatens to overwhelm me, and which, with my latest breath I will say it, I have not deserved.

R. B.

CLXXIX.—To MRS. DUNLOP.

DUMFRIES, *31st December 1792.*

Dear Madam,—A hurry of business, thrown in heaps by my absence, has until now prevented my returning my grateful acknowledgments to the good family of Dunlop, and you in particular, for that hospitable kindness which rendered the four days I spent under that genial roof, four of the pleasantest I ever enjoyed. Alas, my dearest friend! how few and fleeting are those things we call pleasures! on my road to Ayrshire I spent a night with a friend whom I much valued; a man whose days promised to be many; and on Saturday last we laid him in the dust!

Jan. 2nd, 1793.

I have just received yours of the 30th, and feel much for your situation. However, I heartily rejoice in your prospect of recovery from that vile jaundice. As to myself, I am better, though not quite free of my complaint. You must not think, as you seem to insinuate, that in my way of life I want exercise. Of that I have enough; but occasional hard drinking is the devil to me. Against this I have again and again bent my resolution, and have greatly succeeded. Taverns I have totally abandoned: it is the private parties in the family way, among the hard-drinking gentlemen of this country, that do me the mischief—but even this I have more than half given over.

Mr. Corbet can be of little service to me at present; at least I should be shy of applying. I cannot possibly be settled as a supervisor for several years. I must wait the rotation of the list, and there are twenty names before mine. —I might indeed get a job of officiating, where a settled supervisor was ill, or aged; but that hauls me from my family, as I could not remove them on such an uncertainty. Besides, some envious, malicious devil has raised a little demur on my political principles, and I wish to let that matter settle before I offer myself too much in the eye of my supervisors. I have set, henceforth, a seal on my lips, as to these unlucky politics; but to you I must breathe my sentiments. In this, as in everything else, I shall show the undisguised emotions of my soul. War I deprecate: misery and ruin to thousands are in the blast that announces the destructive demon. But....

 R. B.

CLXXX.—To MR. ROBERT GRAHAM OF FINTRY.
DUMFRIES, *Morning of 5th Jan.* 1793.

 Sir,—I am this moment honoured with your letter. With what feelings I received this other instance of your goodness I shall not pretend to describe.

 Now to the charges which malice and misrepresentation have brought against me.[127] It has been said, it seems, that I not only belong to, but head a disaffected party in this town. I know of no party here, republican or reform, except an old Burgh-Reform party, with which I never had anything to do. Individuals, both republican and reform, we have, though not many of either; but if they have associated, it is more than I have the least knowledge of, and if such an association exist it must consist of such obscure, nameless beings as precludes any possibility of my being known to them, or they to me.

 I was in the playhouse one night when *Cà Ira* was called for. I was in the middle of the pit, and from the pit the clamour arose. One or two persons, with whom I occasionally associate, were of the party, but I neither knew of, nor joined in the plot, nor at all opened my lips to hiss or huzza that, or any other political tune whatever. I looked on myself as far too obscure a man to have any weight in quelling a riot, and at the same time as a person of higher respectability than to yell to the howlings of a rabble. I never uttered any invectives against the king. His private worth it is altogether impossible that such a man as I can appreciate; but in his public capacity I always revered, and always will with the soundest loyalty revere the monarch of Great Britain as—to speak in masonic—the sacred keystone of our royal arch constitution. As to Reform principles, I look upon the British Constitution, as settled at the Revolution, to be the most glorious on earth, or that perhaps the wit of man can frame; at the same time I think, not alone, that we have a good deal deviated from the original principles of that Constitution,—particularly, that an alarming system of corruption has pervaded the connection between the Executive and the House of Commons. This is the whole truth of my Reform opinions, which, before I knew the complexion of these innovating times, I too unguardedly as I now see sported with: henceforth I seal up my lips. But I never dictated to, corresponded with, or had the least connection with any political association whatever. Of Johnstone, the publisher of the *Edinburgh Gazetteer*, I know nothing. One evening, in company with four or five friends, we met with his prospectus, which we thought manly and independent; and I wrote to him, ordering his paper for us. If you think I act improperly in allowing his paper to come addressed to me, I shall immediately countermand it. I never wrote a line of prose to *The Gazetteer* in my life. An address, spoken by Miss Fontenelle on her benefit night, and which I called "The Rights of Woman," I sent to *The Gazetteer*, as also some stanzas on the Commemoration of the poet Thomson: both of these I will subjoin for your perusal. You will see they have nothing whatever to do with politics.

 As to France, I was her enthusiastic votary in the beginning of the business. When she came to shew her old avidity for conquest by annexing Savoy and invading the rights of Holland, I altered my sentiments.

 This, my honoured patron, is all. To this statement I challenge disquisition. Mistaken prejudice or unguarded passion may mislead, have often misled me; but when called on to answer for my mistakes, though no man can feel keener compunction for them, yet no man can be more superior to evasion or disguise.—I have the honour to be, Sir, your ever grateful, etc.,

ROBT. BURNS.

[127] Because of what Burns elsewhere called "Some temeraire conduct of mine, in the political opinions of the day."

CLXXXI.—TO MR. ALEX. CUNNINGHAM, W.S., EDINBURGH.

DUMFRIES, *20th Feb.* 1793.

What are you doing? What hurry have you got on your head, my dear Cunningham, that I have not heard from you? Are you deeply engaged in the mazes of the Jaw, the mysteries of love, or the profound wisdom of *politics*? Curse on the word!

Q. What is Politics?

A. It is a science wherewith, by means of nefarious cunning and hypocritical pretence, we govern civil politics (sic) for the emolument of ourselves and adherents.

Q. What is a minister?

A. An unprincipled fellow who, by the influence of hereditary or acquired wealth, by superior abilities or by a lucky conjuncture of circumstances, obtains a principal place in the administration of the affairs of government.

Q. What is a patriot?

A. An individual exactly of the same description as a minister, only out of place.

I was interrupted in my Catechism, and am returned at a late hour just to subscribe my name, and to put you in mind of the forgotten friend of that name who is still in the land of the living, though I can hardly say in the place of hope.

I made the enclosed sonnet[128] the other day. Adieu!

ROBT. BURNS.

[128] "On Hearing a Thrush Sing."

CLXXXIL—To MR. CUNNINGHAM.

3rd March 1793.

Since I wrote to you the last lugubrious sheet, I have not had time to write to you farther. When I say that I had not time, that, as usual, means that the three demons, indolence, business, and ennui, have so completely shared my hours among them, as not to leave me a five minutes' fragment to take up a pen in.

Thank Heaven, I feel my spirits buoying upwards with the renovating year. Now I shall in good earnest take up Thomson's songs. I dare say he thinks I have used him unkindly, and I must own with too much appearance of truth...

There is one commission that I must trouble you with. I lately lost a valuable seal, a present from a departed friend, which vexes me much. I have gotten one of your Highland pebbles, which I fancy would make a very decent one; and I want to cut my armorial bearing on it; will you be so obliging as inquire what will be the expense of such a business? I do not know that my name is matriculated, as the heralds call it, at all; but I have invented arms for myself, so you know I shall be chief of the name; and, by courtesy of Scotland, will likewise be entitled to supporters. These, however, I do not intend having on my seal. I am a bit of a herald, and shall give you, *secundum artem*, my arms. On a field, azure, a holly bush, seeded, proper, in base; a shepherd's pipe and crook, saltier-wise, also proper, in chief. On a wreath of the colours, a wood-lark perching on a sprig of bay-tree, proper, for crest. Two mottoes; round the top of the crest, *Wood notes wild*; at the bottom of the shield, in the usual place, *Better a wee bush than nae bield*. By the shepherd's pipe and crook I do not mean the nonsense of painters of Arcadia, but a *Stock and Horn*, and a *Club* such as you see at the head of Allan Ramsay, in Allan's quarto edition of the "Gentle Shepherd." By-the-bye, do you know Allan? He must be a man of very great genius—Why is he not more known?—Has he no patrons? or do "Poverty's cold wind and crushing rain beat keen and heavy" on him? I once, and but once, got a glance of that noble edition of the noblest pastoral in the world: and dear as it was, I mean dear as to my pocket, I would have bought it; but I was told that it was printed and engraved for subscribers only. He is the *only* artist who has hit *genuine* pastoral *costume*. What, my dear Cunningham, is there in riches, that they narrow and harden the heart so? I think, that were I as rich as the sun, I should be as generous as the

142

day: but as I have no reason to imagine my soul a nobler one than any other man's, I must conclude that wealth imparts a bird-lime quality to the possessor, at which the man, in his native poverty, would have revolted. What has led me to this, is the idea of such merit as Mr. Allan possesses, and such riches as a nabob or government contractor possesses, and why they do not form a mutual league. Let wealth shelter and cherish unprotected merit, and the gratitude and celebrity of that merit will richly repay it.

R. B.

CLXXXIII.—To Miss BENSON, YORK, AFTERWARDS MRS. BASIL MONTAGU.

DUMFRIES, *21st March 1793.*

Madam,—Among many things for which I envy those hale, long-lived old fellows before the flood, is this in particular, that when they met with anybody after their own heart, they had a charming long prospect of many, many happy meetings with them in after-life.

Now, in this short, stormy, winter day of our fleeting existence, when you now and then, in the Chapter of Accidents, meet an individual whose acquaintance is a real acquisition, there are all the probabilities against you, that you shall never meet with that valued character more. On the other hand, brief as this miserable being is, it is none of the least of the miseries belonging to it, that if there is any miscreant whom you hate, or creature whom you despise, the ill-run of the chances shall be so against you, that in the over takings, turnings, and jostlings of life, pop! at some unlucky corner, eternally comes the wretch upon you, and will not allow your indignation or contempt a moment's repose. As I am a sturdy believer in the powers of darkness, I take these to be the doings of that old author of mischief, the devil. It is well known that he has some kind of short-hand way of taking down our thoughts, and I make no doubt that he is perfectly acquainted with my sentiments respecting Miss Benson; how much I admired her abilities and valued her worth, and how very fortunate I thought myself in her acquaintance. For this last reason, my dear Madam, I must entertain no hopes of the very great pleasure of meeting with you again.—I am, etc.

R. B.

CLXXXIV.-To MR. JOHN FRANCIS ERSKINE, OF MAR.

DUMFRIES, 13th *April 1793.*

Sir,—Degenerate as human nature is said to be—and in many instances worthless and unprincipled it is—still there are bright examples to the contrary: examples that, even in the eyes of superior beings, must shed a lustre on the name of Man.

Such an example have I now before me, when you, Sir, came forward to patronise and befriend a distant and obscure stranger, merely because poverty had made him helpless, and his British hardihood of mind had provoked the arbitrary of wantonness and power. My much esteemed friend, Mr, Riddel of Glenriddel, has just read me a paragraph of a letter he had from you. Accept, Sir, of the silent throb of gratitude, for words would but mock the emotions of my soul.

You have been misinformed as to my final dismissal from the Excise; I am still in the service. Indeed, but for the exertions of a gentleman who must be known to you, Mr. Graham of Fintry, a gentleman who has ever been my warm and generous friend, I had, without so much as a hearing, or the slightest previous intimation, been turned adrift, with my helpless family, to all the horrors of want. Had I had any other resource, probably I might have saved them the trouble of a dismissal; but the little money I gained by my publication is almost every guinea embarked to save from ruin an only brother, who, though one of the worthiest, is by no means one of the most fortunate of men.

In my defence to their accusations, I said, that whatever might be my sentiments of republics, ancient or modern, as to Britain, I abjured the idea: That a constitution, which, in its original principles, experience had proved to be every way fitted for our happiness in society, it would be insanity to sacrifice to an untried visionary theory: That, in consideration of my being situated in a department, however humble, immediately in the hands of people in power, I had forborne taking any active part, either personally, or as an author, in the present business of Reform: but that, where I must declare my sentiments, I would say there existed a system of corruption between the executive power and the representative part of the legislature, which boded no good to our glorious constitution, and which every patriotic Briton must wish to see amended. Some such sentiments as these I stated in a letter to my generous patron, Mr. Graham, which he laid before the Board at large; where, it seems, my last remark gave great offence: and one of our supervisors-general, a Mr. Corbet, was instructed to inquire on the spot, and to document me—"that my business was to act, *not to think*; and that whatever might be men or measures, it was for me to be *silent* and *obedient*".

Mr. Corbet was likewise my steady friend; so between Mr. Graham and him I have been partly forgiven; only I understand that all hopes of my getting officially forward are blasted.

Now, Sir, to the business in which I would more immediately interest you. The partiality of my countrymen has brought me forward as a man of genius, and has given me a character to support. In the Poet I have avowed manly and independent sentiments, which I trust will be found in the man. Reasons of no less weight than the support of a wife and family, have pointed out as the eligible, and situated as I was, the only eligible line of life for me, my present occupation. Still my honest fame is my dearest concern; and a thousand times have I trembled at the idea of those *degrading* epithets that malice or misrepresentation may affix to my name. I have often, in blasting anticipation, listened to some future hackney scribbler, with the heavy malice of savage stupidity, exulting in his hireling paragraphs— "Burns, notwithstanding the *fanfaronade* of independence to be found in his works, and after having been held forth to public view and to public estimation as a man of some genius, yet, quite destitute of resources within himself to support his borrowed dignity, he dwindled into a paltry exciseman, and slunk out the rest of his insignificant existence in the meanest of pursuits, and among the vilest of mankind."

In your illustrious hands, Sir, permit me to lodge my disavowal and defiance of these slanderous falsehoods. Burns was a poor man from birth, and an exciseman by necessity; but—I will say it! the sterling of his honest worth no poverty could debase, and his independent British mind, oppression might bend, but could not subdue. Have not I, to me a more precious stake in my country's welfare, than the richest dukedom in it?—I have a large family of children, and the prospect of more. I have three sons, who, I see already, have brought into the world souls ill qualified to inhabit the bodies of slaves.—Can I look tamely on, and see any machinations to wrest from them the birthright of my boys,—the little independent Britons, in whose veins runs my own blood?—No! I will not! should my heart's blood stream around my attempt to defend it!

Does any man tell me that my full efforts can be of no service; and that it does not belong to my humble station to meddle with the concerns of a nation?

I can tell him that it is on such individuals as I that a nation has to rest, both for the hand of support and the eye of intelligence. The uninformed mob may swell a nation's bulk; and the titled, tinsel, courtly throng may be its feathered ornament; but the number of those who are elevated enough in life to reason and to reflect, yet low enough to keep clear of the venal contagion of a court!—these are a nation's strength.

I know not how to apologise for the impertinent length of this epistle; but one small request I must ask of you farther—When you have honoured this letter with a perusal, please to commit it to the flames. Burns, in whose behalf you have so generously interested yourself, I have here, in his native colours, drawn as he is; but should any of the people in whose hands is the very bread he eats, get the least knowledge of the picture, it would ruin the poor bard for ever!

My poems having just come out in another edition, I beg leave to present you with a copy as a small mark of that high esteem and ardent gratitude with which I have the honour to be, Sir, your deeply indebted, and ever devoted, humble servant,

R. B.[129]

[129] This letter was penned in response to the sympathy which Mr. Erskine had expressed for Burns in a letter to Captain Riddell of Carse, when Burns was taken to task by the Board of Excise for his political opinions.

CLXXXV.—To MISS M'MORDO, DRUMLANRIG.

DUMFRIES, *July 1793*.

... Now let me add a few wishes which every man, who has himself the honour of being a father, must breathe when he sees female youth, beauty, and innocence about to enter into this chequered and very precarious world. May you, my young madam, escape that frivolity which threatens universally to pervade the minds and manners of fashionable life, The mob of fashionable female youth—what are they? Are they anything? They prattle, laugh, sing, dance, finger a lesson, or perhaps turn the pages of a fashionable novel; but are their minds stored with any information worthy of the noble powers of reason and judgment? and do their hearts glow with sentiment, ardent, generous, or humane? Were I to poetize on the subject I would call them the butterflies of the human kind, remarkable only for the idle variety of their ordinary glare, sillily straying from one blossoming weed to another, without a meaning or an aim, the idiot prey of every pirate of the skies who thinks them worth his while as he wings his way by them, and speedily by wintry time swept to that oblivion whence they might as well never have appeared. Amid this crowd of nothings may you be something, etc.

R. B.

CLXXXVI.—To JOHN M'MURDO, ESQ., DRUMLANRIG.

This is a painful, disagreeable letter, and the first of the kind I ever wrote. I am truly in serious distress for three or four guineas: can you, my dear sir, accommodate me? These accursed times by tripping up importation have, for this year at least, lopped off a full third of my income;[130] and with my large family this is to me a distressing matter.

R. B.

[130] Never more than 70 UK pounds.

CLXXXVII.—To MRS. RIDDEL.

Dear Madam,—I meant to have called on you yesternight, but as I edged up to your box-door, the first object which greeted my view, was one of those lobster-coated puppies[131] sitting like another dragon, guarding the Hesperian fruit. On the conditions and capitulations you so obligingly offer, I shall certainly make my weather-beaten rustic phiz a part of your box-furniture on Tuesday; when we may arrange the business of the visit.

Among the profusion of idle compliments, which insidious craft, or unmeaning folly, incessantly offer at your shrine—a shrine, how far exalted above such adoration—permit me, were it but for rarity's sake, to pay you the honest tribute of a warm heart and an independent mind; and to assure you that I am, thou most amiable, and most accomplished of thy sex, with the most respectful esteem, and fervent regard, thine, etc.

R. B.

[131] Military officers.

CLXXXVIII.—To MRS. RIDDEL.

I will wait on you, my ever valued friend, but whether in the morning I am not sure. Sunday closes a period of our curst revenue business, and may probably keep me employed with my pen until noon. Fine employment for a poet's pen! There is a species of human genus that I call *the gin-horse class*: what enviable dogs they are! Round, and round, and round they go,—Mundell's ox, that drives his cotton mill, is their exact prototype—without an idea or wish beyond their circle; fat, sleek, stupid, patient, quiet, and contented; while here I sit, altogether Novemberish, a damn'd melange of fretfulness and melancholy; not enough of the one to rouse me to passion, nor of the other to repose me in torpor; my soul flouncing and fluttering round her tenement, like a wild finch, caught amid the horrors of winter, and newly thrust into a cage. Well, I am persuaded that it was of me the Hebrew sage prophesied, when he foretold— "And behold, on whatsoever this man doth set his heart, it

145

shall not prosper!" If my resentment is awaked, it is sure to be where it dare not squeak; and if—....

Pray that wisdom and bliss be more frequent visitors of
R. B.

CLXXXIX.—To MRS. RIDDEL.

I have often told you, my dear friend, that you had a spice of caprice in your composition, and you have as often disavowed it; even perhaps while your opinions were, at the moment, irrefragably proving it. Could any thing estrange me from a friend such as you?—No! To-morrow I shall have the honour of waiting on you.

Farewell, thou first of friends, and most accomplished of women I even with all thy little caprices!
R B.

CXC.—To MRS. RIDDEL.

Madam,—I return your commonplace book. I have perused it with much pleasure, and would have continued my criticisms, but as it seems the critic has forfeited your esteem, his strictures must lose their value.

If it is true that "offences come only from the heart," before you I am guiltless. To admire, esteem, and prize you as the most accomplished of women, and the first of friends—if these are crimes, I am the most offending thing alive.

In a face where I used to meet the kind complacency of friendly confidence, *now* to find cold neglect and contemptuous scorn—is a wrench that my heart can ill bear. It is, however, some kind of miserable good luck, that while *de-haut-en-bas* rigour may depress an unoffending wretch to the ground, it has a tendency to rouse a stubborn something in his bosom, which, though it cannot heal the wounds of his soul, is at least an opiate to blunt their poignancy.

With the profoundest respect for your abilities, the most sincere esteem and ardent regard for your gentle heart and amiable manners, and the most fervent wish and prayer for your welfare, peace, and bliss, I have the honour to be, Madam, your most devoted humble servant,
R. B.

CXCI.—TO MR. CUNNINGHAM.

25th February 1794.

Canst thou minister to a mind diseased? Canst thou speak peace and rest to a soul tost on a sea of troubles, without one friendly star to guide her course, and dreading that the next surge may overwhelm her? Canst thou give to a frame, tremblingly alive to the tortures of suspense, the stability and hardihood of the rock that braves the blast? If thou canst not do the least of these, why wouldst thou disturb me in my miseries, with thy inquiries after me?

For these two months I have not been able to lift a pen. My constitution and frame were, *ab origine*, blasted with a deep incurable taint of hypochondria, which poisons my existence. Of late a number of domestic vexations, and some pecuniary share in the ruin of these cursed times; losses which, though trifling, were yet what I could ill bear, have so irritated me, that my feelings at times could only be envied by a reprobate spirit listening to the sentence that dooms it to perdition.

Are you deep in the language of consolation? I have exhausted in reflection every topic of comfort. *A heart at ease* would have been charmed with my sentiments and reasonings; but as to myself, I was like Judas Iscariot preaching the gospel; he might melt and mould the hearts of those around him, but his own kept its native incorrigibility.

Still there are two great pillars that bear us up, amid the wreck of misfortune and misery. The ONE is composed of the different modifications of a certain noble, stubborn something in a man, known by the names of courage, fortitude, magnanimity. The OTHER is made up of those feelings and sentiments, which, however the sceptic may deny them, or the enthusiast disfigure them, are yet, I am convinced, original and component parts of the human soul; those *senses of the mind* if I may be allowed the expression, which connect us with, and link us to, those awful obscure realities—an all-powerful, and equally beneficent God; and a world to come, beyond death and the grave. The first gives the nerve of combat, while a ray of hope beams on the field: the last pours the balm of comfort into the wounds which time can never cure.

I do not remember, my dear Cunningham, that you and I ever talked on the subject of religion at all. I know some who laugh at it, as the trick of the crafty FEW, to lead the undiscerning MANY; or at most, as an uncertain obscurity which mankind can never know anything of, and with which they are fools if they give themselves much to do. Nor would I quarrel with a man for his irreligion, any more than I would for his want of a musical ear, I would regret that he was shut out from what, to me and to others, were such superlative sources of enjoyment. It is in this point of a view, and for this reason, that I will deeply imbue the mind of every child of mine with religion. If my son should happen to be a man of feeling, sentiment, and taste, I shall thus add largely to his enjoyments. Let me flatter myself that this sweet little fellow, who is just now running about my desk, will be a man of a melting, ardent, glowing heart; and an imagination, delighted with the painter, and rapt with the poet. Let me figure him wandering out in a sweet evening, to inhale the balmy gales, and enjoy the glowing luxuriance of the spring; himself the while in the blooming youth of life. He looks abroad on all nature, and through nature up to nature's God. His soul, by swift delighting degrees, is rapt above this sublunary sphere until he can be silent no longer, and bursts out into the glorious enthusiasm of Thomson,
These, as they change, Almighty Father, these
Are but the varied God. The rolling year
Is full of thee.
And so on, in all the spirit and ardour of that charming hymn. These are no ideal pleasures, they are real delights; and I ask, what of the delights among the sons of men are superior, not to say equal to them? And they have this precious, vast addition, that conscious virtue stamps them for her own; and lays hold on them to bring herself into the presence of a witnessing, judging, and approving God.

R. B.

CXCII.—To MRS. DUNLOP.

CASTLE DOUGLAS, *25th June 1794.*

Here in a solitary inn, in a solitary village, am I set by myself, to amuse my brooding fancy as I may. Solitary confinement, you know, is Howard's favourite idea of reclaiming sinners; so let me consider by what fatality it happens, that I have so long been exceeding sinful as to neglect the correspondence of the most valued friend I have on earth. To tell you that I have been in poor health will not be excuse enough, though it is true. I am afraid that I am about to suffer for the follies of my youth. My medical friends threaten me with a flying gout; but I trust they are mistaken.

I am just going to trouble your critical patience with the first sketch of a stanza I have been framing, as I passed along the road. The subject is Liberty: you know, my honoured friend, how dear the theme is to me. I design it an irregular ode for General Washington's birth-day. After having mentioned the degeneracy of other kingdoms I come to Scotland thus:
Thee, Caledonia, thy wild heaths among,
Thee, famed for martial deed and sacred song,
To thee I turn with swimming eyes;
Where is that soul of freedom fled?
Immingled with the mighty dead!
Beneath the hallowed turf where Wallace lies!
Hear it not, Wallace, in thy bed of death;

Ye babbling winds, in silence sweep,
Disturb ye not the hero's sleep.

You will probably have another scrawl from me in a stage or two.
    R. B.

CXCIII.—To MR. JAMES JOHNSON.
DUMFRIES, 1794.

My Dear Friend,—You should have heard from me long ago; but over and above some vexatious share in the pecuniary losses of these accursed times, I have all this winter been plagued with low spirits and blue devils, so that *I have almost hung my harp on the willow trees.*

I am just now busy correcting a new edition of my poems, and this, with my ordinary business, finds me in full employment.

I send you by my friend, Mr. Wallace, forty-one songs for your fifth volume; if we cannot finish it any other way, what would you think of Scotch words to some beautiful Irish airs? In the meantime, at your leisure, give a copy of the *Museum* to my worthy friend, Mr. Peter Hill, bookseller, to bind for me, interleaved with blank leaves, exactly as he did the Laird of Glenriddel's, that I may insert every anecdote I can learn, together with my own criticisms and remarks on the songs. A copy of this kind I shall leave with you, the editor, to publish at some after period, by way of making the *Museum* a book famous to the end of time, and you renowned for ever.

I have got a highland dirk, for which I have great veneration, as it once was the dirk of *Lord Balmerino.* It fell into bad hands, who stripped it of the silver mounting, as well as the knife and fork. I have some thoughts of sending it to your care, to get it mounted anew.— Yours, etc.,
    R. B.

CXCIV.—To MR. PETER MILLER, JUN., OF DALSWINION.
DUMFRIES, Nov. 1794.

Dear Sir,—Your offer is indeed truly generous, and sincerely do I thank you for it; but in my present situation, I find that I dare not accept it. You well know my political sentiments; and were I an insular individual, unconnected with a wife and a family of children, with the most fervid enthusiasm I would have volunteered my services; I then could and would have despised all consequences that might have ensued.

My prospect in the Excise is something; at least, it is— encumbered as I am with the welfare, the very existence, of near half-a-score of helpless individuals—what I dare not sport with.

In the meantime, they are most welcome to my Ode; only, let them insert it as a thing they have met with by accident and unknown to me. Nay, if Mr. Perry, whose honour, after your character of him, I cannot doubt, if he will give me an address and channel by which anything will come safe from those spies with which he may be certain that his correspondence is beset, I will now and then send him any bagatelle that I may write. In the present hurry of Europe, nothing but news and politics will be regarded; but against the days of peace, which Heaven send soon, my little assistance may perhaps fill up an idle column of a newspaper. I have long had it in my head to try my hand in the way of little prose essays, which I propose sending into the world through the medium of some newspaper; and should these be worth his while, to these Mr. Perry shall be welcome; and all my reward shall be, his treating me with his paper, which, by-the-by, to anybody who has the least relish for wit, is a high treat indeed.

With the most grateful esteem, I am ever, Dear Sir,
    R. B.

[131] He had offered Burns a post on the staff of *The Morning Chronicle*, of which newspaper Mr. Perry was proprietor.

CXCV.—To MRS, RIDDEL

Madam,—I dare say that this is the first epistle you ever received from this nether world. I write you from the regions of hell, amid the horrors of the damn'd. The time and manner of my leaving your earth I do not exactly know, as I took my departure in the heat of a fever of intoxication, contracted at your too hospitable mansion; but, on my arrival here, I was fairly tried, and sentenced to endure the purgatorial tortures of this infernal confine for the space of ninety-nine years, eleven months, and twenty-nine days, and all on account of the impropriety of my conduct yesternight under your roof. Here am I, laid on a bed of pitiless furze, with my aching head reclined on a pillow of ever-piercing thorn, while an infernal tormentor, wrinkled, and old, and cruel—his name I think is *Recollection*—with a whip of scorpions, forbids peace or rest to approach me, and keeps anguish eternally awake. Still, Madam, if I could in any measure be reinstated in the good opinion of the fair circle whom my conduct last night so much injured, I think it would be an alleviation to my torments. For this reason I trouble you with this letter. To the men of the company I will make no apology.—Your husband, who insisted on my drinking more than I chose, has no right to blame me, and the other gentlemen were partakers of my guilt. But to you, Madam, I have much to apologise. Your good opinion I valued as one of the greatest acquisitions I had made on earth, and I was truly a beast to forfeit it. There was a Miss I——too, a woman of fine sense, gentle and unassuming manners—do make, on my part, a miserable damn'd wretch's best apology to her. A Mrs. G——, a charming woman, did me the honour to be prejudiced in my favour; this makes me hope that I have not outraged her beyond all forgiveness.—To all the other ladies please present my humblest contrition for my conduct, and my petition for their gracious pardon. O all ye powers of decency and decorum! whisper to them that my errors, though great, were involuntary—that an intoxicated man is the vilest of beasts—that it was not in my nature to be brutal to any one—that to be rude to a woman, when in my senses, was impossible with me—but—

Regret! Remorse! Shame! ye three hell hounds that ever dog my steps and bay at my heels, spare me! spare me!

Forgive the offences, and pity the perdition of, Madam, your humble slave,

R. B.

CXCVI.—To MRS. DUNLOP.

15th December 1795.

My Dear Friend,—As I am in a complete Decemberish humour, gloomy, sullen, stupid, as even the Deity of Dulness herself could wish, I shall not drawl out a heavy letter with a number of heavier apologies for my late silence. Only one I shall mention, because I know you will sympathise with it: these four months, a sweet little girl, my youngest child, has been so ill, that every day a week or less threatened to terminate her existence. There had much need be many pleasures annexed to the states of husband and father, for, God knows, they have many peculiar cares. I cannot describe to you the anxious, sleepless hours these ties frequently give me. I see a train of helpless little folks; me and my exertions all their stay: and on what a brittle thread does the life of man hang! If I am nipt off at the command of fate! even in all the vigour of manhood as I am—such things happen every day—Gracious God! what would become of my little flock! 'Tis here that I envy your people of fortune. A father on his deathbed, taking an everlasting leave of his children, has indeed woe enough; but the man of competent fortune leaves his sons and daughters independency and friends; while I—but I shall run distracted if I think any longer on the subject!

To leave talking of the matter so gravely, I shall sing with the old Scots ballad—

O that I had ne'er been married,

I would never had nae care;

Now I've gotten wife and bairns,
They cry crowdie evermair.

    Crowdie ance, crowdie twice:
Crowdie three times in a day:
An ye crowdie ony mair,
Ye'll crowdie a' my meal away.
25th, Christmas Morning.

This, my much-loved friend, is a morning of wishes; accept mine—so Heaven hear me as they are sincere! that blessings may attend your steps, and affliction know you not! In the charming words of my favourite author— "The Man of Feeling," "May the Great Spirit bear up the weight of thy grey hairs, and blunt the arrow that brings them rest!"

    Now that I talk of authors, how do you like Cowper? Is not the "Task" a glorious poem? The religion of the "Task," bating a few scraps of Calvinistic divinity, is the religion of God and Nature; the religion that exalts, that ennobles man. Were not you to send me your *Zeluco* in return for mine? Tell me how you like my marks and notes through the book. I would not give a farthing for a book, unless I were at liberty to blot it with my criticisms.

    R. B.

CXCVII.—To MRS. DUNLOP, IN LONDON.
DUMFRIES, *20th December 1795.*

    I have been prodigiously disappointed in this London journey of yours.... Do let me hear from you the soonest possible. As I hope to get a frank from my friend Captain Miller, I shall, every leisure hour, take up the pen and gossip away whatever comes first, prose or poetry, sermon or song. In this last article I have abounded of late. I have often mentioned to you a superb publication of Scottish songs, which is making its appearance in our great metropolis, and where I have the honour to preside over the Scottish verse, as no less a personage than Peter Pindar does over the English.

December 29th.

    Since I began this letter, I have been appointed to act in the capacity of supervisor here, and I assure you, what with the load of business, and what with that business being new to me, I could scarcely have commanded ten minutes to have spoken to you, had you been in town, much less to have written you an epistle. This appointment is only temporary, and during the illness of the present incumbent; but I look forward to an early period when I shall be appointed in full form: a consummation devoutly to be wished! My political sins seem to be forgiven me.

    This is the season (New Year's day is now my date) of wishing, and mine are most fervently offered up for you! May life to you be a positive blessing while it lasts, for your own sake; and that it may yet be greatly prolonged is my wish for my own sake, and for the sake of the rest of your friends! What a transient business is life! Very lately I was a boy; but t'other day I was a young man; and I already begin to feel the rigid fibre and stiffening joints of old age coming fast o'er my frame. With all my follies of youth, and, I fear, a few vices of manhood, still I congratulate myself on having had in early days religion strongly impressed on my mind. I have nothing to say to any one as to which sect he belongs to, or what creed he believes: but I look on the man who is firmly persuaded of infinite Wisdom and Goodness superintending and directing every circumstance that can happen in his lot—I felicitate such a man for having a solid foundation for his mental enjoyment; a firm prop and sure stay, in the hour of difficulty, trouble, and distress; and a never-failing anchor of hope when he looks beyond the grave.

    R. B.

CXVIII.—To THE HON, THE PROVOST, ETC., OF DUMFRIES.
Gentlemen,—The literary taste, and liberal spirit, of your good town has so ably filled the various departments of your schools, as to make it a very great object for a parent to

have his children educated in them. Still, to me, a stranger, with my large family, and very stinted income, to give my young ones the education I wish, at the high-school fees which a stranger pays, will bear hard upon me.

Some years ago, your good town did me the honour of making me an honorary Burgess. Will you allow me to request that this mark of distinction may extend so far, as to put me on a footing of a real freeman of the town, in the schools?

If you are so very kind as to grant my request, it will certainly be a constant incentive to me to strain every nerve where I can officially serve you; and will, if possible, increase that grateful respect with which I have the honour to be, Gentlemen, your devoted humble servant,

R. B.[132]

[132] With the Poet's request the Magistrates of Dumfries very handsomely complied. He was induced to make the request through the persuasions of Mr. James Gray and Mr. Thomas White, Masters of the Grammar School, Dumfries whose memories are still green on the banks of the Nith.—CUNNINGHAM.

CXCIX.—To MRS. DUNLOP.[133]

DUMFRIES, *31st January 1796.*

These many months you have been two packets in my debt—what sin of ignorance I have committed against so highly valued a friend I am utterly at a loss to guess. Alas! Madam, ill can I afford, at this time, to be deprived of any of the small remnant of my pleasures. I have lately drunk deep of the cup of affliction. The autumn robbed me of my only daughter and darling child, and that at a distance too, and so rapidly, as to put it out of my power to pay the last duties to her. [133a] I had scarcely begun to recover from that shock, when I became myself the victim of a most severe rheumatic fever, and long the die spun doubtful; until after many weeks of a sick bed, it seems to have turned up life, and I am beginning to crawl across my room, and once indeed have been before my own door in the street.

R. B.

[133] Cunningham says—"It seems all but certain that Mrs. Dunlop regarded the Poet with some little displeasure during the evening of his days."

[133a] This child died at Mauchline.

CC.—To MR. JAMES JOHNSON.

DUMFRIES, *4th July 1796.*

How are you, my dear friend, and how comes on your fifth volume?[134] You may probably think that for some time past I have neglected you and your work; but, alas! the hand of pain, and sorrow, and care has these many months lain heavy on me! Personal and domestic affliction have almost entirely banished that alacrity and life with which I used to woo the rural muse of Scotia.

You are a good, worthy, honest fellow, and have a good right to live in this world— because you deserve it. Many a merry meeting this publication has given us, and possibly it may give us more, though, alas! I fear it. This protracting, slow, consuming illness which hangs over me will, I doubt much, my dear friend, arrest my sun before he has well reached his middle career, and will turn over the poet to far more important concerns than studying the brilliancy of wit, or the pathos of sentiment! However, hope is the cordial of the human heart, and I endeavour to cherish it as well as I can.

I am ashamed to ask another favour of you, because you have been so very good already; but my wife has a very particular friend, a young lady who sings well, to whom she wishes to present the *Scots Musical Museum.* If you have a spare copy, will you be so obliging as to send it by the very first fly, as I am anxious to have it soon.—Yours ever,

R. B.[135]

[134] Of the *Musical Museum.*

[135] "In this humble manner did poor Burns ask for a copy of a work to which he had contributed, gratuitously, not less than 184 original, altered, and collected songs!"— CROMEK.

CCI—TO MR. CUNNINGHAM.

BROW, *Sea-bathing quarters, 7th July* 1796.

My Dear Cunningham,—I received yours here this moment, and am indeed highly flattered with the approbation of the literary circle you mention; a literary circle inferior to none in the two kingdoms. Alas! my friend, I fear the voice of the bard will soon be heard among you no more! For these eight or ten months I have been ailing, sometimes bedfast and sometimes not; but these last three months I have been tortured with an excruciating rheumatism, which has reduced me to nearly the last stage. You actually would not know me if you saw me. Pale, emaciated, and so feeble, as occasionally to need help from my chair— my spirits fled! fled!—but I can no more on the subject—only the medical folks tell me that my last and only chance is bathing and country quarters, and riding. The deuce of the matter is this—when an exciseman is off duty, his salary is reduced to £35 instead of £50. What way, in the name of thrift, shall I maintain myself, and keep a horse in country quarters, with a wife and five children at home, on 35 pounds? I mention this, because I had intended to beg your utmost interest, and that of all the friends you can muster, to move our Commissioners of Excise to grant me the full salary; I dare say you know them all personally. If they do not grant it me, I must lay my account with an exit truly *en poete*; if I die not of disease, I must perish with hunger.[136]

I have sent you one of the songs; the other my memory does not serve me with, and I have no copy here, but I shall be at home soon, when I will send it you. Apropos to being at home, Mrs. Burns threatens in a week or two to add one more to my paternal charge, which, if of the right gender, I intend shall be introduced to the world by the respectable designation of *Alexander Cunningham Burns*. My last was *James Glencairn*, so you can have no objection to the company of nobility. Farewell.

R. B.

[136] *Not* granted.

CCII.—To MR. GILBERT BURNS.

10th July 1795.

Dear Brother,—It will be no very pleasing news to you to be told that I am dangerously ill, and not likely to get better. An inveterate rheumatism has reduced me to such a state of debility, and my appetite is so totally gone, that I can scarcely stand on my legs. I have been a week at sea-bathing, and will continue there, or in a friend's house in the country, all the summer. God keep my wife and children; if I am taken from their head, they will be poor indeed. I have contracted one or two serious debts, partly from my illness these many months, partly from too much thoughtlessness as to expense when I came to town, that will cut in too much on the little I leave them in your hands. Remember me to my mother.—Yours,

R. B.

CCIII.—To MRS. BURNS.[137]

BROW, *Thursday.*

My Dearest Love,—I delayed writing until I could tell you what effect sea-bathing was likely to produce. It would be injustice to deny that it has eased my pains, and I think has strengthened me; but my appetite is still extremely bad. No flesh nor fish can I swallow: porridge and milk are the only things I can taste. I am very happy to hear, by Miss Jess Lewars, that you are all well. My very best and kindest compliments to her, and to all the children. I will see you on Sunday.—Your affectionate husband,

R. B.

[137] One evening, while at the Brow, Burns was visited by two young ladies. The sun,

setting on the western hills, threw a strong light upon him through the window. One of them perceiving this, proceeded to draw the curtain; "Let me look at the sun, my dear," said the sinking poet, "he will not long shine on me."

CCIV.—To MRS. DUNLOP.

BROW, *Saturday, 12th July 1796.*

Madam,—I have written you so often, without receiving any answer, that I would not trouble you again, but for the circumstances in which I am. An illness which has long hung about me, in all probability will speedily send me beyond that bourne whence no traveller returns. Your friendship, with which for many years you honoured me, was a friendship dearest to my soul. Your conversation, and especially your correspondence, were at once highly entertaining and instructive. With what pleasure did I use to break up the seal! The remembrance yet adds one pulse more to my poor palpitating heart. Farewell!!!

R. B.

CCV.—To MR. JAMES BURNESS, WRITER, MONTROSE.

DUMFRIES, *12th July.*

MY DEAR COUSIN,—When you offered me money assistance, little did I think I should want it so soon. A rascal of a haberdasher, to whom I owe a considerable bill, taking it into his head that I am dying, has commenced a process against me, and will infallibly put my emaciated body into jail. Will you be so good as to accommodate me, and that by return of post, with ten pounds? O James, did you know the pride of my heart, you would feel doubly for me! Alas! I am not used to beg! The worst of it is, my health was coming about finely. Melancholy and low spirits are half my disease. If I had it settled, I would be, I think, quite well in a manner.

R. B.

CCVI.—To HIS FATHER-IN-LAW, JAMES ARMOUR, MASON, MAUCHLINE.[138]

DUMFRIES, *18th July 1799.*

MY DEAR SIR,—Do, for heaven's sake, send Mrs. Armour here immediately. My wife is hourly expecting to be put to bed. Good God! what a situation for her to be in, poor girl, without a friend! I returned from sea-bathing quarters to-day, and my medical friends would almost persuade me that I am better, but I think and feel that my strength is so gone that the disorder will prove fatal to me.—Your son-in-law,

R. B.

[138] Mrs. Burns's father. This is the very last of Burns's compositions, being written only three days before his death.

THE THOMSON LETTERS.
PREFATORY NOTE.

This correspondence began in September 1792, when Burns had already been domiciled nine months in the town of Dumfries, and ended only with his death in July 1796. It originated in the request of a stranger for a series of songs to suit a projected collection of the best Scottish airs. The stranger was George Thomson, a young man of about Burns's own age, and head clerk in the office of the Board of Manufactures in Edinburgh. Thomson outlived his great correspondent by more than half a century. He died so recently as 1851, at the advanced age of ninety-two. Robert Chambers has described him as a most honourable man, of singularly amiable character and cheerful manners. It may interest some people to know that his granddaughter was the wife of Dickens, the famous novelist.

THE THOMSON LETTER.

I.

DUMFRIES, *16th September 1792.*

Sir,—I have just this moment got your letter. As the request you make to me will positively add to my enjoyments in complying with it, I shall enter into your undertaking with all the small portion of abilities I have, strained to their utmost exertion by the impulse of enthusiasm. Only, don't hurry me. "Deil tak the hindmost" is by no means the *crie de guerre* of my muse. Will you, as I am inferior to none of you in enthusiastic attachment to the poetry and music of old Caledonia, and, since you request it, have cheerfully promised my mite of assistance—will you let me have a list of your airs, with the first line of the printed verses you intend for them, that I may have an opportunity of suggesting any alteration that may occur to me? You know 'tis in the way of my trade; still leaving you, gentlemen,[139] the undoubted rights of publishers, to approve or reject at your pleasure, for your own publication. *Apropos* if you are for *English* verses, there is, on my part, an end of the matter. Whether in the simplicity of the ballad, or the pathos of the song, I can only hope to please myself in being allowed at least a sprinkling of our native tongue. English verses, particularly the works of Scotsmen, that have merit, are certainly very eligible. "Tweedside;" "Ah! the Poor Shepherd's Mournful Fate;" "Ah! Chloris, could I now but sit," etc., you cannot mend; but such insipid stuff as "To Fanny fair, could I impart," etc., usually set to "The Mill, Mill, O," is a disgrace to the collections in which it has already appeared, and would doubly disgrace a collection that will have the very superior merit of yours. But more of this in the farther prosecution of the business, if I am to be called on for my strictures and amendments—I say, amendments; for I will not alter, accept where I myself, at least, think that I amend.

As to any renumeration, you may think my songs either above or below price; for they shall absolutely be the one or the other. In the honest enthusiasm with which I embark in your undertaking, to talk of money, wages, fee, hire, etc., would be downright sodomy of soul! A proof of each of the songs that I compose or amend I shall receive as a favour. In the rustic phrase of the season, "Gude speed the wark!"—I am, Sir, your very humble servant,

R. BURNS.

P.S.—I have some particular reasons for wishing my interference to be known as little as possible.

[139] Thomson in his letter spoke of coadjutors, but in less than a year he became sole editor of the collection.

II.

My Dear Sir,—Let me tell you that you are too fastidious in your ideas of songs and ballads. I own that your criticisms are just; the songs you specify in your list have, *all but one*, the faults you remark in them; but how shall we mend the matter? Who shall rise up and say—Go to, I will make a better? For instance, on reading over "The Lea-rig," I immediately set about trying my hand on it, and, after all, I could make nothing more of it than the following, which, Heaven knows, is poor enough:—

When o'er the hill the eastern star
Tells bughtin-time is near, my jo, (etc.)

Your observation as to the aptitude of Dr. Percy's ballad to the air, "Nannie O," is just. It is besides, perhaps, the most beautiful ballad in the English language. But let me remark to you, that in the sentiment and style of our Scottish airs there is a pastoral simplicity, a something that one may call the Doric style and dialect of vocal music, to which a dash of our native tongue and manners is particularly, nay, peculiarly apposite. For this reason, and upon my honour, for this reason alone, I am of opinion (but, as I told you before, my opinion is yours, freely yours to approve or reject as you please) that my ballad of "Nannie, O", might perhaps do for one set of verses to the tune. Now don't let it enter into your head that you are under any necessity of taking my verses. I have long ago made up my mind as to my own reputation in the business of authorship; and have nothing to be pleased or offended at, in your adoption or rejection of my verses. Though you should reject one half of what I give you, I shall be pleased with your adopting the other half, and shall continue to serve you with the same assiduity.

In the printed copy of my "Nannie, O", the name of the river is horridly prosaic. I will alter it,

Behind yon hills where *Lugar* flows.

Girvan is the name of the river that suits the idea of the stanza best, but Lugar is the most agreeable modulation of syllables.

I will soon give you a great many more remarks on this business; but I have just now an opportunity of conveying you this scrawl, free of postage, an expense that it is ill able to pay; so, with my best compliments to honest Allan,[140] goodbye to ye.

Friday night.
Saturday morning.

As I find I have still an hour to spare this morning before my conveyance goes away, I will give you "Nannie, O", at length.

Your remarks on "Ewe-bughts, Marion", are just; still it has obtained a place among our more classical Scottish songs; and what with many beauties in its composition, and more prejudices in its favour, you will not find it easy to supplant it.

In my very early years, when I was thinking of going to the West Indies, I took the following farewell of a dear girl. It is quite trifling, and has nothing of the merits of "Ewe-bughts", but it will fill up this page. You must know that all my earlier love-songs were the breathings of ardent passion, and though it might have been easy in after-times to have given them a polish, yet that polish, to me, whose they were, and who perhaps alone cared for them, would have defaced the legend of my heart, which was so faithfully inscribed on them. Their uncouth simplicity was, as they say of wines, their *race*.

Will ye go to the Indies, my Mary, (etc.)

"Gala Water," and "Auld Rob Morris," I think, will most probably be the next subject of my musings. However, even on *my verses*, speak out your criticisms with equal frankness. My wish is, not to stand aloof, the uncomplying bigot of *opiniâtreté*, but cordially to join issue with you in the furtherance of the work. Gude speed the wark!

Amen.

[140] David Allan, the artist.

III.

November 8th, 1792,

If you mean, my dear Sir, that all the songs in your collection shall be poetry of the first merit, I am afraid you will find more difficulty in the undertaking than you are aware of. There is a peculiar rhythmus in many of our airs, and a necessity of adapting syllables to the emphasis, or what I would call the *feature-notes* of the tune, that cramp the poet, and lay him under almost insuperable difficulties. For instance, in the air, "My Wife's a wanton wee Thing", if a few lines, smooth and pretty, can be adapted to it, it is all you can expect. The enclosed were made extempore to it; and though, on farther study, I might give you something more profound, yet it might not suit the light-horse gallop of the air so well as this random clink.

I have just been looking over the "Collier's bonny Dochter", and if the enclosed rhapsody which I composed the day, on a charming Ayrshire girl, Miss Baillie, as she passed through this place to England, will suit your taste better than the "Collier Lassie", fall on and welcome.

I have hitherto deferred the sublimer, more pathetic airs until more leisure, as they will take, and deserve a greater effort. However, they are all put into your hands, as clay into the hands of the potter, to make one vessel to honour, and another to dishonour. Farewell, etc.

IV.

Inclosing "Highland Mary".—Tune—*Katharine Ogie.*

Ye banks, and braes, and streams around, (etc.)

14th November 1792.

My Dear Sir,—I agree with you, that the song "Katharine Ogie", is very poor stuff, and unworthy, altogether unworthy, of so beautiful an air. I tried to mend it; but the awkward sound "Ogie," recurring in the rhyme, spoils every attempt at introducing sentiment into the piece. The foregoing song pleases myself; I think it is in my happiest manner; you will see at the first glance that it suits the air. The subject of the song is one of the most interesting passages of my youthful days; and I own that I should be much flattered to see the verses set to an air which would ensure celebrity. Perhaps, after all,'tis the still glowing prejudice of my heart that throws a borrowed lustre over the merits of the composition.

I have partly taken your idea of "Auld Rob Morris". I have adopted the two first verses, and am going on with the song on a new plan, which promises pretty well. I take up one or another, just as the bee of the moment buzzes in my bonnet-lug; and do you, *sans ceremonie*, make what use you choose of the productions. Adieu! etc.

V.

26th January 1793.

I approve greatly, my dear Sir, of your plans. Dr. Beattie's essay will of itself be a treasure. On my part, I mean to draw up an appendix to the Doctor's essay, containing my stock of anecdotes, etc., of our Scots songs. All the late Mr. Tytler's anecdotes I have by me, taken down in the course of my acquaintance with him, from his own mouth. I am such an enthusiast, that in the course of my several peregrinations through Scotland, I made a pilgrimage to the individual spot from which every song took its rise, Lochaber and the Braes of Ballendean excepted. So far as locality, either from the title of the air, or the tenor of the song, could be ascertained, I have paid my devotions at the particular shrine of every Scots Muse.

I do not doubt but you might make a very valuable collection of Jacobite songs—but would it give no offence? In the meantime, do not you think that some of them, particularly "The Sow's Tail to Geordie", as an air, with other words, might be well worth a place in your collection of lively songs?

If it were possible to procure songs of merit, it would be proper to have one set of Scots words to every air, and that the set of words to which the notes ought to be set. There is a *naïvetè*, a pastoral simplicity, in a slight intermixture of Scots words and phraseology, which is more in unison (at least to my taste, and, I will add, to every genuine Caledonian taste), with the simple pathos or rustic sprightliness of our native music, than any English verses whatever.

The very name of Peter Pindar is an acquisition to your work. His "Gregory" is beautiful. I have tried to give you a set of stanzas in Scots, on the same subject, which are at your service. Not that I intend to enter the lists with Peter; that would be presumption indeed. My song, though much inferior in poetic merit, has, I think, more of the ballad simplicity in it.
LORD GREGORY.
O mirk, mirk is this midnight hour, (etc.)

Your remark on the first stanza of my "Highland Mary" is just, but I cannot alter it, without injuring the poetry.

VI.

20th March 1793.

My Dear Sir,—The song prefixed ("Mary Morison") is one of my juvenile works. I leave it in your hands. I do not think it very remarkable, either for its merits or demerits. It is impossible (at least I feel it so in my stinted powers) to be always original, entertaining, and witty.

What is become of the list, etc., of your songs? I shall be out of all temper with you by and by. I have always looked on myself as the prince of indolent correspondents, and valued myself accordingly; and I will not, cannot bear rivalship from you, nor anybody else.

VII.

7th April 1793.

Thank you, my dear Sir, for your packet. You cannot imagine how much this business of composing for your publication has added to my enjoyments. What, with my early attachment to ballads, your book, etc., ballad-making is now as completely my hobby-horse as ever fortification was Uncle Toby's; so I'll e'en canter it away till I come to the limit of my race (God grant that I may take the right side of the winning-post!) and then cheerfully looking back on the honest folks with whom I have been happy, I shall say, or sing, "Sae merry as we a' hae been" and raising my last looks to the whole human race, the last words of the voice of Coila shall be, "Good night, and joy be wi' you a'!" So much for my last words; now for a few present remarks as they have occurred at random, on looking over your list.

The first lines of "The last time I came o'er the Moor", and several other lines in it, are beautiful; but in my opinion—pardon me, revered shade of Ramsay!—the song is unworthy of the divine air. I shall try to *make* or *mend*. "For ever, Fortune, wilt thou prove," is a charming song; but "Logan Burn and Logan Braes" are sweetly susceptible of rural imagery; I'll try that likewise, and if I succeed, the other song may class among the English ones. I remember the two last lines of a verse in some of the old songs of "Logan Water" (for I know a good many different ones), which I think pretty—

Now my dear lad maun face his faes,

Far, far frae me, and Logan braes.

"My Patie is a lover gay", is unequal. "His mind is never muddy," is a muddy expression indeed.

Then I'll resign and marry Pate,

And syne my cockernony—

This is surely far unworthy of Ramsay, or your book. My song, "Rigs of Barley", to the same tune, does not altogether please me; but if I can mend it, and thresh a few loose sentiments out of it, I will submit it to your consideration. The "Lass o' Patie's Mill" is one of Ramsay's best songs; but there is one loose sentiment in it, which my much-valued friend, Mr. Erskine, will take into his critical consideration. In Sir J. Sinclair's statistical volumes are two claims, one I think, from Aberdeenshire, and the other from Ayrshire, for the honour of this song. The following anecdote, which I had from the present Sir William Cunningham, of Robertland, who had it of the late John, Earl of Loudon, I can on such authorities believe.

Allan Ramsay was residing at Loudon Castle with the then Earl, father to Earl John; and one forenoon, riding or walking out together, his lordship and Allan passed a sweet romantic spot on Irwine water, still called "Patie's Mill," where a bonnie lass was "tedding hay, bareheaded on the green." My lord observed to Allan, that it would be a fine theme for a song, Ramsay took the hint, and lingering behind, he composed the first sketch of it, which he produced at dinner.

"One day I heard Mary say," is a fine song; but for consistency's sake, alter the name "Adonis." Was there ever such banns published, as a purpose of marriage between Adonis and Mary? I agree with you that my song, "There's nought but care on every hand," is much superior to "Poortith Cauld." The original song, "The Mill, Mill, O," though excellent, is, on account of delicacy, inadmissible; still I like the title, and think a Scottish song would suit the notes best; and let your chosen song, which is very pretty, follow, as an English set. The "Banks of Dee" is, you know, literally "Langolee" to slow time. The song is well enough, but has some false imagery in it, for instance,

And sweetly the nightingale sung from the *tree.*

In the first place, the nightingale sings in a low bush, but never from a tree; and in the second place, there never was a nightingale seen or heard on the banks of the Dee, or on the banks of any other river in Scotland. Exotic rural imagery is always comparatively flat. If I could hit on another stanza equal to "The small birds rejoice," etc., I do myself honestly avow that I think it a superior song. "John Anderson, my jo"—the song to this tune in Johnson's *Museum* is my composition, and I think it not my worst: if it suit you, take it and welcome. Your collection of sentimental and pathetic songs is, in my opinion, very complete; but not so your comic ones. Where are "Tullochgorum," "Lumps o' Puddin'," "Tibbie Fowler," and several others, which, in my humble judgment, are well worthy of preservation? There is also one sentimental song of mine in the *Museum*, which never was known out of the immediate neighbourhood, until I got it taken down from a country girl's singing. It is called "Craigie-burn Wood;" and in the opinion of Mr. Clarke is one of our sweetest Scottish songs. He is quite an enthusiast about it; and I would take his taste in Scottish music against the taste of most connoisseurs.

You are quite right in inserting the last five in your list, though they are certainly Irish. "Shepherds, I have lost my love," is to me a heavenly air—what would you think of a set of Scottish verses to it? I have made one a good while ago, which I think is the best love song[141] I ever composed in my life; but in its original state it is not quite a lady's song. I enclose an altered, not amended copy for you, if you choose to set the tune to it, and let the Irish verses follow.

Mr. Erskine's songs are all pretty, but his "Lone Vale" is divine.—Yours, etc.

Let me know just how you like these random hints.

[141] "Yestreen I had a pint o' wine."

VIII.

April 1793.

My Dear Sir,—I own my vanity is flattered when you give my songs a place in your elegant and superb work; but to be of service to the work is my first wish. As I have often told you, I do not in a single instance wish you, out of compliment to me, to insert anything of mine. One hint let me give you—whatever Mr. Peyel does, let him not alter one *iota* of the original Scottish airs; I mean in the song department; but let our national music preserve its native features. They are, I own, frequently wild, and irreducible to the more modern rules; but on that very eccentricity, perhaps, depends a great part of their effect.

IX.

June 1793.

When I tell you, my dear Sir, that a friend of mine, in whom I am much interested, has fallen a sacrifice to these accursed times, you will easily allow that it might unhinge me for doing any good among ballads. My own loss, as to pecuniary matters, is trifling; but the total ruin of a much-loved friend is a loss indeed. Pardon my seeming inattention to your last commands.

I cannot alter the disputed lines in the "Mill, Mill, O."[142] What you think a defect I esteem as a positive beauty; so you see how doctors differ. I shall now, with as much alacrity as I can muster, go on with your commands.

You know Frazer, the hautboy player in Edinburgh—he is here instructing a band of music for a fencible corps quartered in this country. Among many of the airs that please me, there is one well known as a reel, by the name of "The Quaker's Wife"; and which I remember a grand-aunt of mine used to sing, by the name of "Liggeram Cosh, my bonnie wee lass". Mr. Frazer plays it slow, and with an expression that quite charms me. I became such an enthusiast about it that I made a song for it, which I here subjoin, and inclose Frazer's set of the tune. If they hit your fancy, they are at your service; if not, return me the tune, and I will put it in Johnson's *Museum*. I think the song is not in my worst manner.

Blithe hae I been on yon hill, (etc.)

I should wish to hear how this pleases you.

[142] The lines were the third and fourth—

Wi' mony a sweet babe fatherless,

And mony a widow mourning.

X.

June 25th 1793.

Have you ever, my dear Sir, felt your bosom ready to burst with indignation on reading of those mighty villains who divide kingdom against kingdom, desolate provinces, and lay nations waste, out of the wantonness of ambition, or often from still more ignoble passions? In a mood of this kind to-day I recollected the air of "Logan Water;" and it occurred to me that its querulous melody probably had its origin from the plaintive indignation of some swelling, suffering heart, fired at the tyrannic strides of some public destroyer, and overwhelmed with private distress, the consequence of a country's ruin. If I have done anything at all like justice to my feelings, the following song, composed in three quarters of an hour's meditation in my elbow-chair, ought to have some merit.

[Here follows "Logan Water."]

Do you know the following beautiful little fragment in Witherspoon's *Collection of Scots Songs?*

Air—*Hughie Graham.*

O gin my love were yon red rose,
That grows upon the castle wa',
And I mysel' a drap o' dew
Into her bonnie breast to fa'!

Oh, there beyond expression blest,
I'd feast on beauty a' the night;
Seal'd on her silk saft faulds to rest,
Till fley'd awa by Phoebus light.

This thought is inexpressibly beautiful; and quite, so far as I know, original. It is too short for a song, else I would forswear you altogether, unless you gave it a place. I have often tried to eke a stanza to it, but in vain. After balancing myself for a musing five minutes, on the hind legs of my elbow-chair, I produced the following. The verses are far inferior to the foregoing, I frankly confess; but if worthy of insertion at all, they might be first in place; as every poet, who knows anything of his trade, will husband his best thoughts for a concluding stroke.

O were my love yon lilac fair,
Wi' purple blossoms to the spring;
And I a bird to shelter there,
When wearied on my little wing;

How I wad mourn, when it was torn
By autumn wild, and winter rude!
But I wad sing on wanton wing,
When youthfu' May its bloom renew'd.

XI.

July 1793.

I assure you, my dear Sir, that you truly hurt me with your pecuniary parcel. It degrades me in my own eyes. However, to return it would savour of affectation; but as to any more traffic of that debtor or creditor kind, I swear by that HONOUR which crowns the upright statue of ROBERT BURNS'S INTEGRITY—on the least motion of it, I will indignantly spurn the by—past transaction, and from that moment commence entire stranger to you! BURNS'S character for generosity of sentiment and independence of mind will, I trust, long outlive any of his wants, which the cold, unfeeling ore can supply: at least, I will take care that such a character he shall deserve.

Thank you for my copy of your publication. Never did my eyes behold, in any musical work, such elegance and correctness. Your preface, too, is admirably written; only, your partiality to me has made you say too much: however, it will bind me down to double every eifort in the future progress of the work. The following are a few remarks on the songs in the list you sent me. I never copy what I write to you, so I may be often tautological, or perhaps contradictory.

"The Flowers of the Forest" is charming as a poem; and should be, and must be, set to the notes; but, though out of your rule, the three stanzas, beginning,
I hae seen the smiling o' fortune beguiling,

are worthy of a place, were it but to immortalise the author of them, who is an old lady[143] of my acquaintance, and at this moment living in Edinburgh. She is a Mrs. Cockburn; I forget of what place; but from Roxburghshire. What a charming apostrophe is
O fickle Fortune, why this cruel sporting,

Why, why torment us—*poor sons of a day*!

The old ballad, "I wish I were where Helen lies," is silly, to contemptibility. My alteration of it, in Johnson's, is not much better.

Nee Rutherford, of Selkirkshire. She was then 81 years old.

XII.

August 1793.

That tune, "Cauld Kail," is such a favourite of yours, that I once more roved out yesterday for a gloamin-shot at the muses; when the muse that presides o'er the shores of Nith, or rather my old inspiring dearest nymph, Coila, whispered me the following. I have two reasons for thinking that it was my early, sweet, simple inspirer that was by my elbow, "smooth gliding without step," and pouring the song on my glowing fancy. In the first place, since I left Coila's haunts, not a fragment of a poet has arisen to cheer her solitary musings, by catching inspiration from her; so I more than suspect she has followed me hither, or at least makes me occasional visits; secondly, the last stanza of this song I send you is the very words that Coila taught me many years ago, and which I set to an old Scots reel in Johnson's *Museum*.

Autumn is my propitious season. I make more verses in it than in all the year else. God bless you.

XIII.

Sept. 1793.

You may readily trust, my dear Sir, that any exertion in my power is heartily at your service. But one thing I must hint to you; the very name of Peter Finder is of great service to your publication, so get a verse from him now and then; though I have no objection, as well as I can, to bear the burden of the business.

You know that my pretensions to musical taste are merely a few of nature's instincts, untaught and untutored by art. For this reason, many musical compositions, particularly where much of the merit lies in counterpoint, however they may transport and ravish the ears of your connoisseurs, affect my simple lug no otherwise than merely as melodious din. On the other hand, by way of amends, I am delighted with many little melodies which the learned musician despises as silly and insipid. I do not know whether the old air "Hey tuttie taittie" may rank among this number; but well I know that, with Frazer's hautboy, it has often filled my eyes with tears. There is a tradition, which I have met with in many places of Scotland, that it was Robert Bruce's march at the battle of Bannockburn. This thought, in my solitary wanderings, warmed me to a pitch of enthusiasm on the theme of Liberty and Independence, which I threw into a kind of Scottish ode, fitted to the air, that one might suppose to be the gallant Royal Scot's address to his heroic followers on that eventful morning.
BRUCE TO HIS TROOPS,
On the Eve of the Battle of Bannockburn.
Hey tuttie taittie.
Scots, wha hae wi' Wallace bled, (etc.)

So may God ever defend the cause of Truth and Liberty, as He did that day!—Amen.

160

P.S.—I showed the air to Urbani, who was highly pleased with it, and begged me to make soft verses for it; but I had no idea of giving myself any trouble on the subject, till the accidental recollection of that glorious struggle for freedom, associated with the glowing ideas of some other struggles of the same nature, not quite so ancient, roused my rhyming mania. Clarke's set of the tune, with his bass, you will find in the *Museum*; though I am afraid that the air is not what will entitle it to a place in your elegant selection.

XIV.

September 1793.

I have received your list, my dear Sir, and here go my observations on it.[143]

"Down the burn, Davie." I have this moment tried an alteration, leaving out the last half of the third stanza, and the first half of the last stanza, thus:—

As down the burn they took their way,
And thro' the flowery dale,
His cheek to hers he aft did lay,
And love was aye the tale.

    With "Mary, when shall we return,
Sic pleasure to renew?"
Quoth Mary, "Love, I like the burn,
And aye shall follow you."

"Thro' the wood, laddie." I am decidedly of opinion that both in this and "There'll never be peace till Jamie comes hame," the second or high part of the tune being a repetition of the first part an octave higher, is only for instrumental music, and would be much better omitted in singing.

"Cowden-knowes." Remember in your index that the song in pure English, to this tune, beginning

When summer comes, the swains on Tweed,

is the production of Crawford; Robert was his Christian name.

"Laddie lie near me," must *lie by me* for some time. I do not know the air; and until I am complete master of a tune in my own singing (such as it is), I never can compose for it. My way is: I consider the poetic sentiment correspondent to my idea of the musical expression, then choose my theme, begin one stanza; when that is composed, which is generally the most difficult part of the business, I walk out, sit down now and then, look out for objects in nature around me that are in unison or harmony with the cogitations of my fancy, and workings of my bosom; humming every now and then the air, with the verses I have framed. When I feel my muse beginning to jade, I retire to the solitary fireside of my study, and there commit my effusions to paper; swinging at intervals on the hind legs of my elbow chair, by way of calling forth my own critical strictures, as my pen goes on. Seriously, this, at home, is almost invariably my way. What cursed egotism!

"Gil Morice" I am for leaving out. It is a plaguy length; the air itself is never sung, and its place can well be supplied by one or two songs for fine airs that are not in your list. For instance, "Craigieburn-wood" and "Roy's Wife". The first, besides its intrinsic merit, has novelty; and the last has high merit, as well as great celebrity. I have the original words of a song for the last air in the handwriting of the lady who composed it, and they are superior to any edition of the song which the public has yet seen.

"Highland Laddie". The old set will please a mere Scotch ear best; and the new an Italianised one. There is a third, and what Oswald calls the "Old Highland Laddie", which pleases we more than either of them. It is sometimes called "Jinglan Johnnie", it being the air of an old humorous tawdry song of that name. You will find it in the Museum, "I hae been at Crookie-den", etc. I would advise you in this musical quandary, to offer up your prayers to the muses for inspiring direction; and, in the meantime, waiting for this direction, bestow a libation to Bacchus, and there is not a doubt but you will hit on a judicious choice. *Probatum est.*

"Auld Sir Simon," I must beg you to leave out, and put in its place "The Quaker's Wife".

"Blythe hae I been on yon hill" is one of the finest songs ever I made in my life; and, besides, is composed on a young lady positively the most beautiful, lovely woman in the world. As I purpose giving you the names and designations of all my heroines, to appear in some future edition of your work, perhaps half a century hence, you must certainly include *the bonniest lass in a' the warld* in your collection.

"Daintie Davie" I have heard sung nineteen thousand, nine hundred, and ninety-nine times, and always with the low part of the tune; and nothing has surprised me so much as your opinion on this subject. If it will not suit, as I propose, we will lay two of the stanzas together, and then make the chorus follow.

"Fee him, Father". I enclose you Frazer's set of this tune when he plays it slow; in fact, he makes it the language of despair, I shall here give you two stanzas in that style, merely to try if it will be any improvement. Were it possible, in singing, to give it half the pathos which Frazer gives it in playing, it would make an admirable pathetic song. I do not give these verses for any merit they have. I composed them at the time at which *Patie Allan's mither died*; that was *the back o' midnight*; and by the lee-side of a bowl of punch, which had overset every mortal in the company, except the hautbois and the muse.

Thou hast left me ever, Jamie, (etc.)

"Jockie and Jenny" I would discard, and in its place would put "There's nae luck about the house", which has a very pleasant air; and which is positively the finest love-ballad in that style in the Scottish, or perhaps in any other language. "When she came ben she bobbet", as an air, is more beautiful than either, and in the *andante* way would unite with a charming sentimental ballad.

"Saw ye my father" is one of my greatest favourites. The evening before last I wandered out, and began a tender song, in what I think its native style. I must premise that the old way, and the way to give most effect, is to have no starting note, as the fiddlers call it, but to burst at once into the pathos. Every country girl sings-"Saw ye my father", etc.

My song is just begun; and I should like, before I proceed, to know your opinion of it. I have sprinkled it with the Scottish dialect, but it may be easily turned into correct English.

Fragment.—Tune—"*Saw ye my Father*"
Where are the joys I hae met in the morning, (etc.)

"Todlin hame": Urbani mentioned an idea of his, which has long been mine; and this air is highly susceptible of pathos; accordingly, you will soon hear him, at your concert, try it to a song of mine in the*Museum*—"Ye banks and braes o' bonnie Doon". One song more and I have done: "Auld lang syne". The air is but *mediocre*; but the following song, the old song of the olden times, and which has never been in print, nor even in manuscript, until I took it down from an old man's singing, is enough to recommend any air.[144]

AULD LANG SYNE.
Should auld acquaintance be forgot, (etc.)

Now, I suppose I have tired your patience fairly. You must, after all is over, have a number of ballads, properly so called, "Gil Morice", "Tranent Muir", "M'Pherson's Farewell", "Battle of Sheriff-Muir", or "We ran and they ran" (I know the author of this charming ballad, and his history); "Hardiknute", "Barbara Allan" (I can furnish a finer set of this tune than any that has yet appeared), and besides, do you know that I really have the old tune to which "The Cherry and the Slae" was sung? and which is mentioned as a well-known air in *Scotland's Complaint*, a book published before poor Mary's days. It was then called "The Banks o' Helicon"; an old poem which Pinkerton has brought to light. You will see all this in Tytler's *History of Scottish Music*. The tune, to a learned ear, may have no great merit; but it is a great curiosity. I have a good many original things of this kind.

[143] Songs for his publication. Burns goes through the whole; but only his remarks of any importance are presented here.

162

[144] It is believed to have been his own composition.

XV.

September 1793.

"Who shall decide when doctors disagree?" My ode[145] pleases me so much that I cannot alter it. Your proposed alterations would, in my opinion, make it tame. I am exceedingly obliged to you for putting me on reconsidering it; as I think I have much improved it. Instead of "sodger! hero!" I will have it "Caledonian! on wi' me!"

I have scrutinised it over and over; and to the world some way or other it shall go as it is. At the same time it will not in the least hurt me, should you leave it out altogether, and adhere to your first intention of adopting Logan's verses.

I have finished my song to "Saw ye my Father;" and in English, as you will see. That there is a syllable too much for the *expression* of the air, is true; but allow me to say, that the mere dividing of a dotted crotchet into a crotchet and a quaver is not a great matter; however, in that, I have no pretensions to cope in judgment with you. Of the poetry I speak with confidence; but the music is a business where I hint my ideas with the utmost diffidence.

[145] Scots wha hae.

XVI.

May 1794.

My Dear Sir,—I return you the plates, with which I am highly pleased. I would humbly propose, instead of the younker knitting stockings, to put a stock and horn into his hands. A friend of mine, who is positively the ablest judge on the subject I have ever met with, and though an unknown, is yet a superior artist with the *burin*, is quite charmed with Allan's manner. I got him a peep of the "Gentle Shepherd", and he pronounces Allan a most original artist of great excellence.

For my part, I look on Mr. Allan's choosing my favourite poem for his subject to be one of the highest compliments I have ever received.

I am quite vexed at Pleyel's being cooped up in France, as it will put an entire stop to our work. Now, and for six or seven months, I shall be quite in song, as you shall see by-and-by. I got an air, pretty enough, composed by Lady Elizabeth Heron, of Heron, which she calls "The Banks of Cree." Cree is a beautiful romantic stream, and, as her ladyship is a particular friend of mine, I have written the following song to it:—

Here is the glen, and here the bower, (etc.)

XVII.

Sept. 1794.

I shall withdraw my "On the seas and far away" altogether; it is unequal, and unworthy of the work. Making a poem is like begetting a son; you cannot know whether you have a wise man or a fool, until you produce him to the world and try him.

For that reason I have sent you the offspring of my brain, abortions and all; and as such, pray look over them, and forgive them, and burn them. I am flattered at your adopting "Ca' the yowes to the knowes", as it was owing to me that it ever saw the light. About seven years ago I was well acquainted with a worthy little fellow of a clergyman, a Mr. Clunie, who sung it charmingly: and, at my request, Mr. Clarke took it down from his singing. When I gave it to Johnson, I added some stanzas to the song, and mended others, but still it will not do for you. In a solitary stroll which I took to-day, I tried my hand on a few pastoral lines, following up the idea of the chorus, which I would preserve. Here it is, with all its crudities and imperfections on its head.

Ca' the yowes, (etc.)

I shall give you my opinion of your other newly adopted songs, my first scribbling fit.

XVIII.

19th October 1794.

My Dear Friend,—By this morning's post I have your list, and, in general, I highly approve of it. I shall, at more leisure, give you a critique on the whole. Clarke goes to your town by to-day's fly, and I wish you would call on him and take his opinion in general; you know his taste is a standard. He will return here again in a week or two, so please do not miss asking for him. One thing I hope he will do—persuade you to adopt my favourite, "Craigie-burn wood", in your selection; it is as great a favourite of his as of mine. The lady on whom it was made is one of the finest women in Scotland; and, in fact (*entre nous*), is in a manner to me what Sterne's Eliza was to him—a mistress, a friend, or what you will, in the guileless simplicity of Platonic love. (Now, don't put any of your squinting constructions on this, or have any clishmaclaiver about it among our acquaintances.) I assure you that to my lovely friend you are indebted for many of your best songs of mine. Do you think that the sober gin-horse routine of existence could inspire a man with life, and love, and joy—could fire him with enthusiasm, or melt him with pathos, equal to the genius of your book? No! no! Whenever I want to be more than ordinary *in song*—to be in some degree equal to your diviner airs—do you imagine I fast and pray for the divine emanation? *Tout au contraire!* I have a glorious recipe—the very one that for his own use was invented by the divinity of healing and poetry, when erst he piped to the flocks of Admetus. I put myself on a regimen of admiring a fine woman; and in proportion to the adorability of her charms, in proportion you are delighted with my verses. The lightning of her eye is the godhead of Parnassus, and the witchery of her smile the divinity of Helicon!

To descend to business; if you like my idea of "When she cam ben she bobbit", the enclosed stanzas of mine, altered a little from what they were formerly when set to another air, may perhaps do instead of a worse stanzas.

Now for a few miscellaneous remarks. "The Posie" (in the *Museum*) is my composition; the air was taken down from Mrs. Burns's voice. It is well known in the West Country, but the old words are trash. By-the-bye, take a look at the tune again, and tell me if you do not think it is the original from which "Roslin Castle" is composed. The second part in particular, for the first two or three bars, is exactly the old air. "Strathallan's Lament" is mine; the music is by our right trusty and deservedly well beloved, Allan Masterton. "Donocht head" is not mine; I would give ten pounds if it were. It appeared first in the*Edinburgh Herald*; and came to the editor of that paper with the Newcastle post-mark on it[146]

"Whistle o'er the lave o't" is mine; the music is said to be by a John Bruce, a celebrated violin player in Dumfries, about the beginning of this century. This I know, Bruce, who was an honest man, though a redwud Highlandman, constantly claimed it; and by all the old musical people here is believed to be the author of it.

"Andrew and his cutty gun". The song to which this is set in the *Museum* is mine; and was composed on Miss Euphemia Murray, of Lintrose, commonly and deservedly called the "Flower of Strathmore."

"How lang and dreary is the night." I met with some such words in a collection of songs somewhere, which I altered and enlarged; and to please you, and to suit your favourite air, I have taken a stride or two across the room, and have arranged it anew, as you will find on the other page.

Tune—*Cauld Kail in Aberdeen.*

How lang and dreary is the night, (etc.)

Tell me how you like this. I differ from your idea of the expression of the tune. There is, to me, a great deal of tenderness in it.

I would be obliged to you if you would procure me a sight of Ritson's *Collection of English Songs*, which you mention in your letter. I will thank you for another information, and that as speedily as you please—whether this miserable drawling hotch-potch epistle has not completely tired you of my correspondence.

[146]"Keen blaws the wind o'er Donocht head,

The snaw drives snelly thro' the dale,

164

The Gaberlunzie tirls my sneck,
And, shivering, tells his waefu' tale.
"Cauld is the night, O let me in,
And dinna let your minstrel fa',
And dinna let his winding-sheet
Be naething but a wreath o' snaw."(etc.)

XIX.

November 1794.

Many thanks to you, my dear sir, for your present: it is a book of the utmost importance to me. I have yesterday begun my anecdotes, etc., for your work. I intend drawing it up in the form of a letter to you, which will save me from the tedious dull business of systematic arrangement. Indeed, as all I have to say consists of unconnected remarks, anecdotes, scraps of old songs, etc., it would be impossible to give the work a beginning, a middle, and an end; which the critics insist to be absolutely necessary in a work. In my last, I told you my objections to the song you had selected for "My lodging is on the cold ground". On my visit the other day to my fair Chloris (that is the poetic name of the lovely goddess of my inspiration), she suggested an idea, which I, on my return from the visit, wrought into the following song:—

My Chloris, mark how green the groves, (etc,)

How do you like the simplicity and tenderness of this pastoral? I think it pretty well.

I like you for entering so candidly and so kindly into the story of *ma chère amie*. I assure you, I was never more in earnest in my life than in the account of that affair which I sent you in my last. Conjugal love is a passion which I deeply feel and highly venerate; but, somehow, it does not make such a figure in poesy as that other species of the passion,

Where Love is liberty, and Nature law,

Musically speaking, the first is an instrument of which the gamut is scanty and confined, but the tones inexpressibly sweet; while the last has powers equal to all the intellectual modulations of the human soul. Still, I am a very poet, in my enthusiasm of the passion. The welfare and happiness of the beloved object is the first and inviolate sentiment that pervades my soul; and whatever pleasures I might wish for, or whatever might be the raptures they would give me, yet, if they interfere with that first principle, it is having these pleasures at a dishonest price; and justice forbids, and generosity disdains, the purchase!

XX.

I am out of temper that you should set so sweet, so tender an air, as "Deil tak the wars," to the foolish old verses. You talk of the silliness of "Saw ye my father:" by heavens, the odds is gold to brass! Besides, the old song, though now pretty well modernised into the Scottish language, is, originally, and in the early editions, a bungling low imitation of the Scottish manner, by that genius, Tom D'Urfey; so has no pretensions to be a Scottish production. There is a pretty English song by Sheridan in the "Duenna," to this air, which is out of sight superior to D'Urfey's. It begins,

When sable night each drooping plant restoring.

The air, if I understand the expression of it properly, is the very native language of simplicity, tenderness, and love. I have again gone over my song to the tune as follows.[147]

There is an air, "The Caledonian Hunt's delight", to which I wrote a song that you will find in Johnson. "Ye banks and braes o' bonnie Doon"; this air, I think, might find a place among your hundred, as Lear says of his knights. Do you know the history of the air? It is curious enough. A good many years ago, Mr. James Miller, writer in your good town, a gentleman whom possibly you know, was in company with our friend Clarke; and talking of Scottish music, Miller expressed an ardent ambition to be able to compose a Scots air. Mr. Clarke, partly by way of joke, told him to keep to the black keys of the harpsichord, and preserve some kind of rhythm, and he would infallibly compose a Scots air. Certain it is, that in a few days, Mr. Miller produced the rudiments of an air, which Mr. Clarke, with some touches and corrections, fashioned into the tune in question. Ritson, you know, has the same story of the "Black keys;" but this account which I have just given you, Mr. Clarke informed me of several years ago. Now, to shew you how difficult it is to trace the origin of our airs, I have heard it repeatedly asserted that this was an Irish air nay, I met with an Irish gentleman who affirmed he had heard it in Ireland among the old women; while, on the other hand, a countess informed me, that the first person who introduced the air into this country was a baronet's lady of her acquaintance, who took down the notes from an itinerant piper in the Isle of Man. How difficult then to ascertain the truth respecting our poesy and music! I, myself, have lately seen a couple of ballads sung through the streets of Dumfries, with my name at the head of them as the author, though it was the first time I had ever seen them.

I am ashamed, my dear fellow, to make the request; 'tis dunning your generosity; but in a moment when I had forgotten whether I was rich or poor, I promised Chloris a copy of your songs. It wrings my honest pride to write you this; but an ungracious request is doubly so, by a tedious apology. To make you some amends, as soon as I have extracted the necessary information out of them, I will return you Ritson's volumes.

The lady is not a little proud that she is to make so distinguished a figure in your collection, and I am not a little proud that I have it in my power to please her so much. Lucky it is for your patience that my paper is done, for when I am in a scribbling humour, I know not when to give over.

[147] Our Bard remarks upon it, "I could easily throw this into an English mould; but, to my taste, in the simple and the tender of the pastoral song, a sprinkling of the old Scottish has an inimitable effect."

XXI.

19*th Nov.* 1794.

Tell my friend Allan (for I am sure that we only want the trifling circumstance of being known to one another to be the best friends on earth) that I much suspect he has, in his plates, mistaken the figure of the stock and horn. I have, at last, gotten one; but it is a very rude instrument. It is composed of three parts; the stock, which is the hinder thigh-bone of a sheep, such as you see in a mutton-ham, the horn, which is a common Highland cow's horn, cut off at the smaller end, until the aperture be large enough to admit the stock to be pushed up through the horn, until it be held by the thicker end of the thigh-bone; and, lastly, an oaten reed exactly cut and notched like that which you see every shepherd boy have, when the corn stems are green and full-grown. The reed is not made fast in the bone, but is held up by the lips, and plays loose in the smaller end of the stock; while the stock, with the horn hanging on its larger end, is held by the hands in playing. The stock has six or seven ventiges on the upper side, and one back ventige, like the common flute. This of mine was made by a man from the Braes of Athole, and is exactly what the shepherds wont to use in that country.

However, either it is not quite properly bored in the holes, or else we have not the art of blowing it rightly; for we can make little of it. If Mr. Allan chooses, I will send him a sight of mine; as I look on myself to be a kind of brother-brush with him. "Pride in poets is nae sin", and I will say it, that I look on Mr. Allan and Mr. Burns to be the only genuine and real painters of Scottish costume in the world.

XXII.

January 1795.

I fear for my songs; however a few may please, yet originality is a coy feature in composition, and in a multiplicity of efforts in the same style, disappears altogether. For these three thousand years we poetic folks have been describing the spring, for instance; and, as the spring continues the same, there must soon be a sameness in the imagery, etc., of these said rhyming folks.

166

A great critic, Aikin on Songs, says that love and wine are the exclusive themes for song-writing. The following is on neither subject, and consequently is no song; but will be allowed, I think, to be two or three pretty good prose thoughts, inverted into rhyme.
FOR A' THAT AND A' THAT.
Is there for honest poverty, (etc.)

XXIII.

Ecclefechan,[148] *7th Feb.* 1795.

My Dear Thomson,—You cannot have any idea of the predicament in which I write to you. In the course of my duty as supervisor (in which capacity I have acted of late) I came yesternight to this unfortunate, wicked little village. I have gone forward, but snows of ten feet deep have impeded my progress: I have tried to "gae back the gate I cam again," but the same obstacle has shut me up within insuperable bars. To add to my misfortune, since dinner, a scraper has been torturing catgut, in sounds that would have insulted the dying agonies of a sow under the hands of a butcher, and thinks himself, on that very account, exceeding good company. In fact, I have been in a dilemma, either to get drunk, to forget these miseries; or to hang myself, to get rid of them; like a prudent man (a character congenial to my every thought, word, and deed) I of two evils have chosen the least, and am very drunk at your service!

I wrote you yesterday from Dumfries. I had not time then to tell you all I wanted to say; and Heaven knows, at present I have not capacity.

Do you know an air—I am sure you must know it, "We'll gang nae mair to yon town?" I think, in slowish time, it would make an excellent song. I am highly delighted with it; and if you should think it worthy of your attention, I have a fair dame in my eye to whom I would consecrate it.

As I am just going to bed, I wish you a good night.

[148] The birthplace of Carlyle.

XXIV.

You see how I answer your orders; your tailor could not be more punctual. I am just now in a high fit of poetising, provided that the strait-jacket of criticism don't cure me. If you can, in a post or two, administer a little of the intoxicating potion of your applause, it will raise your humble servant's frenzy to any height you want. I am at this moment "holding high converse" with the Muses, and have not a word to throw away on such a prosaic dog as you are.

XXV.

April 1796.

Alas, my dear Thomson, I fear it will be some time ere I tune my lyre again! "By Babel streams I have sat and wept" almost ever since I wrote you last. I have only known existence by the pressure of the heavy hand of sickness, and have counted time by the repercussions of pain! Rheumatism, cold, and fever have formed to me a terrible combination. I close my eyes in misery, and open them without hope. I look on the vernal day, and say, with poor Fergusson—
Say, wherefore has an all indulgent Heaven
Light to the comfortless and wretched given?

This will be delivered to you by a Mrs. Hyslop, landlady of the Globe Tavern here, which for these many years has been my *howff*, and where our friend Clarke and I have had many a merry squeeze. I am highly delighted with Mr. Allan's etchings. "Woo'd and married and a'", is admirable! The *grouping* is beyond all praise. The expression of the figures, conformable to the story in the ballad, is absolutely faultless perfection. I next admire "Turnim-spike". What I like least is, "Jenny said to Jockey". Besides the female being in her appearance quite a virago, if you take her stooping into the account, she is at least two inches taller than her lover. Poor Cleghorn! I sincerely sympathise with him! Happy am I to think

167

that he yet has a well-grounded hope of health and enjoyment in this world. As for me—but that is a damning subject!

XXVI.

[Probably May 1796.]

My Dear Sir,—Inclosed is a certificate which (although little different from the model) I suppose will amply answer the purpose, and I beg you will prosecute the miscreants[149] without mercy. When your publication is finished, I intend publishing a collection, on a cheap plan, of all the songs I have written for you, The Museum, and others—at least, all the songs of which I wish to be called the author. I do not propose this so much in the way of emolument as to do justice to my muse, lest I should be blamed for trash I never saw, or be defrauded by false claimants of what is justly my own. The post is going.—I will write you again to-morrow. Many thanks for the beautiful seal.

R. B.

[149] For infringement of copyright.

XXVII.

BROW-ON-SOLWAY, *4th July* 1796.

My Dear Sir,—I received your songs; but my health is so precarious, nay, dangerously situated, that, as a last effort, I am here at sea-bathing quarters. Besides an inveterate rheumatism, my appetite is quite gone, and I am so emaciated as to be scarce able to support myself on my own legs. Alas! Is this a time for me to woo the muses? However, I am still anxiously willing to serve your work, and if possible shall try. I would not like to see another employed—unless you could lay your hand upon a poet whose productions would be equal to the rest. Farewell, and God bless you.

R. BURNS.

XXVIII.

BROW, on the Solway Firth, *12th July* 1796.

After all my boasted independence, curst necessity compels me to implore you for five pounds. A cruel wretch of a haberdasher, to whom I owe an account, taking it into his head that I am dying, has commenced a process, and will infallibly put me into jail.

Do, for God's sake, send me that sum, and that by return of post. Forgive me this earnestness, but the horrors of a jail have made me half distracted. I do not ask all this gratuitously; for, upon returning health, I hereby promise and engage to furnish you with five pounds worth of the neatest song-genius you have seen. I tried my hand on · "Rothiemurchie" this morning. The measure is so difficult that it is impossible to infuse much genius into the lines; they are on the other side. Forgive, forgive me![150]

Fairest maid on Devon banks,

Crystal Devon, winding Devon,

Wilt thou lay that frown aside,

And smile as thou wert wont to do? (etc.)

[150] These verses, and the letter inclosing them, are written in a character that marks the very feeble state of their author.

CPSIA information can be obtained
at www.ICGtesting.com
Printed in the USA
FSHW020506040319
56075FS